MEGALOPOLIS

ROLLING NORTHWEST

The Legendary
Illinois Cookbook

Historic and culinary lore from the Prairie State

LAND
BETWEEN THE RIVERS

BREADBASKET FLATLANDS

Agnes M. Feeney
John L. Leckel

GREAT
AMERICAN BOTTOM

LITTLE EGYPT

4

Library of Congress in Publication Data

Feeney, Agnes M.
    The legendary Illinois cookbook.

    Includes index.
    1. Cookery, American—Illinois. 2. Illinois—
History. I. Leckel, John L. II. Title.
TX715.F295   641.59773   82-2517
ISBN 0-89865-199-9   AACR2

Contents

list of illustrations

Preface

The recipes we have included in *The Legendary Illinois Cookbook* have been collected over many years and are from every part of the state. As we were writing the book, we examined more than 150 service club and locally produced cookbooks. In addition, we collected traditional family recipes by requesting them through the "Letters to the Editor" section of every daily newspaper published in Illinois.

From the more than 2,000 recipes we had gathered, we finally selected those that we found to be the most popular today; that were representative of early Illinois cookery; and that were of some interest because of traditional use. We believe, therefore, that we have captured contemporary Illinois cooking and, in a smaller measure, the cooking of Illinois's past. All the recipes have been tested, adjusted, and translated into standard culinary vocabulary. We have made no effort to explain basic cooking techniques.

There is a difference in flavor when substitute ingredients are used in recipes; therefore, we have given specifics to those ingredients which are most often the victims of substitutions. Throughout the book we have used "Lucca" when a recipe calls for olive oil. Lucca, the name of the region in Italy where it is bottled, has a light, fresh flavor that oils from other regions of Italy do not have. Unsalted (sweet) butter is specified in most recipes because the use of salt should be controlled by the cook and not by the butter manufacturer. Food prepared with oleomargarine has an oleaginous taste and lacks that fresh sunshine flavor. Nuts, too, vary the flavor of the food in which they are used. Almonds will give a vastly different flavor from pecans, and pinenuts impart a flavor ethnicworlds apart from walnuts or cashews. We have indicated the kind of cream to use in most recipes. "Heavy" cream by USDA standards cannot contain less than thirty-six percent butterfat. If allowed to set for forty-eight hours in a cool place, it will thicken to a dollop consistency. "Light" cream contains not less than eighteen percent but not more than thirty percent butterfat. Half and Half is pasteurized milk and cream which is at least ten and a half percent but not more than eighteen percent butterfat. Half and Half, therefore, is not a substitute for "light" cream. The cook should find a dairy product store which carries both "heavy" and "light" cream.

The six divisions of Illinois are based on their physical geographic differences. The symbols we have used to represent the divisions are drawn from cultural artifacts which are identified with each of them. All the drawings were made from on-the-spot sketches or from photographs we had taken at times when it was impossible to make sketches. The heirloom photographs we have used were largely gathered from friends and family members who live throughout the state, and occasionally from an Illinoisan we did not know, but who hesitantly let us copy a precious family keepsake.

We wish to thank Joseph and Wynne Feeney, and Dr. Clyde E. Robbins for their tireless proofreading and support; Lockwood E. Wiley who listened and reminisced; Judy Solomon who typed and unscrambled; Bob and Alice O'Donnell, Margaret Leckel, Father Robert Anson, Paul Mueller, William ("Bud") Sherman, Bernice Sons, Helen Below Capdevielle, Aldona Remdzus Gallo, Brian and Sheila Huncke, Jim Conway, Jackie Karvanek, Chet Nichols, Doris Wilhelm, J. Sterling Morton Libraries, School District 100 Libraries, River Forest Public Library, Riverside Public Library, Chicago Public Library, Illinois State Historical Library, Biggsville County Library, and Robyn Browder, our editor, whose perception of our idea helped in its final production.

10

Introduction

Ten thousand years before Marquette's first visit, Indians lived along the streams and rivers of Illinois. Scant traces of their culture remain, only enough to pique the imagination, to tempt one to give full rein to speculation about their life style. Ancient campsites and burial grounds have offered occasional glimpses of primitive pottery, of fresh and salt water shells, and of semi-precious stones more common to the Gulf of Mexico or to the Atlantic Seaboard than to the Midwest. If one allows the mind to transcend time, he can fantasize a breed of people set apart, who traveled freely across an earthly paradise, taking from and giving back to nature all that was natural and good.

The mound-building Indians lived in Illinois before the Algonquin-Illini moved in from the East. We know little about them except for the mounds, some in animal shapes, and scattered traces of villages that have been unearthed. Similar utensils, pottery, and implements have linked the mound builders to Indians of the Southwest. Mineral and animal remains yielded by the burial mound complexes indicate that members of this group, too, were extensive travelers and traders. The contents of the mounds have been scrutinized by modern scientists who have analyzed the skeletal remains and the carefully placed artifacts in an attempt to determine their origin and significance. Both the animal effigy mounds and burial mounds left by these pre-Illini Indians are mysteries yet to be completely unraveled. They rise like giant specters above the land which surrounds them, ancient reminders of a past shrouded by the mists of a lost culture, monumental remains of a civilization which took from the earth only that which it could return to the earth.

The Michigamea, the Moingwena, the Tamaroa, the Peoria, the Cahokia, and the Kaskaskia tribes of Indians were living in Illinois when Père Jacques Marquette first passed through. These tribes were all Algonquin, and Marquette had no trouble in communicating with them in that language. The name Illinois is a French adaptation of Illiniwek, the name that the Indians called themselves. It means "The Men." In his journal, Marquette wrote, "When one speaks the word 'Illinois' it is as if one said in their language, 'the men,' as if the other Savages were looked upon by them merely as animals. It must be admitted that they have an air of humanity which we have not observed in the other nations that we have seen upon our route."

Considerable mobility characterized many of the tribes in the Midwest. The agronomic nature of the Illini was perhaps one of the reasons why they established and maintained large encampments for long periods of time. When European infiltration into the Illinois Territory began, large well-established Indian villages were flourishing near what is now Peoria, at Starved Rock, on the Rock River, and at other sites. The villages consisted of a number of long oval lodges in which as many as five families lived. The floors were covered with mats and the overhead structures were made of uprights of tall tree trunks and branches covered with woven mats.

These Indians thrived on mammals, birds, and fish from the surrounding forests and streams, and nuts, beans, corn, melons, squash, and pumpkins for which they foraged or which they had cultivated themselves. Cooking utensils were made mostly of wood. Some mammal craniums were used as bowls, and mammal stomachs were used for boiling pouches. Native herbs were collected for medicinal purposes as well as for food. The diet was rich and the food plentiful. There was never famine for the Illini, for the earth provided.

The Indians were deeply religious in a manner which the European intruders could not understand. Indian culture was rich in legends, customs, and practices based on an innocent naturalism. This was hardly compatible with European classical theology and philosophy. In the eyes of the Europeans, the Indians were scandalously polygamous while in the mind of the Indian each man simply took as many wives as he could comfortably support. Words such as "polygamous," "marry," "wife," and "husband" were charged with European meanings which had no reality for the Illini. The Indian way of life was so foreign to the European experience that the Europeans could do no better than translate what they thought they saw and heard into European concepts. Consequently, much of what we know of the Illini has been filtered through the distortion of the manners and mores of so-called Western Civilization.

The Indians of Illinois accepted themselves as a part of nature;

so they lived in harmony with the land philisophically and physically. They are all gone; no trace of them remains except in their earthworks and in their mouldering bones, but they will not be forgotten because they were The Illini, The Men!

The Great American Bottom

The Great American Bottom extends roughly from Alton to Chester. Beginning just below the confluence of the Illinois River and the Mississippi River, this crescent of rich, lush farmland was once the flood plain of the Mississippi. Even though dams, levees, and other sophisticated drainage systems have reclaimed it from the surging waters which once filled its curving oxbows and swampy morasses, the American Bottom has lost none of its enthralling beauty.

Describing the Bottom during an 1843 trip through it in his *American Notes*, Charles Dickens said:

> We had a pair of very strong horses, but traveled at the rate of little more than a couple of miles an hour, through one unbroken slough of black mud and water. It had no variety but in depth. Now it was only half over the wheels, now it hid the axle-tree and now the coach sank down in it almost to the windows. The air resounded in all directions with the loud chirping of frogs, who, with the pigs...had the whole scene to themselves.

Dickens was traveling through the Great American Bottom during the drenching spring floods, and his impressions are somewhat exaggerated. Most of the year the flood plain was a paradise for northern or southern migrating birds. Great white herons swooped over the low-lying swampland where the hoarse and bawdy calls of ducks and geese echoed in the stillness. Smaller winged visitors such as grouse, quail, and colorful warblers, like the native cardinal, darted in and out of the rushes and other river growth, while the call of the shypoke shrilled through the dampening air as it dipped and glided over the water below. There were no pheasants, for those birds were not successfully introduced from China into Illinois until the early decades of the Twentieth Century. Native mammals sported and foraged in the foliage at the periphery of the clear fresh waters which supported an extraordinary variety of aquatic life including turtles, eels, fish, and shellfish.

Indians disdained the endless prairie above the bottom land and made their home here where food was plentiful and shelter could be had beneath the cliffs, in the warm coves that fringed the flood plain, and under the limestone bluffs which signaled the beginning of the flatlands extending to the east.

> As we descended the river we saw high rocks with hideous monsters painted on them, and upon which the bravest Indians dare not look. They are as large as a calf, with head and horns like a goat; their eyes red; beard like a tiger; and a face like a man's. Their tails are so long that they pass over their heads and between their fore legs, under their belly, and ending in a fish's tail. They are painted red, green, and black.

Thus Père Marquette described the Piasa birds, the fearsome creatures which turned away fainthearted interlopers. One depiction remains and guards the northern entrance to the Great American Bottom at Alton. The Indians wanted no trespassers in their paradise.

But, undaunted by the frightening Piasa birds or the quivering swamps along the churning Mississippi, they came, the first European settlers of the Bottom, the French voyageur trappers. For the Great American Bottom was vital to their operation. Up the Illinois and across the Chicago Portage they came to travel north and east to the Atlantic. Down the Mississippi they went to travel south to New Orleans and the Gulf. Over and up the wide Missouri they floated to reach the seemingly endless fur trapping lands to the west, finally pushing onward to the Pacific Ocean. Here, indeed, was the central habitable location to form a base of operations and from which to open the sprawling North American continent to settlement.

At the time of their arrival in the seventeenth century, the French began to discover the Indian legacy throughout these Great American Bottom lands. The Cahokia Mounds west of Collinsville were puzzling to both the French and later settlers. The central mound, known as Monk's Mound was named after the Trappist monks who settled there in 1809. This truncated pyramid with four terraces, 104 feet wide and 1,000 feet long, is the largest man-made earth work in the world. Recent excavations at the mound site indicate that the area may have been a "Woodhenge," an Indian astronomical observatory to foretell the coming of eclipses and the changing of the seasons.

Other Indian legacies which have astounded settlers since their discovery are the rock shelters at Modoc near Chester. Here, under the vaulting limestone bluffs which soar above them, the Indians lived for thousands of years. When visited today, the shelters are eerie reminders of the past. No rain water touches their footing in the bottom land. The soft powdery earth billows up with each step. Small shells of long-ago snail species and clam shells from the distant rivers are scattered here and there. Habitation is sparse in this area, and the visitor can feel and see what it must have been like 10,000 years ago.

The French, too, have left their stamp on the land and culture of this terrain. At the town of Cahokia, the first church in Illinois still stands. Built in 1799, the Church of the Holy Family has been preserved and restored as close to its original state as possible. Entering it, one leaves the present and journeys back to another time. Votive lights flicker in the dimness of the interior illuminating testaments in French to the religious fervor of long ago worshippers while here and there saintly images stare with timeless eyes from their places on the walls.

Not far from the church stands the Cahokia Courthouse, reportedly the first house to have been built in Illinois. Its sturdy upright palisade construction and broad sweeping verandah clearly reflect the style of the early French settlers who found their way to Illinois up the Mississippi from the warm climes of the Gulf of Mexico.

Belleville lies astride the steep bluffs at the eastern edge of the Great American Bottom. The land in these environs was a promotion of Illinois Territorial Governor Ninian Edwards. It developed as a rival to the older settlement of Cahokia, finally outstripping Cahokia in political importance to become the seat of St. Clair County. Its emergence as a coal producing center in the mid-nineteenth century drew many German immigrants. The sons and daughters of these early residents make up a large share of its population today.

North of Modoc, tucked back away from any modern road is Fort de Chârtres which was once the strongest French fortress in the entire Mississippi Valley. First built in 1720, the fort was destroyed and rebuilt in 1753, only to be destroyed again. The foundations and grounds of the fort complex, carefully masked by a sentinal line of trees, remain as a tantalizing reminder of a glorious past. The mist swirling in from the river cloaks the terrain eerily, and the susceptible visitor can almost feel the hushed activities of those long-ago French guardians of this prized territory.

The Pierre Menard Mansion situated between Chester and Modoc was built in 1802. Menard was the first officer of the Illinois Territorial Legislature and the first Lieutenant Governor of Illinois. The charm and sophistication of this graceful old home with its authentic furnishings commands an impressive though distant view of the river, which in flood plain times lapped at the very door of the mansion.

The little town of Prairie de Rocher, not far from Modoc, is a relic of one of the bitter disappointments suffered by the French in an eager attempt to realize their dreams of empire on the North American continent. The little town was established in anticipation of great expansion in the New World. But the "Mississippi Bubble," John Law's great plan to return the French economy to financial stability, burst. Prairie de Rocher became simply another French outpost, never more than a small farming community scarcely distinguishable from its counterparts which, with less ambitious beginnings, sprang up around it in the bountiful Bottom.

There is a sense of "Middle Earth" about the Great American Bottom. Friendly ghosts of the past comfortably cohabit this historic land with exponents of industry and progress which represent modern day Illinois. Although the surface activity is late twentieth century, one has only to scratch that surface to reveal the ecology, geography, and geneology of Illinois as it was, as it is, and as it always will be.

Appetizers

The Church of the
Holy Family—Cahokia

Spiced Cheese Ball

Yield: 8 servings
1 cup grated Cheddar cheese
1 8-ounce package cream cheese
½ cup chopped chutney
2 teaspoons curry

½ teaspoon dry mustard
Salt and pepper to taste
6 ounces slivered almonds, toasted
   and chopped

Cream cheese until softened. Add chutney and spices. Mix well.
Shape into a ball. Roll in almonds. Serve with party crackers.

Glen Carbon was founded by the Madison Coal Company and named after that carboniferous substance. When the mines closed in 1931, the village was left with no industry as it remains today.

Cheese Ball

Yield: 1 ball

1 8-ounce package cream cheese, at
   room temperature
¼ pound crumbled Bleu cheese, at
   room temperature
½ pound sharp Cheddar cheese,

   grated
1 medium onion, minced
1 tablespoon Worcestershire sauce
½ cup chopped pecans
Parsley, finely chopped, for coating

Beat cheeses with an electric mixer until well mixed. Add onion and
Worcestershire sauce and beat well. Stir in nuts. Chill 3 to 4 hours.
Shape mixture into a ball and roll in parsley. Chill until firm.

> *Not a trace of Benbowe City remains. It was a construction camp and
> had all the attributes and faults of a lawless town of the Old West.
> Standard Oil bought its site and tore down every building and dwelling to
> make room for a large refinery.*

Ham and Cheese Ball

Yield: About 2½ cups

4 ounces shredded Cheddar cheese,
   at room temperature
8 ounces cream cheese, at room
   temperature

1 4½-ounce can deviled ham
½ cup chopped black olives
½ cup chopped pecans
Parsley flakes for coating

Blend cheese together. Add ham and black olives. Chill. Shape into a
ball and roll in chopped nuts and parsley flakes. Serve with crackers.

> *Poag in Madison County is the largest muskmelon growing region in
> the state. The drained Bottom Land's rich soil produces melons of prize-
> winning size and quality.*

Sherried Cheese

Yield: 4 cups

1 pound sharp Cheddar cheese,
   grated
¼ pound butter, at room temperature
¼ teaspoon dry mustard

Dash hot pepper sauce
½ cup dry sherry
1 cup chopped pecans

Place cheese in mixing bowl. Add remaining ingredients except nuts
and whip until smooth. Pack into a large crock. Cover with nuts,

pressing them firmly into cheese mixture. Cover with foil. Refrigerate.

> *Brooklyn was once the largest all-black community in the state. It was platted in 1837 and originally named Lovejoy. Nine railroads converge here today.*

Sherry Cheese Paté

Yield: 8 servings

6 ounces cream cheese, at room
  temperature
1 cup shredded sharp Cheddar
  cheese
4 teaspoons sherry

½ teaspoon curry powder
¼ teaspoon salt
1 8-ounce jar chutney, minced
2 scallions, chopped

Beat together cream cheese, Cheddar cheese, sherry, curry powder, and salt. Spread on a serving platter. Chill until firm. At serving time, spread with chutney and sprinkle with scallions. Serve with cocktail crackers.

21

> *Sugar Loaf is listed on no map of Illinois. It is an Indian-built mound of earth on the bluff just north of Collinsville. From here the Indians could survey their lands, the prairie to the east, and the fertile Bottom to the west.*

Cheese Cake Appetizer

Yield: about 4 cups

2 cups crushed cheese crackers
1 3-ounce package cream cheese, at
  room temperature
2 cups sour cream
½ cup chopped celery
¼ cup chopped green pepper
½ cup chopped pimiento-stuffed

  olives
¼ cup chopped capers
2 tablespoons chopped onion
1½ teaspoons Worcestershire sauce
1 teaspoon salt
4 drops hot pepper sauce

Butter bottom and sides of angel food cake pan and press on some cracker crumbs. Blend the cream cheese and sour cream; add remaining ingredients to sour cream and mix thoroughly. Spread mixture about ½ inch thick on pan bottom. Put in remaining cracker crumbs, then the rest of the sour cream mixture. Cover and refrigerate for 24 hours. Turn out on a tray. Serve with crackers.

Monroe City has had a long and honorable history at the edge of the Great Bottom as James' Mill, Monrovia, Noser, and Woodville.

Baked Cheese Dip

Yield: 1½ cups

1 2½-ounce jar chipped beef
1 8-ounce package cream cheese, at
 room temperature
3 tablespoons minced onion

3 tablespoons minced green pepper
2 tablespoons light cream
½ cup sour cream
¼ teaspoon pepper

Preheat oven to 350 degrees F. Cut chipped beef into small pieces. Whip cream cheese well; add cut up chipped beef, onion, green pepper, cream, sour cream, and pepper. Put in a 1-quart casserole and bake 20 minutes. Serve with corn chips.

Venice, part of the Granite City complex, was first platted in 1841 and got its name because its streets were so often flooded by the Mississippi.

22

Canoes on the River

Stuffed Cocktail Biscuits

Yield: about 2 dozen

1 cup biscuit mix
1 cup grated sharp Cheddar cheese
3 tablespoons light cream
2 tablespoons butter, melted

¼ teaspoon thyme
¼ teaspoon sweet basil
24 pimiento-stuffed green olives

Preheat oven to 400 degrees F. Combine first 6 ingredients. Mold a teaspoon of dough around each olive. Bake for 12 to 15 minutes.

Roxana is the home of a giant Shell Oil Refinery which was established in 1917. The not unpleasant smell of oil gives the town a distinctive odor, and the burn pipes and round oil domes give its skyline a futuristic look at night.

Cheese Crisps

Yield: 3 dozen

1 cup (2 sticks) butter, at room
    temperature
2 cups grated sharp cheese
2 cups flour

1 teaspoon salt
¼ teaspoon cayenne
2 cups crisped rice cereal

Cream together butter and cheese. Add flour, salt, and cayenne. Fold in rice cereal. Chill. Preheat oven to 350 degrees F. Drop by teaspoonfuls on cookie sheets. Bake for 15 minutes.

New Hanover, originally called Hanover, is now part of the Waterloo complex of towns and villages. It had its own post office in 1875, but it was discontinued in 1917.

Cheese Nibbles

Yield: 6 dozen

½ cup (1 stick) butter, at room
    temperature
1 cup grated sharp Cheddar cheese
1 cup flour

1 teaspoon salt
¾ cup chopped pecans
1½ teaspoons Worcestershire sauce
1½ cups crisped rice cereal

Preheat oven to 400 degrees F. Mix together butter and Cheddar cheese. Add flour, salt, pecans, Worcestershire sauce, and cereal.

Mix well. Roll into balls. Place close together on a cookie sheet. Flatten with a fork. Bake 10 minutes until lightly browned.

The East St. Louis Levee acts as a protective barrier for ninety-six square miles of Bottom that before its construction were swampy marshes. Now rich fields of corn, soy beans, and horseradish replace the sodden soil.

Cheese Temptations

Yield: 9 dozen
½ pound grated Cheddar cheese
½ pound (2 sticks) butter, at
   room temperature
2 cups flour

¼ teaspoon red pepper or a dash of
   hot pepper
1 egg white, slightly beaten

Preheat oven to 425 degrees F. Blend cheese and butter. Gradually work in flour and pepper. Roll out on floured board to ¼ inch thickness. Cut into 1-inch rounds, brush each with egg white. Place on unbuttered cookie sheet. Bake for 6 to 8 minutes.

24

Fort de Chârtres in Randolph County was first built of wood and was one of the finest forts in the country. When the British took possession of it in 1763, it was renamed Fort Cavendish. It has been partially reconstructed as a state memorial.

Olive Cheese Puffs

Yield: 24 pieces
1 cup grated sharp cheese
3 tablespoons butter
½ cup flour

¼ teaspoon salt
½ teaspoon paprika
24 stuffed olives

Combine all ingredients except olives into a dough. Wrap 1 teaspoon dough around each olive. Chill. Preheat oven to 400 degrees F. Bake on unbuttered cookie sheets for 10 to 15 minutes or until brown.

> *Bluff Road runs from Edwardsville to French Village, tight against the base of the ancient banks of the Mississippi. Before the flood plain was reclaimed, it was the only dry passage through this area of the Bottom.*

Cheese Fondue

Yield: 4 servings
1 garlic clove, split
1 cup dry white wine
1 pound Swiss cheese, grated
2 tablespoons cornstarch
1 teaspoon rosemary

4 tablespoons Kirsch
Freshly ground black pepper to taste
2 loaves French bread, cut in 1-inch
 cubes

Rub fondue pot with garlic. Add wine and heat on stove until bubbles begin to rise. Do not boil. Toss cheese with cornstarch and rosemary. Add to wine, a handful at a time, cooking over heat until cheese is melted and smooth, stirring constantly with a wooden spoon. Stir in Kirsch and sprinkle with pepper. Light burner; set pot on unit. Dip bread cubes into mixture with fondue forks.

> *At the confluence of the Wood River and the Mississippi, directly east of the confluence of the Mississippi and Missouri Rivers, is the Lewis and Clark Memorial Park. From here Lewis and Clark launched their exploratory expedition of the Pacific Northwest.*

Flaming Cheese

Yield: 6 servings
1 pound soft kasseri or kefalotiri
 cheese
2 tablespoons butter or margarine,

melted
2 tablespoons brandy
¼ lemon

Heat broiler. Cut cheese into three wedges; arrange on a buttered pan. Pour melted butter on cheese. Broil 4 to 6 inches from heat until cheese is bubbly and light brown. Cut cheese wedges in half and arrange on six fireproof serving plates. Pour brandy quickly over hot cheese; ignite immediately. Squeeze juice from lemon over cheese as flame begins to die. Serve.

Cheese in Pastry

Yield: 1 dozen

2 pounds dry curd cottage cheese
2 eggs
4 tablespoons melted butter

½ small onion, minced
4 tablespoons sugar
Salt to taste

Crust

2 cups flour
¼ teaspoon salt

½ cup (1 stick) butter
½ cup minus 1 tablespoon cold water

Place cheese in a mixing bowl. Blend in eggs. Sauté onion in butter until the onion is transparent; add to cheese. Add sugar and salt to taste.

Blend flour, salt, butter, and water. Preheat oven to 425 degrees F. Divide dough into twelve sections. Roll each piece thinly. Place a generous spoonful of cheese mixture in the center and pinch dough together over it. Place on a buttered cookie sheet. Brush each thoroughly with melted butter. Bake for 20 to 25 minutes, or until browned. Serve with sugar and sour cream.

Cheese Croquettes

Yield: 6 servings

1 pound cottage cheese
1 tablespoon sugar
¼ cup flour

1 egg
¼ teaspoon salt
Flour for coating

Drain cheese. Add remaining ingredients except for flour and shape into croquettes. Roll in flour. Fry in deep fat at 375 degrees F. until browned. Serve with sour cream.

Polynesian Rib Kabobs

Yield: 8 to 10 servings

3 pounds small back ribs or spare ribs, cut in 2 to 2½-inch pieces
¼ cup brown sugar

2 teaspoons liquid smoke
Polynesian Barbecue Sauce

Polynesian Barbecue Sauce

½ cup soy sauce
½ cup catsup
3 tablespoons brown sugar

1 teaspoon ground ginger
1 teaspoon accent

Rub ribs on both sides with liquid smoke and sugar; let stand 2 hours. Brush with sauce, and let stand an hour longer. Preheat oven to 450 degrees F. Place ribs meaty side up on a rack in a shallow pan. Bake for 15 minutes. Spoon off fat. Lower heat to 350 degrees F. and continue baking 1 hour or until done, turning ribs and brushing with barbecue sauce a few times.

Mix sauce ingredients; let stand overnight before using.

27

Kabob Appetizers

Yield: 2 dozen

½ cup soy sauce
1 teaspoon ground ginger
1 teaspoon sugar
2 garlic cloves, crushed
1 pound sirloin steak, 1 inch thick, cut

into 24 cubes
1 8-ounce can pineapple cubes
1 8-ounce jar pimiento-stuffed green olives

Combine soy sauce, ginger, sugar, and garlic. Add steak cubes. Cover. Marinate overnight. Drain steak; place on wooden appetizer stick one steak cube and one pineapple chunk. Continue until all are skewered. Broil 3 minutes. Turn; broil 3 minutes more. Add olive to each stick; serve immediately.

> At Cahokia Mounds on the flood plain of the Mississippi stands the largest man-made earthwork in the world: Monks Mound. Other mounds surround it, giving the Bottom a palpable link with the past.

28

Interior of Pierre Menard House—Fort Kaskaskia State Park

Steak Tartare

Yield: 8 servings

1 pound beef tenderloin, ground
1 egg yolk
1 teaspoon Worcestershire sauce
1 teaspoon brandy
1 teaspoon capers
4 pimiento olives, thinly sliced
Juice of half a lemon

4 tablespoons grated onion
1 teaspoon salt
½ teaspoon pepper
¼ teaspoon dry mustard
2 teaspoons minced parsley
1 tablespoon anchovy paste, optional

Combine all ingredients; thoroughly blend to a paste-like consistency. Spread on platter. Serve chilled with rye rounds.

The 650-pound Liberty Bell of the West was a gift by Louis XV to the French colonists in Illinois. It was rung in joy when George Rogers Clark liberated Kaskaskia from British rule. It hangs there now in a memorial building.

Rye Appetizers

Yield: 5 dozen

1 3-ounce package sliced smoked
  beef, chopped
4 ounces (1 cup) shredded natural
  Cheddar cheese
1 can pitted ripe olives, drained and

  chopped
1 cup mayonnaise
1 11-ounce box pumpernickel
  crackers

Preheat oven to 375 degrees F. Combine ingredients and spread on crackers. Bake 5 to 7 minutes.

Waterloo was first settled in 1781 and is considered to be the oldest "American" settlement in Illinois. It gets its name from the defeat of Napolean at Waterloo in 1815.

Dried Beef Dip

package dried beef   room temperature
our cream   ¼ cup chopped green pepper
nce package cream cheese, at   3 tablespoons chopped onions

eheat oven to 350 degrees F. Combine all ingredients. Heat for 20 minutes. Serve in a fondue dish with crackers.

> *Merrimac is a tiny settlement in Monroe County which was left behind when main-traveled roads were moved to the prairie above the Great Bottom.*

Beef Cup Appetizer

Yield: 10 servings
¾ pound lean ground beef
½ cup barbecue sauce
1 tablespoon minced onion
2 tablespoons brown sugar

1 8-ounce can refrigerator tender, flakey biscuits
¾ cup shredded, aged Cheddar cheese

Brown meat; drain; add sauce, onion, and sugar. Preheat oven to 400 degrees F. Separate biscuit dough; with each biscuit form a cup in unbuttered muffin tin. Press dough on bottom and sides. Spoon meat mixture into cups; sprinkle with cheese. Bake about 14 minutes.

> *Kaskaskia was founded in 1703 as a Jesuit mission and became an important French village. In 1763 Kaskaskia was under British rule. In 1778 George Rogers Clark captured the village, and it became part of Virginia. Kaskaskia was the first state capital of Illinois. By 1910 floods had destroyed the old settlement.*

Pizza Pinwheels

Yield: 8 slices
2 loaves frozen white bread dough
1½ pounds ground beef
Salt and pepper to taste
1 medium onion, chopped
½ pound mushrooms, sliced
4 tablespoons butter

½ teaspoon sweet basil
½ teaspoon fennel seeds
1 15-ounce can tomato sauce
8 ounces Mozzarella cheese, grated
Melted butter for brushing

Knead bread into a soft ball. Place in a large buttered bowl; cover and let rise in a warm place until doubled. Sauté ground beef, salt, pepper, onion, and mushrooms in butter. Drain. Add basil, fennel seeds, and tomato sauce. Simmer 5 minutes. Turn bread onto floured board and gently roll into a 10-by-14-inch rectangle. Leaving 3 inches empty on one end, spread remaining dough with meat sauce. Sprinkle with cheese. Roll dough toward empty end. Fold ends under slightly and pinch to seal. Place lengthwise on a cookie sheet and cut 3 diagonal slits in the top. Brush with butter. Cover and refrigerate 1 hour. Preheat oven to 350 degrees F. Place in oven and bake 55 minutes. Remove and slice.

> *Grafton, snuggled tightly between the Mississippi and the bluff, with Elsah forms the very top point of the Great Bottom. Grafton was settled before 1834 and was first called Musick's Ferry.*

Pizza Bread

Yield: 12 slices

1 loaf Vienna bread
1 pound ground beef
¾ cup hot chili sauce

1 teaspoon salt
⅛ teaspoon pepper
½ cup shredded Mozzarella cheese

Preheat oven to 375 degrees F. Cut bread in half lengthwise. Mix beef, chili sauce, salt, and pepper. Spread evenly on each half of bread. Broil 12 minutes. Remove from broiler and sprinkle with cheese. Return to broiler until cheese bubbles. Remove and slice diagonally into serving pieces. Garnish with parsley and radishes.

> *Collinsville was settled in 1817 by the Collins Brothers who established a store, a blacksmith shop, a shoe shop, a wagon shop, a sawmill, a distillery, and a small church. Collinsville spills over the bluff into the Bottom.*

Meatballs in Wine Sauce

Yield: 4 servings

1 pound ground beef
¾ cup breadcrumbs
1 small onion, minced
1 egg, beaten
1 teaspoon chopped mint leaves
½ teaspoon allspice
¾ cup milk

1 teaspoon salt
3 tablespoons flour
4 tablespoons butter
2 cups red wine
1 cup water
Salt and pepper to taste

Combine meat, crumbs, onion, egg, mint leaves, allspice, milk, and salt. Shape into small balls. Roll in flour and drop into hot oil in skillet, a few at a time. Brown well and put into a bowl. Make a roux of the flour and butter; stir in wine, water, salt, and pepper. Cook and stir until smooth. Add meatballs and simmer about 20 minutes.

> *Wartburg, whose first post office was established in 1881, is a tiny settlement of about fifty people. It was first known as Beaver Pond.*

Barbecued Cocktail Meat Balls

Yield: 5 dozen

1 pound ground beef
¾ cup instant dry milk
½ cup water
1½ cups soft breadcrumbs

1 medium onion, minced
1 egg, beaten
½ teaspoon salt
Dash pepper

Sauce

½ lemon, sliced
1 small onion, minced
Dash chili powder
1½ teaspoons celery seed
2 tablespoons firmly packed brown
   sugar

2½ tablespoons vinegar
1 teaspoon Worcestershire sauce
Few drops tabasco sauce
½ cup Ketchup
¾ cup hot water

Combine ingredients. Shape into ¾-inch balls. Place in a 15-by-10-by-1-inch pan. Preheat oven to 325 degrees.

Combine sauce ingredients. Pour over meat balls. Bake 25 minutes.

Wanda had its own post office in 1859, but since then it has become a rural delivery route from Edwardsville. It was also known as Old Salem and Gillham.

Deviled Meat Balls

Yield: 6 servings

1½ slices fresh bread
1 pound ground beef
1 egg, slightly beaten
2½ tablespoons minced green
   pepper
1 teaspoon horseradish

1 teaspoon dry mustard
2 teaspoons Worcestershire sauce
½ teaspoon salt
Pepper to taste
¼ cup ketchup
2 tablespoons butter or shortening

Gravy

2 tablespoons flour
1½ cups light cream
½ teaspoon salt
Pepper to taste

½ teaspoon Worcestershire sauce
½ teaspoon concentrated meat
   extract

33

Break bread into fine crumbs. Add to ground beef with egg and green pepper. Mix well. Stir together horseradish, mustard, Worcestershire sauce, salt, pepper, and ketchup. Add to meat mixture. Shape into 12 balls. Melt butter in skillet. Add meat balls and brown evenly for 15 to 20 minutes.

Stir flour into drippings in pan. Cook until it bubbles. Add cream, salt, pepper, Worcestershire sauce, and meat extract. Cook, stirring constantly, until thickened. Add meat balls, cover skillet and cook 10 minutes.

Swansea in St. Clair County was named after the seacoast town in Wales. Once the village was known for its brick yards and coal mines, but today it is largely a "bedroom" community for nearby Scott Air Force Base.

Sausage Puffs

Yield: 3½ dozen
1 pound pork sausage
1 pound Cheddar cheese, grated
2½ to 3 cups biscuit mix

Preheat oven to 400 degrees F. Combine all ingredients. Form into balls 2 inches in diameter. Bake for 15 minutes. Serve hot.

> *Caseyville was a going concern in 1853 when its first post office opened. It was named for Zadok Casey, Lieutenant Governor of Illinois in 1830.*

Homemade Summer Sausage

Yield: 2 1-pound sausages
4 pounds hamburger
4 teaspoons quick cure meat salt
½ teaspoon garlic salt
1 teaspoon dry mustard
1 teaspoon liquid smoke
1½ teaspoons coarse ground pepper

Mix ingredients thoroughly and form into 2 rolls. Wrap tightly in foil and refrigerate 24 hours. Preheat oven to 350 degrees F. Put 2 inches of water in a pan. Place foil wrapped meat in water. Bake 1 hour. Remove foil. Let meat drain and cool. Refrigerate.

> *Alorton was incorporated as a village in 1944. Cahokia Downs Race Track is here, as are lumber mills, a chemical company, and a grease plant. Alorton was formerly known as Alcoa.*

Sweet-Sour Sausages

Yield: 4 to 6 servings
1 8-ounce can pineapple chunks
2 8-ounce packages pre-cooked
   sausage links
4 teaspoons cornstarch
⅛ teaspoon salt
½ cup maple-flavored syrup
⅓ cup water
⅓ cup vinegar
1 large green pepper, cut in squares
½ cup drained maraschino cherries

Drain pineapple, reserving syrup. Cut sausages in thirds crosswise; brown in skillet. Blend cornstarch, salt, reserved pineapple syrup, maple syrup, water, and vinegar. Heat to boiling, stirring constantly, add pineapple, sausage, pepper, and cherries. Cook 5 minutes. Keep warm in chafing dish.

Liver Sausage Nut Ball

Yield: 8 to 10 servings
1 pound liver sausage
1/4 cup mayonnaise
2 tablespoons dill pickle juice
1 1/2 teaspoons Worcestershire sauce
2 drops hot pepper sauce
1/2 teaspoon garlic salt
1 8-ounce package cream cheese, at room temperature
1/3 cup minced onion
1/2 cup chopped cashews

Mash sausage until smooth. Add mayonnaise, dill pickle juice, Worcestershire sauce, hot pepper sauce, garlic salt and $1/3$ of the cream cheese. Blend until smooth. Stir in onion. Pack firmly into a 2-cup mixing bowl. Chill for several hours. Turn out onto a serving tray. Frost with remaining cream cheese. Chill well. Just before serving, cover with cashews.

35

Liverwurst-Cucumber Slices

Yield: 4 cups
2 8-ounce packages liverwurst spread
2 3-ounce packages cream cheese, at room temperature
2 cups minced radishes
3 tablespoons grated onion
4 large cucumbers

In a small bowl, mix the liverwurst and cream cheese until smooth. Stir in radishes and onion. Thickly slice cucumbers and spread mix on top of each slice. Refrigerate before serving.

Chopped Liver

Yield: 2 cups
1 pound chicken livers
1 to 2 onions, chopped
4 tablespoons chicken fat

3 hard-boiled eggs
Salt and pepper to taste

Sauté chicken livers and onions in chicken fat. Sprinkle with salt and pepper. Grind with the hard-boiled eggs. Form into a ball.

36

Liver-Cheese Paté in Aspic

Yield: 8 servings
¾ pound chicken livers
2 tablespoons butter
4 ounces Madeira
6 ounces cream cheese

Salt to taste
2 packages gelatin
2 9½-ounce cans chicken consomme

Sauté livers in the butter until browned. Mash with a fork. Blend with juices and Madeira until smooth. Mix with the cream cheese, salt to taste, and refrigerate. Soften and combine gelatin with consommé. Pour 1 tablespoon in an oiled mold and chill. Place paté, shaped in a ball, on top. Pour remaining consommé all around, and chill until firm and unmold. Serve with party crackers.

The Piasa Bird—Indian Rock Painting—Elsah

Chicken and Nut Puffs

Yield: 75 puffs
1 cup chicken broth
½ cup (1 stick) butter
1 cup flour
4 eggs
1 tablespoon parsley
2 teaspoons seasoned salt
2 teaspoons Worcestershire sauce
½ teaspoon paprika
⅛ teaspoon cayenne
1 5-ounce can boned chicken,
    drained and chopped
¼ cup chopped almonds

In a saucepan, combine broth and butter; bring to a boil. Stir in flour. Cook, beating until mixture leaves sides of pan and forms a smooth ball. Remove from heat. Preheat oven to 400 degrees F. Add eggs, one at a time, beating well after each until mixture is shiny. Stir in parsley, seasonings, chicken, and almonds. Drop by rounded teaspoon on unbuttered baking sheets. Bake for 18 minutes or until brown. Serve hot.

Chicken Wing Appetizer

Yield: about 15 pieces
3 pounds chicken wings or more
½ cup (1 stick) butter
1 cup soy sauce
1 cup brown sugar

¾ cup water
½ teaspoon dry mustard
¼ teaspoon cinnamon

Arrange wings in a shallow 11-by-7-by-2-inch baking pan. Heat butter, soy sauce, sugar, water, mustard, and cinnamon until butter and sugar melt. Cool. Pour over wings and marinate 2 hours. Preheat oven to 375 degrees F. Bake in same pan 1½ hours, turning occasionally. Drain on paper towels.

Rumaki

Yield: 1 dozen
6 chicken livers, cut in half
1 5-ounce can water chestnuts, cut into 12 slices

6 slices bacon, cut in half
¼ cup brown sugar

Oriental Sauce

¼ cup soy sauce
¼ cup vegetable oil
2 tablespoons ketchup

1 tablespoon vinegar
¼ teaspoon pepper
2 garlic cloves, crushed

Pour sauce over chicken livers and water chestnuts in baking dish. Cover dish with plastic wrap; refrigerate 4 hours. Remove chicken livers and water chestnuts from marinade. Wrap 1 liver and water chestnut slice in 1 piece of bacon; secure with a wooden toothpick. Roll in brown sugar. Broil 3 inches from heat 10 minutes, turning occasionally, until bacon is crisp.

Mix all sauce ingredients.

Ham Balls I

Yield: 3 dozen
1 cup cottage cheese
½ cup deviled ham
1 tablespoon prepared horseradish
¼ cup sour cream

¼ teaspoon salt
⅛ teaspoon pepper
½ cup chopped watercress
2 tablespoons chopped chives

Combine all ingredients except watercress and chives. Form into small balls and roll in a mixture of the watercress and chives. Chill and serve.

39

Ham Balls II

Yield: about 3½ dozen
1 pound ground ham
1½ pounds ground lean pork
2 cups dry breadcrumbs
2 eggs, beaten

1 cup light cream
¼ cup grated Romano cheese
Pepper and salt to taste

Sauce

1½ cups brown sugar
½ cup water

½ cup vinegar
1 teaspoon dry mustard

Preheat oven to 300 degrees F. Mix first 7 ingredients and roll into small balls. Bake 1 hour or until done.

Combine sauce ingredients and boil for 1 minute. Serve ham balls covered with sauce in chafing dish.

Edwardsville, the seat of Madison County, was platted in 1813 and named after Ninian Edwards, third governor of the state. Five other governors of Illinois had homes in Edwardsville: Edward Coles, Charles S. Deneen, John Reynolds, Thomas Carlin, and Thomas Ford.

Ham and Cheese Appetizers

Yield: 20 pieces

1 3-ounce package cream cheese, cubed
6 large pimiento-stuffed olives
2 tablespoons mayonnaise

½ teaspoon prepared mustard
Dash hot pepper sauce
4 thin slices cold boiled ham

Put first 5 ingredients in blender and mix until smooth. Spread mixture on ham slices. Roll each slice as for a jelly roll. Wrap in aluminum foil. Chill for 2 hours. Slice in ¼ inch slices. Place slices on small crackers to serve.

Chester is the seat of Randolph County and was settled in 1819 as a rival to Kaskaskia. The cartoon "Popeye" was created here and was based on local people. Chester was also known as Smith's Landing.

Prune Rumaki

Yield: 2 dozen
24 large prunes, pitted
12 water chestnuts, halved
12 strips bacon, halved

Preheat oven to 350 degrees F. Stuff each prune with half a water chestnut. Wrap each in ½ slice bacon. Secure with toothpick. Bake until bacon is crisp. Drain on paper toweling. Serve hot.

Kaskaskia Island is a memorial to old Kaskaskia and is the only piece of Illinois that lies west of the Mississippi. It is a remnant of the town which was inundated when the Mississippi moved into the channel of the Kaskaskia River.

Souse

Yield: 8 servings

3 pigs feet, about 2 pounds, scraped, washed, and cleaned
2 onions chopped
½ cup chopped celery

3 tablespoons cider vinegar
¾ teaspoon salt
Pepper to taste
5 thin slices lemon

Place feet in stew pan with onion and celery. Cover with cold water. Boil. Reduce heat and simmer until meat is tender and falls from the bones. Pick meat from the bones and strain liquid, which should measure a scant three cups. (If less add water.) Put meat and liquid in a bowl. Add vinegar, salt, pepper, and lemon slices. Chill overnight. Remove surplus fat from the top. Serve on a platter garnished with parsley.

Centreville was incorporated as a city in 1957. It is an example of the rapid settlement of the Bottom after World War II with the final drainage of the marshes.

41

Ford de Chârtres—Fort Chârtres State Park

Shrimp Mold Appetizer

Yield: 5 cups

1½ envelopes unflavored gelatin
½ cup cold water
1 cup hot undiluted tomato soup
1 8-ounce package cream cheese, at
   room temperature

1 cup mayonnaise
2 4-ounce cans shrimp, crumbled
1 cup chopped celery
¾ teaspoon chopped onion
¼ teaspoon tarragon

Soften gelatin in water and add to hot soup. Combine cheese and mayonnaise; stir into soup mixture. Add remaining ingredients. Pour into oiled 2 -quart fish mold and chill 2 or 3 hours. Unmold and serve with crackers.

> *Dupo's name is a contraction of Prairie Du Pont, and it was incorporated as a village in 1907. Dupo is four and one-half miles long and only one thousand feet wide.*

Shrimp Puffs

Yield: 30 to 40 pieces

½ cup (1 stick) butter
1 onion, minced
1 6-ounce can shrimp

2 tablespoons curry powder
½ teaspoon cumin
2 cups quick biscuit dough

Melt butter and sauté onion until golden. Add shrimp which has been drained, rinsed, and mashed with a fork. Season to taste with curry powder and cumin; cook until flavors are blended. Make 1 recipe of biscuit dough. Roll out very thin and form into bite-size balls with a bit of shrimp mixture in the center. Fry in deep fat until golden.

> *Brooks, though on the map, is little more than a memory. Its first post office was established in 1887, but was discontinued in 1903. It lingers in the Bottom, a ghost of another time.*

Shrimp Toast

Yield: 6 servings
½ medium onion
½ pound raw shrimp, shelled and
   deveined
⅛ teaspoon ground ginger
½ teaspoon salt

Dash pepper
1 egg white
6 slices white bread, stale
½ cup fine, dry breadcrumbs
½ cup vegetable oil

Put onions and shrimp through food grinder or processor. Add ginger, salt, and pepper. Beat egg white lightly; combine with the shrimp mixture. Remove crusts from slices of bread and cut each slice diagonally. Spread shrimp mixture on bread triangles. Heap breadcrumbs on top, patting them down. Heat oil until very hot and fry shrimp toast for 1 minute on each side. Drain on paper towels and serve.

> *National City was known as National Stock Yards when its first post office opened in 1875. It was incorporated in 1907 with its present name.*

43

Quiche Appetizer

Yield: 12 servings
Pastry for 2-crust pie
¾ cup chopped cooked shrimp
¼ cup sliced scallion
4 ounces (1 cup) shredded Swiss
   cheese

½ cup mayonnaise
2 eggs
⅓ cup heavy cream
¼ teaspoon salt
¼ teaspoon sweet basil

Preheat oven to 400 degrees F. Roll pastry and cut into 12 4-inch circles. Fit into twelve 2½-inch muffin pan cups. Fill each with some shrimp, onion, and cheese. Beat remaining ingredients. Pour over cheese. Bake for 15 minutes or until browned.

> *The Goshen Road between Shawneetown and Edwardsville was completed in 1814. It was one of the most traveled roads of the early 1800s and was named after the tiny settlement of Goshen near Edwardsville.*

Crab Stuffed Mushrooms

Yield: 1½ to 2 dozen pieces

1 pound fresh mushrooms
5 tablespoons butter
½ cup fine dry breadcrumbs
2 eggs, beaten
1 tablespoon chopped parsley

1½ tablespoons snipped chives
¼ teaspoon nutmeg
Salt and pepper to taste
1 6-ounce package crabmeat

Preheat oven to 375 degrees F. Remove stems from mushrooms and chop. Heat butter in a skillet and sauté them. Combine other ingredients. Fill each mushroom cap with crab mixture. Bake in an 11-by-7-by-2-inch buttered pan 20 minutes.

> *The Cahokia Court House in Cahokia was first used as a private dwelling when it was built in 1737, but was used as a county building from 1793 to 1814. It is open for inspection.*

Smoked Oysters in Cheese

Yield: 14 servings

16-ounces cream cheese, at room
    temperature
1½ teaspoons Worcestershire sauce
1½ teaspoons lemon juice

½ teaspoon white pepper
1 cup sour cream
1 3⅔-ounce can smoked oysters,
    drained

Combine the cheese, Worcestershire, juice, pepper, and sour cream. Stir in oysters. Chill and serve with taco chips.

> *New Design is now a part of Burkesville and part of the larger area of Waterloo: New Design was founded in 1790.*

Oyster Kabobs

Yield: 8 servings

3 cups breadcrumbs
Salt and pepper, to taste
40 large oysters

3 eggs, slightly beaten
4 tablespoons melted butter

Mix crumbs, salt, and pepper. Drain oysters. Dip in eggs, then roll in crumb mixture until well coated. Place 5 oysters on each skewer and arrange skewers across the top of a pan. Pour a little butter on each oyster. Broil and brown quickly, about 3 or 4 minutes. Serve at once on skewers.

> *Burkesville, whose first post office was established in 1857 but is now discontinued, was known as Corne de Carl prior to that date.*

Clam and Cheese Ball

Yield: 26 servings

1 8-ounce can minced clams, drained
1 8-ounce package cream cheese, at room temperature
1 tablespoon lemon juice
2 teaspoons grated onion

1 teaspoon horseradish
¼ teaspoon salt
¼ teaspoon liquid smoke
½ cup chopped pecans
3 tablespoons snipped parsley

Combine all ingredients except nuts and parsley. Chill several hours. Shape in a ball. Roll in nuts and parsley. Serve with crackers.

> *Elsah, a charming village of houses made of native stone, was first known as Jersey Landing and was set up to rival St. Louis. It and Grafton make up the northern beginning point of the Bottom.*

Clam Filled Puffs

Yield: 4 dozen

2 6½-ounce cans clams
¾ cup water
⅔ cup butter
1½ cups flour
6 eggs

1 8-ounce package cream cheese, whipped
2 teaspoons chopped onions
Salt and pepper to taste
1 tablespoon parsley, chopped

Preheat oven to 400 degrees F. Reserving juice, drain clams. Heat clam juice, water, and butter to rolling boil. Stir in 1½ cups flour all at once. Let cool one minute. Beat in eggs, one at a time. Drop by teaspoon on cookie sheets and bake 30 minutes. Make slit in each puff. Combine cream cheese, onion, salt, pepper, parsley, and drained clams. Fill puffs.

Garrison Hill is in Fort Kaskaskia State Park. Here is all that remains of the early settlers of Kaskaskia whose caskets were removed to this location when the flood swamped the original site.

Anchovy Dip

Yield: 1 cup

½ cup (1 stick) butter
4 tablespoons Lucca olive oil
1-ounce tin anchovies

4 garlic cloves, crushed
Raw cauliflower, celery, carrots

Place first four ingredients in a fondue pan and heat until anchovies disintegrate. Cut the cauliflower into flowerettes, and the celery and carrots into sticks. Serve surrounding the fondue pan.

Prairie Du Rocher, meaning prairie of rocks, is one of the oldest towns in Illinois. Remnants of the culture of its first French settlers remain in names of residents, foods, and local celebrations. Prairie Du Rocher was founded in 1722.

Anchovy Cheese Spread

Yield: about 1 cup

1 8-ounce package cream cheese, at
  room temperature
¼ cup sour cream
4 tablespoons butter, at room
  temperature
2 teaspoons anchovy paste

2 teaspoons capers, drained
2 scallions, chopped
2 teaspoons caraway seeds
½ teaspoon dry mustard
2 tablespoons dry white wine

Place all ingredients in blender and whip until smooth. Chill and serve with thin slices of pumpernickel.

The Eads Bridge at East St. Louis was an architectural wonder when it was built back in 1869 to 1874. It was the first bridge to use steel and contained the longest fixed metal arch in the world.

Herring Mold

Yield: 3 cups

1 12-ounce jar herring fillets in wine sauce
2 slices white bread, trimmed
1 onion, sliced
1 apple, peeled, cored and sliced
3 hard cooked eggs, chopped
1 teaspoon sugar
1 teaspoon tarragon
3 tablespoons vinegar

Drain herring and rinse. Use onions from jar. Combine herring, bread, onion, and apple; blend until smooth. Add eggs, sugar, tarragon, and vinegar; blend again until smooth. Pack into a 3-cup mold. Chill. Unmold and serve with party bread.

> *The Kaskaskia River is also known as the Okaw from the French pronunciation "Aux Kaw Kaw." It was once the home of eel, mussels, and spoon-billed catfish, but in the wake of progress it is left with little but gar and carp.*

Beet-Herring Toss

Yield: 8 to 10 servings

1 12-ounce jar pickled beets, drained and chopped
1 7½-ounce jar pickled herring, drained and chopped
1 apple, peeled, cored, and diced
½ cup sour cream
4 tablespoons chopped onion
2 tablespoons pimiento-stuffed olives, chopped
2 dashes white pepper
Salt to taste

Toss all ingredients together gently but thoroughly. Chill 2 hours. Serve with cocktail bread.

> *Père Marquette State Park at the junction of the Illinois and Mississippi River at Grafton commemorates the explorer and provides one of the most striking views in Illinois.*

Herring Spread

Yield: 1 cup
2½ tablespoons heavy cream
Dash hot pepper sauce
3 tablespoons chopped chives
¼ teaspoon dill weed

6 ounces cream cheese, at room
  temperature
1 6-ounce jar marinated herring in
  wine sauce, drained

Blend all ingredients together until smooth, stirring occasionally.
Serve with crackers.

Columbia was settled before 1800; however, it is the German immigrants who moved here in the 1850s who give the city its flavor. There are still lederhosen, Bavarian costumes, and oompah bands to be seen at the annual Strassenfest.

Salmon Spread

Yield: 8 to 10 servings
1 10½-ounce can red salmon
1 cup mayonnaise
1 large onion, chopped
½ cup pickle relish, drained

Juice of 1 lemon
¼ teaspoon mace
½ teaspoon garlic powder

Mix together all ingredients except the salmon. Place salmon in a
shallow bowl and pour the mixture over it. Chill several hours.
Serve with crackers.

Ellisgrove is the southern terminus of St. Leo's Road. This area on the bluff has been settled since the early 1800s, but was not officially recognized until 1853 when it was called Ellis Grove.

Salmon Ball

Yield: 1 ball
15½ ounces canned salmon
1 8-ounce package cream cheese, at
  room temperature
1 tablespoon lemon juice

2 tablespoons grated onion
1 teaspoon horseradish
½ (scant) teaspoon liquid smoke
½ cup chopped cashews

Drain salmon. Remove skin and bones and flake. Add all remaining
ingredients except cashews. Blend well and chill. Form into a ball
and roll in cashews. Serve with assorted snack crackers.

> *Canteen Creek which winds through bottom land is an example of changing Illinois names. The creek was named for the settlement Cantine which was first called, by the French, Quentine.*

Taramasalata (Greek Fish Roe Dip)

Yield: 2 cups
3 ounces red fish roe
1 small onion, finely grated
⅔ cup Lucca olive oil

5 slices white bread, trimmed
Juice of 3 lemons

Mash roe and onion. Add 2 tablespoons olive oil. Beat to a smooth paste. Moisten bread with water and squeeze out excess. Beat mixture, alternately adding small bits of bread, oil, and lemon juice. Beat until creamy and pink. Serve as a dip with Greek bread.

> *Bloody Island, in East St. Louis, was a Mississippi sandbar used for illegal boxing bouts, cock fights, and duels. Charles Dickens visited there and proclaimed that its name was derived from a bloody duel whose participants shot each other to death "and some rational persons may think . . . they were no great loss to the community."*

Egg and Caviar Mold

Yield: 1 quart
18 hard cooked eggs, chopped
6 bacon slices, cooked, and crumbled
3 medium onions, chopped
½ cup (scant) mayonnaise

Salt and pepper to taste
1 cup sour cream
1 jar black caviar, drained
1 2-ounce jar red caviar, drained

Mix eggs, bacon, and onions with just enough mayonnaise to hold together. Season with salt and pepper. Pack in a large bowl. Chill overnight. Unmold onto a serving platter. Frost with sour cream. Spoon black caviar in a ring around the top; mound red caviar in the center. Serve with party bread.

> *Shadrach Bond was the first governor of Illinois. He was a resident of Kaskaskia and is buried in the Evergreen Cemetery in Chester, where a marble shaft marks his grave as a state memorial.*

Quiche Lorraine

Yield: 4 to 6 servings
6 slices bacon
1 unbaked 9-inch pie crust
¾ cup onions, thinly sliced
¾ cup chopped Swiss cheese
1½ cups heavy cream

3 eggs
3 tablespoons flour
¼ teaspoon salt
Dash pepper

Preheat oven to 350 degrees F. Fry bacon until crisp and crumble it. Sprinkle on crust. Sauté onion in bacon drippings until limp and sprinkle on crust. Add cheese. Blend cream, eggs, flour, salt, and pepper. Pour over all other ingredients. Bake until custard is set and top is golden brown, about 35 minutes.

> *Modoc, on St. Leo's Road, is the site of the Ancient Rock Shelters. It is now the home of about 150 people who farm the rich alluvial soil of the Great Bottom that was the long ago home of ancient Indians who lived off the fish, mammals, and fruits that the land provided.*

Spinach Dip

Yield: serves 8
1 10-ounce package chopped
  spinach, frozen
1 teaspoon salt
½ cup chopped parsley

2 cups mayonnaise
1 teaspoon chopped onion
1 garlic clove, crushed

Thaw spinach. Squeeze out water carefully. Mix spinach with other ingredients. Chill. Serve with fresh vegetables.

> *Roots was never officially named. Typical of areas served by a post office which had no other designation, mail came directly in the postmaster's name. So this settlement became known as Roots after its first postmaster, John P. Roots.*

Avocado Dip

Yield: 2 cups

2 ripe avocados, mashed
1½ tablespoons minced onion
1 garlic clove, minced
¼ teaspoon chili powder
¼ teaspoon salt

Dash pepper
⅓ cup mayonnaise
6 slices crisp cooked bacon, crumbled

Combine mashed avocado, onion, garlic, and seasonings in bowl. Spread top with mayonnaise, sealing to edges of bowl. Chill. To serve, stir in the mayonnaise and all but 1 tablespoon bacon. Top with additional crumbled bacon.

> *Horse Shoe Lake in Madison County is an oxbow of the Mississippi which is rapidly filling with vegetation. It was originally called Marais Mensoui and is a summer home for great white herons.*

Chili Con Queso Dip

Yield: 2 cups

1 medium onion, chopped
2 small jalapeno peppers, chopped
Dash each of salt, pepper, and garlic powder
½ teaspoon cumin

½ cup (1 stick) butter
1 heaping tablespoon flour
1 15-ounce can whole tomatoes, drained
1 pound American cheese, grated

Sauté onions, peppers, and seasonings in butter. Add flour to thicken. Stir in tomatoes. Gradually add cheese until melted and the dip is smooth.

> *The Jarrot House in Cahokia was built in 1798 of locally made bricks, with windows and doors imported from France. Its supporting timbers are of native black walnut.*

Bloody Mary Dip

Yield: 2 cups

2 cups sour cream
2 2½-ounce envelopes Bloody Mary
    Cocktail Mix

2 tablespoons chopped chives
1 teaspoon tarragon
2 tablespoons capers, drained

Combine all ingredients. Refrigerate. Serve as a dip for raw vegetables.

> *In 1800 with 266 residents, Bellefontaine was the third largest settlement in the Illinois country. Its site is now encompassed by the town of Waterloo.*

Coconut Fruit Dip

Yield: 1½ cups

1 cup sour cream
¼ cup flaked coconut
2 tablespoons chopped English

walnuts
3 tablespoons apricot preserves

52

Combine ingredients in a small bowl. Serve as a dip for fruits.

> *Harrisonville, whose post office existed for one hundred and one years (1810 to 1911), once had these charming names: Brashear's Fort, Carthage, and Walnut Grove.*

Eggplant Caviar

Yield: 2 cups

1 medium eggplant
1 cup onions, minced
1 4-ounce jar pimientos, minced

3 tablespoons Lucca olive oil
½ teaspoon sugar
Salt and pepper to taste

Preheat oven to 350 degrees F. Perforate top of eggplant 2 or 3 times with a fork and bake 45 minutes. Cool, peel, and chop. Add chopped onions and pimientos. Combine olive oil, sugar, salt, and pepper. Whip with a fork. Combine with eggplant mixture and blend well. Chill thoroughly.

> *The Pierre Menard Home was built in 1800 by the first Lieutenant Governor of the Illinois Territory. It is of French Colonial architecture and is open to the public.*

The Old Cahokia Courthouse

Stuffed Cherry Tomatoes

Yield: 2½ dozen
1 quart cherry tomatoes
¼ pound smoked salmon, chopped
1 onion, chopped
1 green pepper, chopped
½ teaspoon tarragon
⅛ teaspoon white pepper

Remove tops of cherry tomatoes. Scoop out seeds and pulp. Combine the pulp with other ingredients and stuff tomatoes. Chill thoroughly before serving.

Nameoki was named after an Indian tribe. Its first post office was established in 1876. It has now been absorbed by Granite City.

Asparagus Canapes

Yield: 12 servings
12 thin slices bread
12 thin slices packaged ham
Prepared mustard to taste

12 asparagus spears
2 tablespoons mayonnaise
2 tablespoons butter

Trim crust from bread and roll flat. Trim ham to fit bread slices and paint with mustard. Dip an asparagus spear, cut to fit bread, in mayonnaise; lay on ham and roll up. Spear with a toothpick and paint with butter. Broil until golden. Serve hot.

Maryville's first post office opened its doors in 1903. The village was incorporated in 1902 and serves Donkville and Winters.

Mushroom Canapes

Yield: 24 pieces
18 to 24 large mushrooms
3½ tablespoons butter
½ cup chopped onion
½ teaspoon salt
½ teaspoon pepper

1 garlic clove, crushed
1 tablespoon flour
6 tablespoons milk
½ cup breadcrumbs, buttered
½ cup Parmesan cheese

Preheat oven to 350 degrees F. Remove stems from mushrooms. Chop stems coarsely and sauté in butter and onion until onion is tender. Add salt, pepper, and garlic and simmer for 5 minutes. Stir in flour. Add milk. Fill mushroom caps with mixture and place in a buttered 9-by-9-inch baking dish. Mix breadcrumbs with Parmesan cheese and sprinkle over mushrooms. Bake for 15 minutes.

French Village's post office opened in 1841, but its history begins before statehood when the first house was erected and the village was called Petit Village Français.

Onion Butter Canapes

Yield: 4 dozen
24 slices white bread, trimmed
1 pound (4 sticks) butter, at room

temperature
2 envelopes dry onion soup mix

Preheat oven to 375 degrees F. Cut each slice of bread into 2 triangles. Cream butter and soup mix together. Spread on bread.

Place on unbuttered cookie sheet. Bake for 10 minutes or until brown.

> *Fort Kaskaskia State Park sits high on the bluff overlooking the confluence of the Kaskaskia and Mississippi Rivers. This is one of the most beautiful and melancholy vistas in Illinois.*

Artichoke Cheese Squares

Yield: 2 dozen

⅓ cup chopped onion
1 garlic clove, crushed
2 tablespoons butter
4 eggs, well beaten
1 14-ounce can artichoke hearts,
  drained and chopped

¼ cup coarse dry breadcrumbs
½ pound Cheddar cheese, shredded
2 tablespoons minced parsley
1 teaspoon salt
½ teaspoon oregano
¼ teaspoon pepper

Preheat oven to 325 degrees F. Sauté onion and garlic in butter. Add to eggs, artichoke hearts, crumbs, cheese, parsley, and seasonings. Turn into a buttered 11-by-7-by-1-inch pan. Bake for 30 minutes or until set. Cut into 1-inch squares and serve hot.

> *The Cahokia-Kaskaskia Trace linked the two settlements and Fort de Chârtres in a line down the Mississippi. The Trace was originally an Indian path.*

Pickled Mushrooms and Olives

Yield: 8 servings

2 pounds fresh mushrooms, sliced
⅓ cup Lucca olive oil
1½ cups white wine
2 tablespoons lemon juice
2 garlic cloves, halved

1¼ teaspoons salt
½ teaspoon pepper
½ teaspoon ground coriander
½ teaspoon thyme leaves
1 cup pimiento-stuffed olives, halved

Combine mushrooms, oil, white wine, lemon juice, and seasonings in large saucepan. Bring to boil and cook for 5 minutes. Place in a bowl; add olives and cool to room temperature. Cover and chill. Drain before serving.

Garlicky Curried Popcorn

Yield: 2 quarts
1 cup popcorn kernels
1 12-ounce can mixed salted nuts
½ pound (2 sticks) butter

1 teaspoon salt
2 teaspoons curry powder
½ teaspoon garlic powder

Pop kernels according to package directions. Combine with nuts. Melt butter with salt, curry powder, and garlic. Pour butter over popcorn-nut mixture.

56

Toasted Pumpkin Seeds

Yield: 2 cups
2 cups pumpkin seeds
1½ teaspoons salt

Preheat oven to 200 degrees F. Spread seeds on cookie sheet. Sprinkle with salt and bake for 30 minutes.
NOTE: Squash seeds may be substituted.

Garlic Olives

Yield: 8 to 10 servings
1 8½-ounce can large black olives
⅔ cup vegetable oil

⅓ cup vinegar
3 garlic cloves, chopped

Drain olives. Add oil, vinegar, and garlic. Cover and chill for 2 days.

> *Fairmont City was given life in 1910 by the building of the round-house for the Pennsylvania Railroad. Its original name was Willow Town after the trees which flourished in the marshy soil surrounding it.*

Almond Appetizer

Yield: 12 servings
2 tablespoons unsalted butter
1½ tablespoon chili powder
2 large garlic cloves, crushed

2½ cups unblanched almonds
Salt to taste

Preheat oven to 250 degrees F. Place butter in a shallow pan. When it is melted, stir in the garlic and chili powder. Add the almonds and turn with a spoon until they are coated. Bake for about 1½ hours, stirring occasionally.

> *John Law's Mississippi Bubble resulted in a speculation disaster for France when 250 years ago he organized a company to exploit the Louisiana Territory. Six thousand whites and 3,000 blacks were to be sent to the territory centered in Prairie du Rocher. It failed and all his investors were financially ruined.*

Seasoned Salt

Yield: 1½ cups
1 cup salt
1 teaspoon crushed, dried thyme
  leaves
1½ teaspoons crushed, dried
  oregano leaves

1 teaspoon garlic powder
1 teaspoon curry powder
2 teaspoons dry mustard
½ teaspoon onion powder
¼ teaspoon dill

Combine all ingredients and mix well. Store in jars.

> *Fults, with less than one hundred residents, has had an active post office since 1903. It was incorporated as a village in 1937, and one railroad, the Missouri-Pacific, chugs through it.*

58

A Great American Bottom Scrapbook

Little Egypt

Little Egypt is that southern delta of Illinois washed by the waters of the Mississippi on the west, the Wabash on the east, the Ohio on the south, and enclosed by a phantom line drawn roughly from Alton to Palestine on the north. One can travel through this sparsely populated area and recapture the Illinois of the early nineteenth century French settlers, for this beautiful delta has remained largely untouched by the encroachments of "progress." It is breathtaking in its geographical splendors, encompassing the Shawnee National Forest with its mistletoe-laden trees and its bewitching "Garden of the Gods"; Cave-in-Rock, the hiding place of river pirates; the sleepy town of Cairo, which sits on a literal point of land at the confluence of two mighty rivers rushing headlong to the sea; Elizabethtown, whose Rose Hotel sits on a high, stark bluff overlooking the Ohio River below; and Salem, with its unexpected oilfields.

During the last glaciation, the monolithic ice sheets which scoured much of the rest of Illinois into Breadbasket Flatlands began to lose their potency in Little Egypt and left it with rolling and rollicking hillocks which make up the Mount Vernon Hill Country. Further south, the Illinois Ozarks or Shawnee Hills cover 204,000 acres in the Shawnee National Forest.

Little Egypt lies on the same latitude as southern Virginia and Death Valley in California. Therefore, its winters are mild, its summers hot, and its Indian summers of such memorable grace and gentleness that one remembers them with cobwebby deliciousness so gossamer and fragile that they drift hazily through the consciousness.

Old Shawneetown was the bustling first-city of the Illinois Territory. Now it is but a ghostly forgotten outpost of decaying grandeur languishing on the banks of the Ohio River. On the riverfront, lovely old tumbled-down houses of past charm and elegance have vainly resisted the trespass of time. Trumpet creepers, grasses, and weeds have overgrown their verandahs and have masked the designs of their graceful old balustrades. Signs of life are reduced to an occasional errant Monarch butterfly, paused in its colorful flight to inspect the decay and the ravages of time.

Crumbling to ruin here is the first bank building in Illinois, built in 1812. Officials of the bank refused a loan to the tiny village of Chicago "because Chicago was too far from Shawneetown to ever amount to much." Shawneetown had been the gateway to the Illinois Territory to those immigrants pouring in from the South and the Southeast, but it depended on the river to maintain its strategic importance and soon the coming of the railroad made river travel less important to the homesteader and Old Shawneetown began its gradual decline. The devastating flood of 1937 finished Old Shawneetown as a habitable location and its few remaining townspeople moved to safer locations away from the reach of the capricious Ohio River.

The area surrounding Old Shawneetown is rich in Illinois history. Nigger Riffle, in the stream outside the town, is the site of the state's first important industry. For centuries before the advent of the white settler, Indians from miles around had come to use the springs to get their salt supply. The Saline Industry became so important to the new state of Illinois that in 1818 the State Legislature set aside 180,000 acres of woodland to stoke the fires needed to evaporate the water of the Riffle for its salt content.

Traveling one of the black-topped roads near the Riffle today one can catch a glimpse of traces of the old timbers that were used as linings for the salt pits, all but hidden from sight by an overgrowth of weeds and native violets. A sudden glint of sunlight might also reveal a shard or two of Indian pottery, mementos of a past all but obliterated by the vagaries of time.

Cave-in-Rock is a tiny Ohio River town named after a great cave whose mouth faces the river. The cave was once used for liquor storage and as the hiding place for brigands who would lure a

60

flatboat to shore with the promise of provisions only to plunder it of its contents.

Cairo, situated at the very southern tip of Illinois, became prominent during the Civil War as a holding station for soldiers and supplies which were funnelled into the western battles of the Civil War. By 1867, Cairo had 3,700 steamboats docked on its doorstep, which made the doomsayers' predictions of the quick demise of river traffic seem ridiculous. But, very shortly, rail cartage took over the steamboat's business and Cairo began its descent into genteel poverty. Today, Cairo's evanescent beauty, its faintly Southern flavor, and relics of its bustling past make it one of Illinois's most attractive cities.

Olney is a typical Illinois farm community. The city, like many other towns in Little Egypt, is laid out around a square, and fine old mansions line its streets. What makes Olney unique is that in 1902 a pair of albino squirrels were introduced into the ecology of the city. The squirrels flourished amidst the native oak trees and reproduced startlingly well in their new environment, giving Olney the distinction of becoming "The White Squirrel Capital of the World." A recent resident of the White House asked for a pair of the snowy creatures to complement the White House lawn. Olney kindly and wisely refused, keeping its unique reputation and its white squirrel population intact.

Mount Vernon, the seat of Jefferson County, is a handsome old city with graceful tree-shaded streets defining its residential area. It rests in rich coalfields in the central part of Little Egypt. The courthouse in the center of town is beautifully preserved and is a delightful example of Greek Revival architecture. Settled by immigrants from the South, Mount Vernon is characterized by gracious, porticoed houses with a Southern flavor which reminds one that Illinois has ties to the South as well as to the North.

Located in the heart of the lucrative fruit producing region of Little Egypt is Centralia. Like many other Illinois towns, Centralia prospered with the expansion of the railroads. Located near rich coal deposits, Centralia became a shipping center for the fruits grown in surrounding areas after the railroad barons finally overcame the problem of how to use coal for fuel for the Iron Horses.

Although its magnolia trees make Metropolis seem more a city below the Mason-Dixon Line than one in Illinois, it is similar to many of the towns in Little Egypt, with one glamorous exception. Several years ago the town of Metropolis claimed a rather unique "famous son": Superman. The famous King Features Syndicate personality was known to all the world for his activities in Metropolis both as reporter and hero. So, the little town, not far from the site of old Fort Massac and near the mouth of the Ohio River, proudly boasts that it is "The Home of Superman." Signs, memorials, and other trappings remind the visitor of the simple beginnings of its ultrabalistic urbanite.

Not far from the Wabash River in the eastern reaches of Little Egypt is the town of Albion. It was settled by a group of British immigrant seekers of the American Dream. A small band of Englishmen left their homeland and arrived in Southern Illinois in the second decade of the nineteenth century. The settlers of Albion were unlike many other immigrant groups who began life in Illinois in the nineteenth century. For the most part they were well educated and by existing standards relatively affluent. The settlement was well organized and its inhabitants were determined to maintain a certain high level of culture. Unlike the French and Southern influence demonstrated in other towns of Little Egypt, the architecture of the homes in Albion reflects the influence of the Georgian England which these settlers had left behind.

Little Egypt is the mother of Illinois. It is a womb of mythic beginning, the very soul of our collective subconscious. This is the land of glaciers' end, of migrant Indian movement into the Eastern and Western regions of the country, and of the fringes of memory of times before the glacier. This is Little Egypt, the fertile delta, the birthplace of the state.

Bread, Sweet Breads and Preserves

Drop Biscuits

Yield: 1 dozen
2 cups flour, sifted
2 teaspoons baking powder
1 teaspoon salt

4 tablespoons butter
1 cup milk

Preheat oven to 450 degrees F. Sift dry ingredients together; cut in butter. Add milk; mix to a soft dough. Drop by spoonful onto a baking sheet. Bake 12 to 15 minutes.

> *Galatia was the home of the Webber Brothers who were the largest buyers and processors of Illinois-grown tobacco in the state. During just one year, they exported 1,500,000 pounds of tobacco.*

Colorful Biscuits

Yield: 1 dozen
2 cups sifted flour
2 teaspoons baking powder
½ teaspoon salt
½ cup (1 stick) butter
1½ tablespoons minced green

pepper
1½ tablespoons minced pimiento
¾ cup milk
2 tablespoons minced onion

Preheat oven to 450 degrees F. Sift dry ingredients together. Cut in butter. Add green pepper and pimiento. To milk, add onion. Add to dry ingredients; mix to soft dough. Knead slightly for 30 seconds. Roll to 1 inch thick; cut with a 2½-inch biscuit cutter. Bake on a cookie sheet 12 to 15 minutes.

> *Norris City, in a rich coal mining district, was incorporated in 1884. The first house in the area was built by Grover Harper in 1871 and still stands as a local landmark.*

Buttermilk Biscuits

...en
...d flour
...n salt
...on baking soda

1 teaspoon baking powder
4 tablespoons butter
¾ cup buttermilk

...eat oven to 450 degrees F. Sift together dry ingredients. Cut in
...ter. Add milk; mix to soft dough. Knead lightly for 30 seconds.
Roll out to 6-by-8-inch rectangle ¾-inch thick. Allow dough to rest
1 minute. Cut with a 2-inch biscuit cutter. Bake on a cookie sheet 12
to 15 minutes.

> *Centralia, once "the strawberry capital" of Illinois, was named after
> the Illinois Central Railroad and was platted by that company in 1853.*

Sour Cream Biscuits

Yield: 1 dozen
2 cups sifted flour
2 teaspoons baking powder
½ teaspoon baking soda

1 teaspoon salt
1 tablespoon butter
1 cup plus 2 tablespoons sour cream

Preheat oven to 450 degrees F. Sift dry ingredients; cut in butter.
Add sour cream; mix to a soft dough. Roll out to 6-by-8-inch
rectangle ¾ inch thick. Cut with a 2-inch biscuit cutter. Bake on a
cookie sheet 12 to 15 minutes.

> *Brookport was once a center for the mussel shell button industry. A
> bridge crosses the Ohio River here to Paducah.*

Mayonnaise Biscuits

Yield: 8 servings
2 cups self-rising flour
1 cup milk
2 heaping tablespoons mayonnaise

Preheat oven to 350 degrees F. Combine ingredients and pour into 8
buttered muffin cups. Bake 25 to 30 minutes or until golden.

Popovers

Yield: 10 popovers
2 eggs
1 cup milk
1 cup sifted flour

½ teaspoon salt
1 tablespoon butter, melted

Preheat oven to 400 degrees F. Beat eggs slightly; add milk. Sift flour and salt together. Add to egg mixture. Beat until smooth. Add butter; beat until blended. Butter 10 muffin cups very lightly on bottom and half way up the sides. Pour batter into cups. Place cups on rack in oven. Bake 30 minutes. Pierce each popover with a sharp knife; bake 5 minutes longer. Remove from cups. Serve at once.

Vergennes, whose post office serves Finney and Grubbs, was incorporated as a village in 1887. It was formerly known as Middletown.

65

Corn Muffins

Sina Lockwood Wiley, of Stonington and Champaign, in Breadbasket Flatlands, used this recipe which came from the Lockwood side of her family who came to Illinois from Maryland after the War of 1812.

Yield: 1 dozen
¾ cup cornmeal
1⅔ cups flour
2 teaspoons baking powder
½ teaspoon baking soda
2 tablespoons sugar

¾ teaspoon salt
1 egg
1 cup sour milk
3 tablespoons butter, melted

Preheat oven to 400 degrees F. Sift dry ingredients into a large bowl. Mix the liquid ingredients and add to the dry ingredients. Stir well, but do not beat. Pour into buttered muffin tins and bake about 35 minutes or until golden.

—Sina Lockwood Wiley

> *Coulterville was settled in 1829 by James and George Coulter. Their house still stands as a landmark for the town.*

"Poppin" Biscuits

Mrs. Glastetter of Freeport in Rolling Northwest reports "These are good served with lima beans made with extra juice and thickened with flour and water. This was a recipe of Mary Ann Bangasser who was born in Germany in 1816. She came to Buffalo, New York, as a young girl, married and came to Stephen County in 1843. Mrs. Bangasser and her husband homesteaded in a region near a good supply of spring water. They ran a creamery, shipping butter to Chicago. The farm is still owned by a grandson, Edwin."

Yield: 2 dozen biscuits
1 recipe white bread dough
Lard for frying

After first rising of dough, roll out and cut with biscuit cutter. Let rise 30 minutes. Heat lard until sizzling in Dutch oven. Put 4 biscuits in hot lard, holding lid over. Add 1 tablespoon of cold water. Cover. Turn biscuits, adding 1 tablespoon water and tightly covering each time. Each side takes about 2 minutes. Remove. Continue until all biscuits are cooked.

—*Mrs. C. B. Glastetter*

> *Central City was incorporated in 1857 by German immigrants. The first post office there was established in 1854.*

Monkey Puzzle Bread

Yield: one loaf
½ cup (1 stick) butter, melted
½ cup boiling water
⅓ cup sugar
1 teaspoon salt
1 package dry yeast

½ cup lukewarm water
1 egg
3 cups flour
Melted butter for dipping

Combine butter, boiling water, sugar, and salt in bowl. Cool. Dissolve yeast in lukewarm water. Beat egg and add to yeast mixture. Add yeast mixture to butter mixture. Gradually add flour. Mix thoroughly. Cover and let rise 1 hour. Punch dough down. Roll out on floured surface. Cut into various shapes. Dip each shape into melted butter and place pieces into tube pan. Let rise about 1 hour in a warm place. Preheat oven to 350 degrees F. Bake 35 minutes. Cool about 5 minutes and turn out.

> *Venedy in Washington County was incorporated as a village in 1881. Its post office, established in 1861, served the surrounding communities of Johannesburg, Stone Fort, and Venedy Station.*

The Rose Hotel—Cairo

67

Whole Wheat Bread

Yield: 2 loaves

1⅓ cups boiling water
⅔ cup evaporated milk
1 package yeast, compressed or dry
2 teaspoons light brown sugar
¼ cup water, lukewarm
2 tablespoons butter, at room

temperature
⅓ cup molasses
2 teaspoons salt
4 cups stone ground whole wheat
  flour
1½ cups sifted flour, divided

Add boiling water to evaporated milk. Cool to lukewarm. Place yeast, sugar, and lukewarm water in bowl. Stir until yeast is dissolved. Stir in lukewarm milk, butter, molasses, and salt. Mix in whole wheat flour and 1 cup all-purpose flour. Use remaining flour for kneading. Turn out dough; knead until smooth and elastic. Place in buttered bowl. Turn dough to butter top. Cover. Let rise until double in bulk, about 1½ hours. Punch down; let rise again until double in bulk, 1 to 1½ hours. Shape into 2 loaves. Place each in buttered 1 pound loaf pan, 8¾-by-4⅝-by-2½ inches. Let rise until double in size, about ¾ hour. Preheat oven to 400 degrees F. Bake 35 to 40 minutes.

68

> *Palestine was one of six land offices in the state in 1830 when there were only thirty families in residence in the area.*

Cornbread

Yield: 8 servings

1½ cups self-rising cornmeal
2 eggs
¾ cup butter, melted

1 medium onion, chopped
1 cup sour cream
1 8-ounce can cream style corn

Preheat oven to 350 degrees F. Combine all ingredients and mix well. Pour into buttered 9-inch iron skillet and bake uncovered for 45 minutes.

> *Dowell was founded in 1916 and was named after George Dowell who was legal advisor to the Progressive Miners of America.*

Rye Bread

Mrs. Lindquist of Galesburg in Land Between the Rivers comments, "Rye bread recipe was given to me by Anna Walberg. She lived in Galesburg for eighty years. She appeared on the Art Linkletter Show in the 1960s. She baked 40 loaves of bread a week."

Yield: 3 loaves

2 packets dry yeast
¼ cup warm water
3 cups boiling water
2 tablespoons lard
1 tablespoon salt
¾ cup molasses
1½ cups rye flour
4 to 5 cups white flour

Dissolve yeast in warm water. Let stand for 10 minutes. In a 6-quart bowl, pour boiling water over lard, salt, and molasses. Mix well. Add rye flour and stir thoroughly. Cool to lukewarm. Add yeast mixture and enough white flour to make a soft dough. Knead until elastic and not sticky. Place in a large buttered bowl; cover and let stand twenty minutes. Make into 3 loaves and place in 7-by-3-by-2-inch pans. Preheat oven to 325 degrees F. Let rise until bread reaches above top of pan. Bake 50 minutes. Turn pans and bake an additional 30 minutes or until browned.

—*Thressa W. Lindquist*

> *Elkville, at an altitude of 400 feet, sustained its greatest tragedy in the spring of 1936 when a fire burned most of the town's business district.*

Soda Bread

Yield: 1 loaf

3 cups flour
1 teaspoon salt
1½ teaspoon baking soda
¼ cup sugar
3 teaspoons baking powder
4 tablespoons butter
1 egg
1 cup raisins
1½ cups buttermilk
2 tablespoons caraway seeds

Preheat oven to 400 degrees F. Sift together dry ingredients. Cut butter into dry mixture. Add remaining ingredients. Turn dough onto a floured board. Knead lightly. Shape into an 8-inch circle and place in a well-buttered 8-inch round pan. Bake for 40 minutes.

Herb Bread

Yield: 1 loaf

½ cup milk
1½ tablespoons sugar
1 teaspoon salt
1 tablespoon butter
1 package dry yeast
½ cup warm water

2¼ cups whole wheat flour
1 medium onion, minced
½ teaspoon dried dill weed
1 teaspoon crushed rosemary
1 teaspoon sweet basil

Scald milk. Dissolve sugar, salt, and butter in milk. Cool to lukewarm. In large bowl, dissolve the yeast in warm water. Add lukewarm milk mixture to yeast. Stir in flour, onion, and herbs. When batter is smooth, cover the bowl and let rise until triple. Stir down batter and beat vigorously for a few minutes. Place a buttered 9-by-5-by-3-inch loaf pan. Let rise until double. Preheat oven to 350 degrees F. Bake for 45 minutes or until bread sounds hollow when tapped.

Egg Bread

Yield: 2 loaves

1 package active dry yeast or 1 cake
   compressed yeast
¼ cup lukewarm water
½ cup (1 stick) butter
2½ tablespoons sugar

1½ teaspoons salt
1 cup milk, scalded
5 to 5½ cups unsifted flour, divided
2 eggs
1 beaten egg for brushing

Soften yeast in ¼ cup warm water. Add butter, sugar, and salt to hot milk. Stir until lukewarm. Stir in 2 cups flour. Beat well. Add softened yeast and 2 eggs. Mix. Add enough flour to make a soft dough, reserving some flour for kneading. Turn out on floured surface. Let rest for 15 minutes. Knead 10 minutes or until dough is smooth. Place in lightly buttered bowl, turning once. Cover and let rise in warm place until double, about 1½ hours. Turn out again on lightly floured surface and divide into six equal parts. Cover and let rest for 10 minutes. Shape each ball into a long strip, about 15 inches long. For each loaf place three strips side by side. Without stretching dough, braid strips together tucking ends under. Cover. Let rise in warm place 1 hour. Brush with well-beaten egg. Preheat oven to 325 degrees F. Bake on lightly buttered baking sheet for 50 minutes.

> *Sparta was first named Columbia when it was settled in 1826. The town calls itself "The Comic Book Capital of the World" because of a large comic book printing concern there.*

Honey Bread

Yield: 2 loaves
1½ cup warm milk
½ cup honey
4 tablespoons butter, melted
2 teaspoons salt

2 packages active dry yeast
1 cup warm water
5½ cups sifted flour

Combine milk, honey, butter, and salt. Set aside. Combine yeast and warm water; mix well. Blend with milk mixture. Stir in flour. Let rest covered for 20 minutes. Knead until smooth and elastic. Let rise in buttered bowl until doubled, about 60 minutes. Form into loaves and let rise until doubled in 9-by-5-by-3-inch loaf pans. Preheat oven to 375 degrees F. Bake for 35 to 40 minutes.

> *Residents of Kinmundy in Marion County tell a story about the origin of their town's name: When there was but one store there and the settlers were hardpressed for money, it was not uncommon to hear, "I can't pay you today, but I kin Monday."*

Beer Bread

Yield: 1 loaf
3 cups self-rising flour
⅓ cup sugar
1 12-ounce can beer

Preheat oven to 350 degrees F. Mix ingredients together and pour into a buttered 9-by-5-by-3-inch loaf pan. Bake for 50 minutes.

> *Giant City State Park was established in 1927. It was so named for the huge blocks of sandstone which rise skyscraper fashion from water-eroded street-like troughs at their bases. The park contains one of the seven earliest Indian forts found in Little Egypt.*

Sour Cream and Onion Bread

Yield: 6 to 8 servings
2 cups biscuit mix
½ cup light cream
4 tablespoons chopped scallions, greens and all
1 pint sour cream
2 eggs

Preheat oven to 350 degrees F. Butter bundt pan heavily. Combine all ingredients and pour into pan. Bake 50 minutes until done. Turn out at once.

> *Fairfield was founded in 1819. While staying at the Jackson Hotel there, Lew Wallace wrote many chapters of his famous novel, Ben Hur.*

Wine Cheese Bread

Yield: 8 servings
2 cups biscuit mix
1 tablespoon sugar
2 tablespoons minced onion
½ teaspoon crushed basil
4 tablespoons butter, melted
½ cup dry white wine
1 egg, beaten
½ cup light cream
½ cup grated Parmesan cheese

Preheat oven to 400 degrees F. Combine biscuit mix, sugar, onion, and basil. Add melted butter, wine, egg, and cream. Beat until blended, and pour into a buttered 8-inch round cake pan. Sprinkle cheese generously over top. Bake for 20 to 25 minutes.

Casserole Bread

Yield: 1 loaf

1 package dry or compressed yeast
¼ cup warm water
1 cup lukewarm creamed cottage cheese
2 tablespoons sugar
1 tablespoon minced onion

1 tablespoon butter
2 teaspoons dill seed
1 teaspoon salt
¼ teaspoon baking soda
1 unbeaten egg
2¼ to 2½ cups flour

Soften yeast in water. In mixing bowl combine cottage cheese, sugar, onion, butter, dill seed, salt, soda, egg, and softened yeast. Add flour gradually to form stiff dough, beating well after each addition. Cover. Let rise in a warm place until light and double in size, 50 to 60 minutes. Punch down dough. Turn into a well buttered 8-inch round 2-quart casserole. Preheat oven to 350 degrees F. Let rise in warm place until light, 30 to 40 minutes. Bake for 40 to 50 minutes until golden brown. Brush with soft butter and sprinkle with salt.

73

Corn Bread Cheese Casserole

Yield: 4 to 6 servings

5 cups corn bread, baked and cooled
1 pint heavy cream
½ teaspoon tarragon
1 tablespoon sugar

1 large onion, chopped
Dash of hot pepper sauce
10 ounces Cheddar cheese, grated

Preheat oven to 350 degrees F. Crumble corn bread and mix with the remaining ingredients. Pour into buttered casserole and bake 30 minutes.

Casserole Spoon Bread

Yield: 4 servings
½ cup yellow cornmeal
1 pint heavy cream
2 tablespoons butter, melted

2 eggs, well beaten
1 teaspoon salt
1 heaping teaspoon baking powder

Preheat oven to 350 degrees F. Cook cornmeal in cream until thickened. Cool slightly. Beat in butter and eggs. Add salt and baking powder and pour into buttered 1½-quart casserole. Place casserole in pan of hot water and bake for 30 to 35 minutes.

74

Flatboat on the River

Brown Sugar Bread

Yield: 8 to 10 servings
2 cups flour
1 teaspoon baking powder
½ teaspoon baking soda
1 teaspoon salt
1 cup brown sugar, firmly packed

¾ cup pecans, chopped
2 eggs, beaten
1 cup buttermilk
3 tablespoons butter, melted

Preheat oven to 350 degrees F. Sift dry ingredients together. Add sugar and nuts and stir. Combine eggs, buttermilk, and butter and stir into dry ingredients. Do not beat. Pour into a 9-by-5-by-3-inch buttered loaf pan. Bake for 60 minutes or until a toothpick comes out clean.

Wetaug is named for a tribe of the Cherokee Indians who camped at the site of a spring on their "Trail of Tears" march from Georgia to Oklahoma. In 1896 an earthquake stopped the flowing of the spring as if in retribution for this tragic exodus.

Sweet Nut Bread

Yield: 1 loaf
2 cups sifted flour
2 teaspoons baking powder
½ cup sugar
½ teaspoon salt

1 cup walnuts or pecans, chopped
1 cup light cream
1 egg, beaten slightly

Preheat oven to 325 degrees F. Butter and flour a 9-by-5-2¾-inch loaf pan. Sift together flour, baking powder, sugar, and salt. Add nuts; mix well. Mix together cream and egg; stir into dry ingredients to blend. Pour in prepared pan. Let stand 20 minutes. Bake 1 hour.

Oblong's name was derived from the shape of its original site as laid out in 1883. The apocryphal headline from a local newspaper—"Oblong Man Marries Normal Girl,"—is a legendary joke to residents.

Date Oatmeal Nut Bread

Yield: 1 loaf

1 egg, beaten slightly
1 cup buttermilk
2 tablespoons butter
½ cup firmly packed brown sugar, sieved
1 cup sifted flour

1 teaspoon baking soda
½ teaspoon salt
1 cup rolled oats
1 cup dates, chopped
½ cup chopped walnuts

Preheat oven to 325 degrees F. Butter and flour a 9-by-5-by-2¾-inch loaf pan. Mix together egg, milk, and butter. Stir in sugar. Sift together flour, baking soda, and salt; add rolled oats. Add to egg mixture; stir to blend. Stir in dates and nuts. Pour in prepared pan. Bake for 1¼ hours. Let stand before slicing.

Highland was the home of John Mayenard, who in 1884 brought with him the process for creating evaporated milk. The town was settled in 1804 and got its name from the fact that it is 127 feet higher than the floor of the nearby Great American Bottom.

76

Apple Cheddar Nut Bread

Yield: 8 to 10 slices

3 cups biscuit mix
¾ cup sugar
½ teaspoon cinnamon
⅛ teaspoon nutmeg
1 egg

½ cup light cream
2 cups apples, chopped and peeled
¾ cup chopped pecans
1 cup shredded Cheddar cheese

Preheat oven to 350 degrees F. Combine biscuit mix, sugar, spices, egg, and cream. Stir vigorously 30 seconds. Blend in apples, nuts, and cheese. Pour into buttered 9-by-5-by-3-inch loaf pan. Bake 55 to 60 minutes. Cool before slicing.

Mount Carmel, laid-out in 1818, was once the home of the mussel industry in Illinois. More than $1 million in fresh water pearls were gathered there when the industry was in its prime.

Blueberry Nut Bread

Yield: 2 loaves
2 eggs, well beaten
1 cup sugar
3 tablespoons butter, melted
1 cup buttermilk
3 cups sifted flour
1 teaspoon salt
3 teaspoons baking powder
1 cup fresh blueberries (or frozen, drained)
½ cup chopped walnuts

Preheat oven to 350 degrees F. Mix eggs, sugar, butter and buttermilk. Add sifted dry ingredients. Stir until blended. Fold in blueberries and nuts. Pour mixture into 2 buttered 9-by-5-by-3-inch loaf pans. Bake 50 minutes.

> *Alto Pass at 748 feet commands one of the most impressive views in Little Egypt. Almost six hundred square miles may be seen from this vantage point.*

Pineapple Date Bread

Yield: 1 loaf
2 cups sifted flour
1 tablespoon baking powder
½ teaspoon salt
¾ cup sugar
4 tablespoons butter, at room temperature
¾ cup drained crushed pineapple
½ teaspoon vanilla extract
2 eggs
1 cup chopped dates

Preheat oven to 325 degrees F. Butter and flour a 9-by-5-by-2¾-inch loaf pan. Sift together flour, baking powder, salt, and sugar. Add butter, pineapple, and vanilla; mix well. Beat 2 minutes. Add eggs; beat 2 minutes. Add dates; mix. Pour in prepared pan. Bake 1½ hours.

> *Pinckneyville is the seat of Perry County and was platted in 1829. It was named for Charles Cotesworth Pinckney, a Revolutionary War veteran who helped draft the United States Constitution.*

Apricot Bread

af
...iling water
...ried apricots
..., beaten slightly
...p buttermilk
...2 cups sifted flour

2 teaspoons baking powder
½ teaspoon baking soda
¾ teaspoon salt
½ cup sugar
¼ cup butter, melted

Pour water over apricots and let stand overnight. Put drained apricots through food chopper. Preheat oven to 375 degrees F. Butter and flour a 9-by-5-by-2¾-inch loaf pan. Mix egg and milk. Stir into sifted dry ingredients; add butter. Add apricots; stir to blend. Pour in prepared pan. Let stand 20 minutes. Bake 60 to 70 minutes.

Marissa's first post office opened in 1846. The town moved to its present site in 1871 to be directly on the route of the Cairo Short Line Railroad. It is "dry."

78

Banana Bread

Yield: 1 loaf
3 cups sifted flour
¾ cup sugar
1 teaspoon salt
2 teaspoons baking powder
1 teaspoon baking soda
1¼ cups mashed slightly under-ripe

bananas
1 egg
1 egg yolk
½ cup buttermilk
⅓ cup butter, melted
1 teaspoon grated lemon peel

Butter and flour a 9-by-5-by-2¾-inch loaf pan. Preheat oven to 325 degrees F. Sift together flour, sugar, salt, baking powder, and baking soda. Add remaining ingredients; mix thoroughly. Pour in prepared pan. Let stand 20 minutes. Bake 1 hour.

Old Marissa, the root town of Marissa, still remains on Route 13 away from the railroad. It is "wet": the very reason the two towns have never merged.

Cherry Bread

Yield: 2 loaves
4 cups sifted flour
2 teaspoons baking powder
1 teaspoon baking soda
1 teaspoon salt
1¼ cup sugar
⅔ cup butter, at room temperature

3 eggs
1 17-ounce can applesauce
1 cup chopped pecans or walnuts
1 16-ounce can red sour pitted
  cherries, drained
2 teaspoons almond extract

Preheat oven to 350 degrees F. Sift together flour, baking powder, soda, and salt. Blend sugar and butter until fluffy. Add eggs and beat smooth. Add flour mix alternately with applesauce. Stir in nuts, cherries, and extract. Pour into 2 buttered 9-by-5-by-3-inch loaf pans. Bake for 50 to 60 minutes or until toothpick comes out clean.

> *At 8 a.m. on July 22, 1871, Sandoval ceased being a busy railway terminal because at that moment the Baltimore and Ohio Railroad switched to standard gauge track, and there was no longer any need to stop there to switch track gauge.*

Orange Bread

Yield: 1 loaf
2 cups sifted flour
2 teaspoons baking powder
1 cup sugar
⅛ teaspoon salt

4 tablespoons butter
1 tablespoon grated orange peel
⅔ cup orange juice
1 egg, beaten slightly

Preheat oven to 325 degrees F. Butter and flour a 9-by-5-by-2¾-inch loaf pan. Sift together flour, baking powder, sugar, and salt. Cut in butter. Mix together orange peel, juice, and egg. Add to dry ingredients; stir to blend. Pour in prepared pan. Let stand 30 minutes. Bake 1¼ hours.

> *Steeleville was named for John Steele, who settled there in 1807. The town still prospers because of the strip mines which provide employment for many of the residents.*

Pumpkin Bread

Yield: 2 loaves

⅔ cup butter, at room temperature
2⅔ cups sugar
4 eggs
1 16-ounce can pumpkin
⅔ cup water
3⅓ cups flour
½ teaspoon baking powder

2 teaspoons baking soda
1½ teaspoons salt
1 teaspoon cinnamon
1 teaspoon ground cloves
¾ cup chopped pecans
⅔ cup raisins

Preheat oven to 350 degrees F. Cream butter and sugar thoroughly. Mix in eggs, pumpkin, and water. Sift together flour, baking powder, soda, salt, and spices. Add to pumpkin mixture. Stir in nuts and raisins and pour into 2 buttered 9-by-5-by-3-inch loaf pans. Bake for 1 hour.

> *Greenville is the seat of Bond County and was settled in 1815. Greenville College was originally Almira College which was founded in 1855 as one of the state's first all-female schools.*

80

Farm Windmill

Fresh Strawberry Fritters

Yield: 6 servings
1 cup buttermilk pancake mix
⅔ cup water
2 pints fresh whole strawberries,
hulled, washed, and dried
Oil for deep frying
Confectioners' sugar for dusting

Mix pancake mix and water until smooth. Dip berries in batter. Fry in hot oil at 400 degrees F. until golden, about 30 seconds. Drain. Dust with confectioners' sugar. Serve with whipped cream for dipping.

> *Marion is the seat of Williamson County and was the pre-Civil War home of Robert G. Ingersoll and John Logan whose flamboyant oratory won over southern Illinois' sympathies to the Northern cause.*

Apple Fritters

Yield: 3 dozen
1 egg, beaten
1 cup light cream
1 cup apples minced, peeled, and cored
¼ cup sugar
¼ teaspoon salt
1 teaspoon grated orange peel
3 tablespoons orange juice
½ teaspoon vanilla extract
2 cups flour
1 tablespoon baking powder
Vegetable oil for frying
Sifted confectioners' sugar for dusting

In mixing bowl combine egg, cream, apple, sugar, salt, orange peel, orange juice, and vanilla. Sift together flour and baking powder; fold into egg mixture, stirring only until all flour is moistened. Drop batter by rounded teaspoons into deep hot oil (350 degrees F.) and fry a deep golden brown, about 3 minutes, turning once. Drain fritters thoroughly. Roll in sifted confectioners' sugar.

> *Cave-In-Rock is named after a natural cave in the river bluff which was the hideout for brigands who lured travelers on the river to it and pirated their belongings. A state park, established in 1929, now commemorates the cave.*

French Doughnuts

Yield: 2 dozen
½ cup (1 stick) butter
1 cup boiling water

1 cup sifted flour
4 eggs

Add butter to boiling water in saucepan. Return to boiling point; add flour all at once. Stir vigorously until mixture leaves sides of pan. Remove from heat; add eggs, one at a time, beating vigorously after each addition. Put mixture through pastry bag with star tube; squeeze onto rounds of waxed paper about 2½ inches in diameter. Place with paper side up into hot oil. Remove paper. Fry until golden brown, turning. Drain on absorbent paper.

> *Cobden, the home of the Apple-Knockers, was the birthplace of Parker Earl who was instrumental in the development of the refrigerated railroad car.*

Syrup Doughnuts

Yield: 4 dozen
1 ¼-ounce package dry yeast
3 cups lukewarm water
1 cup warm milk
1 tablespoon salt
2 eggs, beaten

6 cups flour, as needed
Shortening for frying
Syrup for dipping
2 tablespoons cinnamon
1 cup sugar

Syrup

1 cup honey
3 tablespoons rose water

1 cup water
2 cups sugar

Soften yeast in a little warm water. Combine remaining water and milk. Stir in yeast, salt, and beaten eggs. Beat in enough flour to make a sticky batter. Cover and set in a warm place for 2 hours to rise. Stir batter down. Drop from a tablespoon into hot, deep frying oil until brown on all sides. Remove from oil and drain. Dip in hot syrup. Roll in cinnamon and sugar.

   To make syrup combine honey, rose water, water, and sugar; boil 15 minutes.

Pumpkin Doughnuts

Yield: 3 dozen

5 cups flour
½ cup sugar
2 teaspoons baking powder
1 teaspoon baking soda
1 teaspoon salt
½ teaspoon cinnamon

1 teaspoon ground ginger
1 egg, well beaten
1 cup canned pumpkin
1 cup milk or buttermilk
1 tablespoon butter, melted
Confectioners' sugar for dusting

Sift dry ingredients together 3 times. Beat egg. Add pumpkin, milk, and butter. Mix well. Add sifted dry ingredients and blend thoroughly. Roll out on floured board to ¼ inch thickness. Cut with floured doughnut cutter. Fry a few at a time in deep hot fat until browned. Turn and brown other side. Drain on paper towels. While still warm, dust with sugar.

83

New Grand Chain was named for a chain of rocks stretching out into the Ohio River upon whose banks it once stood. It was moved to its present site in 1872 with the coming of the Big Four Railroad.

Breakfast Puffs

Yield: 14 muffins

⅓ cup butter, at room temperature
½ cup sugar
1 egg
1½ cups sifted flour
1½ teaspoons baking powder
½ teaspoon salt

¼ teaspoon nutmeg
½ cup light cream
⅓ cup butter, melted
½ cup sugar
1 teaspoon cinnamon

Preheat oven to 350 degrees F. Cream ⅓ cup butter and ½ cup sugar. Add egg, mixing well. Sift together the flour, baking powder, salt, and nutmeg and add alternately with cream. Fill buttered muffin cups ⅔ full. Bake for 20 to 25 minutes until golden brown. Immediately roll in melted butter, then in mixture of the sugar and cinnamon.

Apple Spice Muffins

Yield: 1 dozen
¾ cup light cream
1 egg, beaten
4 tablespoons butter, melted
2 cups flour
½ cup sugar

1 tablespoon baking powder
½ teaspoon salt
1 teaspoon cinnamon
1 cup minced apples
¼ cup raisins

Preheat oven to 400 degrees F. Add cream to egg; stir in butter. Mix dry ingredients; stir in apples and raisins. Add egg mixture and stir until moistened. Batter should be lumpy. Fill buttered muffin tins ⅔ full. Bake 20 to 25 minutes or until golden brown.

Orange Baking Powder Biscuits

Yield: 15 biscuits
2 cups sifted flour
2 teaspoons baking powder
3½ tablespoons sugar
½ teaspoon salt
2 teaspoons grated orange rind

4 tablespoons butter
½ cup milk
¼ cup orange juice
1 tablespoon orange juice
1 teaspoon sugar

Preheat oven to 450 degrees F. Sift together flour, baking powder, 3½ tablespoons sugar, and salt. Add orange rind. Cut in butter; add milk and ¼ cup orange juice. Mix to a soft dough. Knead a few seconds. Roll out ½ inch thick. Cut with a 2-inch cutter. Place on an unbuttered cookie sheet. Brush biscuits with 1 tablespoon orange juice; sprinkle with 1 teaspoon sugar. Bake 12 to 15 minutes.

Butter Horns

Yield: 3½ dozen
1 cup warm light cream
1 package yeast
1 cup (2 sticks) butter, melted
4½ cups flour
¾ cup sugar
½ teaspoon salt

3 eggs
Grated rind of 1 lemon
½ cup (1 stick) butter, melted
Sugar for dusting
Chopped pecans or walnuts

Dissolve the yeast in the cream. When dissolved combine with 1 cup melted butter, flour, sugar, salt, eggs, and lemon rind. Mix well to a soft dough. Cover and let rise until double in a warm draft-free place. Then refrigerate for 3 hours. Preheat oven to 375 degrees F. Roll out some dough as for a pie crust ¼ inch thick. Brush with remaining melted butter and sprinkle with sugar. Cut the dough into pie shaped slices and sprinkle each with nuts. Roll each piece from the wide end and place on buttered baking sheet. Let rise again and bake for 15 minutes.

> *Belle Rive's first post office was established in 1872. It was named after Louis Groston, dit St. Ange, dit Bellerive, who was the last commander of Fort de Châtres.*

Cluster Coffee Cake

Miss Solomon's mother, of Summit, in Megalopolis would also scatter red and green maraschino cherries between the layers for holiday breakfasts. "We never cut this cake; we just pulled off a piece with a fork."

Yield: 8 to 10 servings
1 package dry yeast
¼ cup warm water
1¼ cups milk, scalded and cooled
1 cup flour
4 egg yolks, beaten
½ cup sugar
½ cup (1 stick) butter, melted

1 teaspoon salt
3½ to 4 cups flour
½ cup (1 stick) butter, melted
¾ cup sugar
2 teaspoons cinnamon
¾ cup chopped pecans
½ cup raisins

Soften yeast in water for 5 minutes. Add milk and 1 cup flour, beating thoroughly. Let mixture stand 20 minutes or until light and bubbly. Blend egg yolks, ½ cup sugar, ½ cup butter, and salt together. Add to yeast mixture, mixing well. Work in remaining flour and knead until smooth and elastic. Place in a buttered bowl, cover, and let rise until double in bulk. Turn out on well floured pastry cloth and divide in half. Form each half into a long roll and cut each roll into 24 pieces. Roll each piece into a ball. Dip in melted butter, then in sugar-cinnamon mixture and chopped nuts. Place balls in a large buttered tube pan, close together and in layers. Sprinkle raisins between the layers. Let stand about 45 minutes or until light. Preheat oven to 350 degrees F. Bake for 45 minutes.

—*Judith Solomon*

Troy is the result of a combination of three vanished villages: Columbia, Mechanicsburg, and Brookside.

Cinnamon Coffee Ring

Yield: 6 to 8 slices

2½ cups sifted flour
½ cup sugar
1½ teaspoons salt
½ cup (1 stick) butter
1 cake yeast, crumbled
1 teaspoon sugar

¼ cup milk
½ cup sour cream
3 eggs
1 teaspoon vanilla extract
½ cup sugar
1 tablespoon cinnamon

Topping

4 tablespoons flour
4 tablespoons butter

½ cup sugar
1 teaspoon cinnamon

Resift flour with sugar and salt into a large mixing bowl. Cut in butter until mixture resembles fine meal. Combine yeast, 1 teaspoon sugar, and milk and add to flour mixture with sour cream, eggs, and vanilla. Blend. Beat hard until smooth and elastic. Cover and let rise about 1 hour, or until double in bulk. Knead dough thoroughly. Cover and let rise again until double. Punch down, cover, and place in the refrigerator overnight. Preheat oven to 325 degrees F. Mix ½ cup sugar with cinnamon. Turn out dough onto a lightly floured board and roll to a 14-inch square, ½ inch thick. Dough will be very soft and difficult to handle. Sprinkle with sugar and cinnamon mixture. Roll up as for jelly roll and lift into a buttered 9-inch tube pan, overlapping the ends. Cover and again let rise until light. Brush milk over the top and sprinkle with crumb topping made by combining the topping ingredients. Bake for 1 hour or until done.

> The town of Muddy bore earlier names of Little Ridge and Robinson's Ford. Although its post office was established in 1908, it was not incorporated as a village until 1955.

Fruit and Nut Coffee Cake

Yield: one 9-inch square coffee cake

Batter

⅓ cup butter
½ cup sugar
2 eggs
1 cup light cream
2 cups sifted flour

3 teaspoons baking powder
1 teaspoon salt
½ teaspoon mace
½ teaspoon cinnamon

Fruit and Nut Filling

87

½ cup prunes, chopped and cooked
½ cup chopped dates

½ cup chopped nuts
⅓ cup sugar

Topping

¼ cup flour
⅔ cup brown sugar, firmly packed
⅛ teaspoon mace
⅛ teaspoon cinnamon

3 tablespoons butter, at room temperature
½ cup blanched almonds, chopped

Preheat oven to 350 degrees F.
Batter
Cream butter and sugar. Beat in eggs, one at a time, beating well after each addition. Add cream alternately with sifted dry ingredients. Turn ½ of batter into a 9-inch square buttered and floured baking pan. Cover evenly with Fruit and Nut Filling and pour remaining batter evenly over top. Sprinkle with Topping and then with chopped almonds. Bake 1 hour. Serve warm.
Fruit and Nut Filling
Combine prunes, dates, and nuts. Add sugar; mix.
Topping
Mix flour, sugar, mace, almonds and cinnamon. Cut in butter.

Apple Coffee Cake

Yield: 6 servings

1½ cups flour, sifted
3 teaspoons baking powder
½ teaspoon salt
2 tablespoons butter, at room
    temperature
½ cup milk
1 egg

2 cups apples, peeled, cored, and
    sliced
4 tablespoons brown sugar
3 tablespoons butter, at room
    temperature
1 teaspoon cinnamon
½ teaspoon nutmeg

Preheat oven to 375 degrees F. Mix dry ingredients. Add butter, milk, and egg and blend thoroughly. Butter an 8-inch cake tin. Pour batter into tin. Mix apples with sugar, butter, cinnamon, and nutmeg. Arrange apple slices on dough. Bake for 35 minutes, until done.

88

Banana Coffee Cake

Yield: 8 pieces

½ cup (1 stick) butter, at room
    temperature
1 cup sugar
2 eggs
1 cup mashed banana
½ teaspoon vanilla, extract
½ cup sour cream

2 cups sifted flour
1 teaspoon baking powder
1 teaspoon baking soda
¼ teaspoon salt
¼ cup sugar
½ cup chopped nuts
½ teaspoon cinnamon

Preheat oven to 350 degrees F. Cream butter and sugar until fluffy. Beat in eggs, banana, and vanilla. Fold in sour cream. Sift together flour, baking powder, soda, and salt. Gently fold into cream mixture; stirring just to blend. Mix together nuts, ¼ cup sugar, and cinnamon. Sprinkle half the nuts into a well buttered springform pan. Spoon in half the batter. Sprinkle with remaining nuts. Add the rest of batter. Bake for 45 minutes or until done. Let stand for 5 minutes.

Pineapple Coffee Cake

Yield: 1 coffee cake
1½ cups sifted flour
2 teaspoons baking powder
¼ teaspoon salt
2 tablespoons sugar
1 egg
½ cup milk

⅓ cup butter, melted
⅓ cup well drained, crushed
  pineapple
2 tablespoons honey
1 tablespoon butter, melted

Preheat oven to 400 degrees F. Sift together flour, baking powder, salt, and sugar. Beat egg. Add milk and ⅓ cup butter. Pour into flour mixture; stir only until dry ingredients are moistened. Turn into a buttered and floured 8-inch round layer cake pan. Mix pineapple, honey, and butter together. Spoon pineapple topping over batter. Bake 30 minutes. Serve warm.

Raisin Coffee Cake

Yield: 1 coffee cake
1½ cups sifted flour
½ teaspoon salt
6 tablespoons sugar
2 teaspoons baking powder
½ teaspoon cinnamon
¾ cup milk

1 egg
3 tablespoons butter, melted
½ cup raisins
¼ cup sugar
1 teaspoon cinnamon

Preheat oven to 350 degrees F. Sift together flour, salt, 6 tablespoons sugar, baking powder, and ½ teaspoon cinnamon. Add milk, egg, and butter. Mix thoroughly. Stir in raisins. Pour into a buttered and floured 9-inch layer cake pan. Mix together ¼ cup sugar and 1 teaspoon cinnamon. Sprinkle over top of cake. Let stand 5 minutes. Bake for 30 minutes. Cool slightly. Serve.

...e of 505 feet, is surrounded by the fragrant
...ear orchards.

Native Birds

Easy Pickles

Yield: 5 pints
24 medium-sized cucumbers,
   cleaned and sliced
12 onions, peeled and sliced
1½ cups salt
8 quarts water

4 cups vinegar
2 cups sugar
1 tablespoon turmeric
2 teaspoons celery seed
2 teaspoons mustard seed

Soak cucumbers and onions 2 hours in brine made of salt and water.
Drain. Bring remaining ingredients to a boil. Add cucumbers and
onions; bring again to boil. Cook 10 minutes. Put into hot sterilized
jars. Seal.

*Vienna, at an altitude of 400 feet, has been the seat of Johnson County
since 1818.*

Dill Pickles

Yield: 4 quarts
20 to 25 cucumbers, about 4 inches
   long
½ teaspoon powdered alum
4 garlic cloves
8 heads dill

4 small, hot red peppers
4 cups vinegar
1 cup pickling salt
3 quarts water

Wash fresh cucumbers thoroughly; drop into cold water and soak for 1 hour. Remove from water; wipe dry and pack into 4 sterilized jars. To each quart jar, add ⅛ teaspoon alum, 1 clove garlic, 2 heads dill, and 1 red pepper. Boil together vinegar, pickling salt, and water. Pour over cucumbers while hot.

> *In 1805 Saint Francisville was settled high on a bluff overlooking the Wabash River by Joseph Tougas. It was named for Saint Francis Xavier.*

Icicle Pickles

Yield: 12 half pints
1 cup salt
1 gallon cucumbers, cut lengthwise
1 tablespoon alum
1 quart hot vinegar

4 pints sugar
1 teaspoon celery seed
1 teaspoon mustard seed

Dissolve salt in ½ gallon boiling water. Pour over cucumbers. Stir every day for 1 week; drain and cover with clear boiling water. Let stand 24 hours. Drain; pour in ½ gallon boiling water in which 1 tablespoon alum has been dissolved. Let stand 24 hours; drain. Combine vinegar, sugar, and spices; pour over cucumbers. Drain and reheat liquid each day for 4 days. Place pickles in hot sterilized jars and pour hot strained vinegar mixture over pickles; seal.

91

> *Mascoutah was founded in 1837. Its name is the Algonquin Indian word for "prairie."*

Cucumber Slices

Yield: 1½ quarts
2 cups sugar
1 cup vinegar
1 teaspoon salt

6 cups fresh cucumber slices
1 cup thinly sliced onions
1 cup chopped green pepper

Combine sugar, vinegar, and salt. Mix with the cucumbers, onions, and green pepper. Store in a covered jar in the refrigerator.

> *Red Bud is named for the groves of trees that once grew in profusion about it. South of the town is Horse Prairie where wild horses once roamed.*

Sweet Pickles

Yield: 3 pints

2 quarts small cucumbers
¾ cup salt
4½ quarts water, divided
2¼ teaspoons powdered alum,
   divided

2 cups vinegar
2⅔ cups sugar, divided
5 teaspoons mixed pickling spices
¼ teaspoon celery seed

Select small firm cucumbers 2 to 3 inches long. Wash and scrub; drain well. Add salt to 1½ quarts water. Bring to boil; pour over cucumbers boiling hot. Put plate over cucumbers to keep them under brine. Let stand 7 days. In hot weather skim daily. On the 8th day drain cucumbers. To 1 quart water add ¾ teaspoon alum. Bring to boiling point; pour over drained cucumbers boiling hot. Let stand overnight. Drain. On the 9th day make a fresh solution of 1 quart water and ¾ teaspoon alum; pour boiling hot over cucumbers. Repeat the 10th day with a fresh boiling hot alum solution; let stand overnight. On the 11th day drain off alum solution. Mix together vinegar, 1⅔ cups sugar, pickling spices and celery seed. Heat to boiling point; skim and pour boiling hot over pickles. Let stand overnight. On the 13th day, drain syrup; add ⅓ cup sugar. Heat to boiling point. Pack pickles into hot sterilized jars; pour over boiling hot syrup.

92

> *Albion was founded in 1818 as a haven for members of the English working class who wished to escape from the poor economic conditions in England following the Napoleanic Wars.*

Watermelon Rind Pickles

Yield: 6 pints

5½ pounds watermelon rind, cut up
4 tablespoons salt
8 quarts water, divided
3 tablespoons alum

11 cups sugar
2 cups white vinegar
2 tablespoons whole cloves
3 sticks cinnamon

Leave a small amount of red flesh on rind when cutting. Add salt to rind; cover with water. Let stand overnight. Drain; rinse well. Add 4 quarts water and alum; cook to a boil. Reduce heat; simmer 35 minutes. Drain and rinse again. Simmer in 4 more quarts water until tender. Water should cover rind; add more if necessary. Add sugar; cook until transparent. Add vinegar and cook 30 minutes more. Add cloves and cinnamon; cook 5 minutes. Pack in jars.

New Athens was founded in 1836 by French settlers from the nearby Bottom and brings a little bit of ancient Greece to Egypt.

Chow-Chow Mustard Pickles

Yield: 8 quarts

1 quart 2-inch-long green cucumbers
1 quart large green cucumbers, chopped
1 pint green tomatoes, chopped
3 small hot red peppers, chopped
2 stalks celery, chopped
½ head cabbage, chopped
3 pints small white onions, chopped
2 heads cauliflower, in flowerettes
Salt

Water
1 pound ground mustard
1 tablespoon turmeric
1 cup flour
2 quarts vinegar, divided
½ teaspoon mixed pickling spices
2 cups brown sugar
1½ teaspoons celery seed
1 teaspoon mustard seed

Soak vegetables in brine made from 1 cup salt to 1 gallon water. Scald them in brine after they have soaked for 24 hours. Drain well. Mix mustard, turmeric, and flour with 1 cup vinegar, stirring mixture to a smooth paste. Add remaining vinegar and heat mixture, stirring constantly until it is thickened. Add spices, brown sugar, and remaining ingredients. Cook for 10 minutes; pour boiling hot into sterilized jars.

Clay City, settled in the early 1830s, originally was known as Maysville.

A Road in Little Egypt

93

Pickled Hen-of-the-woods

Mr. Zielinski of Peoria in Land Between the Rivers says that the Hen-of-the Woods is a large fungus found in the fall before the first frost at the base of living oak trees. Its scientific name is Polyperous Frondosis. Raw supermarket mushrooms may be substituted.

Yield: 8 to 10 pints

8 to 10 pounds Hen-of-the-Woods mushrooms, washed and sliced	5 garlic cloves, minced
Water to cover	20 whole cloves
1 tablespoon salt	14 whole allspice
2½ quarts wine vinegar	1 cup sugar
	10 bay leaves

Boil the mushroom slices in water and salt for 10 minutes. Drain. Rinse in cold water and pat dry. Place the rest of the ingredients except the bay leaves in a large pot. Boil for 5 minutes. Add the mushrooms and boil for an additional 10 minutes. Remove the mushrooms from the cooking liquid and pack loosely into sterilized jars. Add one bay leaf per jar. Strain the cooking liquid and pour over mushrooms. Add 2 of the whole cloves to each jar. Lid the jars and seal them.

—*Steve Zielinski*

94

> *McLeansboro is the seat of Hamilton County and was named after Dr. William McLean. In 1809 the town site was settled by families of Revolutionary War veterans.*

Pickled Peppers

Yield: 4 half pints

3 large red peppers	1½ cups white vinegar
3 large green peppers	1½ tablespoons mustard seed
1 large onion	1½ tablespoons celery seed
¾ cup sugar	

Wash peppers and remove seeds; cut into strips. Slice onion into rings. Cover peppers and onion with boiling water; let stand 3 minutes. Drain; pack into hot pint jars. Boil sugar, vinegar, and spices together 6 minutes; pour over peppers and onions. Seal.

Pickled Beets

Yield: 11 pints

1 gallon small whole beets, boiled and peeled
3 cups red vinegar
3 cups water

3 cups sugar
1 stick cinnamon
1½ tablespoons allspice

Drain beets. Mix all other ingredients and boil 5 minutes. Add beets; simmer 15 minutes longer. Pack in sterile jars; cover with liquid. Seal.

95

Pickled Pineapple Chunks

Yield: 4 to 6 servings

1 8-ounce can pineapple chunks
¾ cup vinegar
1¼ cups sugar

Pinch salt
6 to 8 whole cloves
1 stick cinnamon

Drain syrup from pineapple. In a saucepan, combine syrup, vinegar, sugar, salt, cloves, and cinnamon. Simmer uncovered 10 minutes. Add pineapple chunks. Bring to a boil. Cool. Refrigerate for one week before serving.

Spiced Pickled Pears

Yield: 6 pints

3 cups light brown sugar
3 cups white corn syrup
2 cups white vinegar

2 cinnamon sticks
2 tablespoons whole cloves
4 quarts quartered pears

Cook sugar, corn syrup, vinegar, and spices for 18 minutes. Pour syrup into large, glass sterilized jar. Add pears and cook in boiling water bath until almost tender. Pour cooked syrup into enameled pan and cook until thick. Place a few cooked pears into hot pint jars, adding thick syrup and pears alternately.

> *O'Fallon was developed in 1854 along the Baltimore and Ohio Railroad. It was incorporated as a city in 1865. One of its famous residents, Billy Needles, later became known as William Holden.*

Quick Peach Pickle

Yield: 6 servings

1 No. 2½ can peach halves
¾ cup packed brown sugar
½ cup vinegar

2 3-inch sticks cinnamon
1 teaspoon whole cloves
1½ teaspoons whole allspice

Drain syrup from peaches; combine syrup, brown sugar, vinegar, and spices. Boil mixture for 5 minutes. Add peach halves and simmer 5 minutes longer. Let stand overnight in refrigerator.

> *Nashville was settled in 1830 by Tennesseans, thus its name. The local library is housed in one of the town's most interesting buildings which had been a residence for one of Nashville's early citizens.*

Polynesian Chutney

Yield: 3 pints

4 cups crushed pineapple
2 cups chopped seedless golden
  raisins
½ cup brown sugar, packed
3 tablespoons white vinegar
1 teaspoon salt
½ cup sugar

¼ teaspoon ground ginger
⅛ teaspoon cayenne pepper
¾ teaspoon ground allspice
¼ teaspoon ground cloves
¼ teaspoon cinnamon
Few drops hot sauce
⅓ cup chopped almonds

In a large saucepan combine pineapple, raisins, brown sugar, vinegar, and salt. In a bowl combine white sugar, ginger, cayenne pepper, allspice, cloves, cinnamon, and hot sauce. Stir spice mixture into pineapple mixture. Cook, stirring constantly, over low heat for 40 minutes or until mixture becomes clear. Remove from heat; add almonds. Pour into hot sterilized pint jars; seal.

> *Irvington's annual strawberry crop was once so huge that the Illinois Central ran special non-stop trains to Chicago with the precious cargo.*

Peach Chutney I

Yield: 4 pints

4 quarts peaches, peeled, pitted, and chopped
5 cups vinegar, divided
½ cup minced onion
½ cup sugar
⅓ pound raisins
¼ cup white mustard seed
2 ounces grated ginger root
1 red pepper, minced
1 garlic clove, minced

Mix peaches with 4 cups of vinegar. Cook over medium heat until soft. Add 1 cup vinegar, onion, sugar, raisins, mustard seed, ginger, red pepper, and garlic. Mix. Cook 15 minutes. Fill hot sterilized jars.

> *Jonesboro is the oldest town in Union County. It was laid out in 1816 and named after Dr. Jones, an early settler.*

Peach Chutney II

Yield: 5 pints

1 medium onion, minced
1 garlic clover, minced
1 cup raisins, minced
1 cup minced ginger root
2 tablespoons chili powder
2 tablespoons mustard seed
1 quart cider vinegar
1 tablespoon salt
2¼ cups brown sugar
20 medium peaches, peeled and chopped

Combine all ingredients and mix well. Bring to a boil, stirring until sugar dissolves. Reduce heat and simmer 1 hour or until thick and deep brown. Ladle into jars.

> *New Burnside was founded in 1872 and was named after Major General Ambrose Burnside, president of the Big Four Railroad.*

Dried Fruit Chutney

Yield: 4 pints

4 pounds apples
1 quart cider vinegar
2 cups apple juice
1 cup thinly sliced pitted dates
¾ cup currants
¾ cup raisins

2 pounds brown sugar
3 tablespoons salt
1 tablespoon chopped, crystallized
   candied ginger
⅓ teaspoon cayenne

Peel and core apples; chop them coarsely. Place apples in large kettle; pour vinegar and apple juice over. Add dates, currants, and raisins; let stand for 24 hours. Stir in brown sugar, salt, ginger, and cayenne. Simmer, stirring occasionally, for 50 minutes or until thickened. Pack into steriliized pint jars; seal.

> *Shattuc in Clinton County was until recently the population center of the United States. A marker in a cornfield outside of town still attests to its evanescent fame.*

Mincemeat

Yield: 7 quarts

2 pounds lean beef
10 cups peeled, chopped Jonathan
   apples
1 15-ounce box raisins
1 15-ounce box currants
1 lemon, seeded and ground
2 cups sorghum

4 cups sugar
4 cups apple cider
1 cup vinegar
1 tablespoon cinnamon
1 teaspoon each ground cloves,
   allspice, and nutmeg
2 8-ounce jars apple jelly

Cook beef in salted water. When tender, chop fine. Combine all ingredients in big kettle and slowly bring to a boil, stirring often to prevent sticking. Turn heat to simmer and cook until apples are tender, about 45 minutes.

> *Carlyle was the site of John Hill's Fort which in 1812 protected the settlers from the hostile Indians who inhabited the area.*

Cranberry Relish

Yield: 8 to 10 servings

1 16-ounce package fresh
   cranberries
1 cup water
2 cups sugar
1 cup orange juice
1 cup white raisins

1 cup chopped pecans
1 cup chopped celery
1 apple, peeled and chopped
1 tablespoon grated orange rind
1 teaspoon ground ginger
1 teaspoon nutmeg

Boil cranberries, stirring frequently. Reduce heat; simmer for 12 minutes. Add remaining ingredients. Mix and refrigerate.

Du Quoin was named for Jean Baptiste Du Quoigne, a chief of the Kaskaskia tribe who was of French heritage.

Cranberry Orange Relish

Yield: 1 quart
4 cups cranberries
2 oranges
2 cups sugar

Pick over, wash, and drain cranberries; put through food chopper. Peel and chop 1 orange very fine, removing seeds. Wash, dry, and cut remaining orange, unpeeled, into eights. Remove seeds; put through food chopper twice. Mix oranges, sugar, and cranberries. Chill.

Anna, at an altitude of 629 feet, is situated on route 146 and surrounded by apple orchards which in the spring are breathtaking in their flowery beauty.

Pepper Relish

Yield: 16 half pints

12 tomatoes, unpeeled
12 apples, unpeeled
12 medium onions
3 green peppers
4 red peppers
3 cups sugar
3 cups vinegar

3 tablespoons salt
2 sticks cinnamon
8 whole cloves
2 whole nutmeg
1 teaspoon celery seed
1 teaspoon mustard seed

Grind tomatoes, apples, onion, and peppers coarsely. Mix sugar, vinegar, and salt. Put spices in cloth bag. Bring to a boil. When syrup is boiling hard, add ground ingredients and boil 30 minutes. Put into sterilized jars while hot and seal.

Germantown was once known as Hanover. Situated in Clinton County, its first post office was established in 1846. It was incorporated as a village in 1874.

Corn Relish

Yield: 6 pints
12 ears sweet corn
4 cups chopped cabbage
3 sweet green peppers
3 sweet red peppers
2½ teaspoons dry mustard
1½ tablespoons celery seed

1 teaspoon turmeric
2 cups sugar
½ cup flour
1 teaspoon salt
1 quart white vinegar

Cut corn from cob. Chop other vegetables fine. Mix spices, sugar, flour, salt, and vinegar. Add chopped vegetables and corn. Boil 12 minutes. Pack into sterilized jars and seal.

Flora came into existence in 1854 as a railroad town. It was named after a daughter of one of its founders.

India Relish

Yield: 3 pints
12 large green tomatoes
1 red pepper
1 green pepper
4 large onions
1 cup sugar

1 cup vinegar
1 tablespoon mustard seed
1 tablespoon celery seed
1 tablespoon salt

Put tomatoes, peppers, and onions through food chopper, coarsely chopping. Drain well, reserving juice for soup or beverage. Add remaining ingredients; mix well. Cook until vegetables are tender and relish thickens, about 15 minutes. Turn into hot sterilized jars; seal.

Eldorado was a mining town. During the Great Depression there was a migration of its young people to the industrial areas in the Bottom to look for work. Eldorado mothers used to frighten their children when they behaved poorly by telling them that they couldn't go to East St. Louis when they grew up.

Pediment Detail of Old Shawneetown Bank—Old Shawneetown

Apple Butter

Yield: 6 pints
2 quarts apple cider
4 quarts apples
2 cups sugar

2 cups dark corn syrup
1 teaspoon cinnamon

Boil cider until reduced by half. Pare and core the apples and slice thin. Put apples into the cider and cook very slowly, stirring frequently until it begins to thicken. Add sugar, syrup, and cinnamon and continue to cook until thickened. Seal in sterilized jars.

> *Carrier Mills was named for William H. Carrier who started a sawmill there in 1870.*

Blackberry Jam

Yield: 4 half pints
2 cups blackberries, crushed
2 cups sugar
1 teaspoon butter

Combine all ingredients in a 4-quart saucepan; bring to a boil, stirring until sugar is dissolved. Continue cooking rapidly, stirring occasionally, until mixture sheets from a spoon. Remove from heat; pour into 4 hot sterile jars and seal.

> *The town of Bridgeport was the center of the first Illinois oil boom. It was incorporated as a village in 1865.*

Strawberry Jam

Yield: 4 half pints
4 cups strawberries, crushed
1½ tablespoons lemon juice

4 cups sugar
1 teaspoon butter

Put berries in a 4-quart kettle with lemon juice; boil for three minutes, stirring occasionally. Remove from heat; add sugar and butter. Boil for ten minutes. Let stand overnight. Place in sterilized jars and seal.

> *Wamac was incorporated in 1913, and its name is derived from the three counties whose boundaries meet there: Washington, Marion, and Clinton. Wamac boomed once as the only "wet" community in a group of "dry" towns.*

Paw Paw Jam

Yield: 4 6–ounce glasses
¼ cup water
1¾ cup paw paw pulp
1½ tablespoons lemon juice

6 ounces pectin
2¾ cups sugar

Mix first 4 ingredients in a 2-quart saucepan. Bring to a boil. Add sugar, mixing thoroughly to dissolve. Bring to a rolling boil. Continue boiling for 3 minutes. Pour into hot sterilized jelly jars. Seal.

> *Lebanon was laid out in the 1820s and is the home of McKendree College, one of the three oldest colleges in Illinois.*

Raspberry Jam

Yield: 3 half pints

1 quart (4 cups) raspberries, cleaned and drained	4 cups sugar ½ cup fresh lemon juice

Put berries in a 10 or 12-quart kettle; cover with sugar. Let stand 4 hours. Heat slowly to full rolling boil; boil 2 minutes longer, stirring constantly. Skim off any froth. Turn into hot sterilized jars. Seal.

> *1898 saw the incorporation of Cisne as a village, although an office providing postal service had been established in 1871.*

103

Plum Jam

Yield: 4 pints
4 quarts plums
1 quart water
Sugar

Wash and drain plums; cut in halves. Drop into 10 or 12-quart kettle. Add water. Cook gently 15 minutes after boiling point is reached. Cool slightly; remove pits. Measure pulp and juice. Add ¾ cup sugar for each cup. Stir; boil gently 20 minutes. Turn into hot sterilized jars and seal.

> *Patoka was named after an Indian chieftain, and just before World War II it had a giant oil boom.*

Tomato Jam

Yield: 9 half pints
2¼ pounds ripe tomatoes
2 teaspoons grated lemon rind
¼ cup lemon juice

6 cups sugar
1 6-ounce bottle pectin

Scald, peel, and chop tomatoes. Bring to a boil; simmer 10 minutes. Measure 3 cups into a large saucepan. Add grated lemon rind, lemon juice, and sugar. Mix well; bring to a rolling boil. Boil hard 1 minute, stirring. Remove from heat; add pectin all at once and stir in. Stir and skim by turns for 5 minutes. Pour into hot sterilized glasses. Cover with melted paraffin.

First settled in 1796, Metropolis is the seat of Massac County. It combined with the city of Massac in 1892 to form the present community.

Rose-Hip Jelly

Yield: 4 half pints
2 cups water
2 pounds rose-hips
Sugar

Pick rose-hips from a roadside wild rose bush. Add water to rose hips. Simmer until tender. Put through a sieve and weigh the pulp. Add an equal amount of sugar. Simmer until thickened and pour into hot sterilized jars. Seal.

Carmi was laidout in 1816 as the seat of White County.

Hot Pepper Jelly

Yield: 6 pints
2 large green peppers, chopped
2 long green chili peppers, chopped
1½ cups cider vinegar

5½ cups sugar
6 ounces liquid fruit pectin
4 to 8 drops green food coloring

Combine green peppers and chili peppers in a small bowl. Place half the mixture in a blender with ½ cup vinegar. Blend until smooth and pour into a large kettle. Blend the remaining mixture with another

½ cup vinegar and pour into kettle. Rinse the blender with the last ½ cup vinegar and pour into kettle. Stir in the sugar. Bring to a boil and stir 1 minute. Remove from kettle, skim the top, and add food coloring. Add the pectin. Cool 5 minutes and ladle into sterilized jars.

> *Olney, named for John Olney who was a lieutenant in the Civil War, has the largest white squirrel population in the world.*

Corncob Jelly

Yield: 4 pints
12 red corncobs
2 quarts water

1 package jelly thickener
3 cups sugar

Boil broken cobs in water for 30 minutes. Remove from heat; strain juice to make 3 cups. Add jelly thickener; bring to a rolling boil. Add sugar; boil 5 minutes or to jelly stage. Ladle into sterilized glasses. Pour ¼ inch paraffin on top.

> *Beckemeyer was founded in 1904 when a coal mine opened for business there. The town is named for a family who owned large amounts of land in the area.*

Apricot Conserve

Yield: 6 pints
1½ pounds dried apricots
2 15½-ounce cans crushed pineapple
4½ cups sugar

¾ teaspoon salt
1 cup chopped walnuts

Soak apricots overnight. Drain. Cut into small pieces and put into large kettle. Add pineapple, sugar, salt, and nuts. Bring to a boil and simmer for 1 hour or until soft. Pour into sterilized jars and refrigerate.

> *Crab Orchard Lake ranks with the most beautiful lakes in Illinois. It was a project of the WPA and was completed in 1939.*

Six Fruit Conserve

half pints
peaches
plums
h pineapple
und white grapes

1 orange
1 lemon
Sugar
1 pound blanched almond meats

Wash fruits. Prepare peaches, plums, and pineapple and cut into small pieces. Halve grapes. Remove seeds. Slice orange and lemon very thin. Cook fruits over low heat until soft. Measure and add ¾ cup sugar for each cup of fruit. Cook over low heat 20 minutes. Add almonds. Cook slowly, stirring occasionally until thick and clear for 2 hours. Seal in hot, sterilized jars.

> *Williams Hill at 1,065 feet altitude is the highest elevation in all of Egypt.*

Pear Preserves

Yield: 8 pints
5 pounds cooking pears thinly sliced
5 pounds sugar
2 lemons, sliced thin

Wash sliced pears and dry well. Place in a 5-quart cooking pot. Add sugar and mix well. Cover and let stand overnight. Add sliced lemons, bring to a boil; turn heat to low temperature and cook until pears are tender and syrup is golden about 2½ hours. Place into sterile jars.

> *Mount Vernon has been the seat of Jefferson County since 1819 and was settled by Southern families. The city reflects their influence in architecture and traditions.*

Strawberry Preserves

Yield: 5 half pints
8 cups strawberries, hulled
Water
6 cups sugar, divided

Wash and drain berries. Cover with boiling water and let stand 2 minutes. Drain. Put berries in an 8-quart kettle; add 4 cups sugar; mix. Bring slowly to full rolling boil. Boil vigorously 3 minutes. Take off heat. Let stand 5 minutes; add 2 cups sugar. Bring again to full rolling boil; boil 7 minutes. Cover; let stand several hours or overnight. Pack cold preserves into hot sterilized jars. Process 15 minutes in boiling water.

The village of New Minden in Washington County was incorporated in 1877. Nine years earlier, in 1868, the little community had opened its first post office.

Trumpet Creeper—Native Wildflower

Spiced Cherries

Yield: 12 half pints

7 pounds tart cherries
4 pounds sugar
2 cups cider vinegar

1 tablespoon cinnamon
1 teaspoon ground cloves
½ teaspoon nutmeg

Place all the ingredients in a large kettle. Bring to a boil and boil gently until cherries are soft. Remove cherries and boil syrup until thickened. Add cherries and bring to a boil. Fill sterile jars and seal.

> *In 1937, after another devastating flood, many residents of Old Shawneetown moved away from the banks of the river and settled Shawneetown which sits watchfully over the river-ravaged grandeur of the old town.*

Glazed Spiced Orange Slices

Yield: 1 quart

4 seedless oranges
2 cups sugar
½ cup cider vinegar

¼ cup water
5 whole cloves
1 3-inch cinnamon stick

Slice oranges ¼ inch thick. Place in a heavy saucepan. Cover with water. Simmer 30 minutes covered. Drain and rinse well. Return slices to pan. Add rest of ingredients and simmer 1 hour, uncovered. Pack oranges in sterilized jars and fill with hot syrup. Refrigerate.

> *Salem was settled in 1813 on the St. Louis-Vincennes stage coach route and was the childhood home of William Jennings Bryan.*

Orange Glaze

Yield: 1 cup

¾ cup frozen orange juice
   concentrate, thawed

¼ cup orange marmalade
3 tablespoons bottled meat sauce

Combine all ingredients in a small saucepan. Heat slowly, stirring until mixture is blended. Remove from heat. Use with rock cornish hens, ducks, or turkey.

Apple-Horseradish Sauce

Yield: 3 cups

1 cup unsweetened applesauce, drained
1 cup horseradish, drained

½ cup mayonnaise
1 cup heavy cream, whipped

Combine the ingredients. Serve with meat.

Cairo is the end of the line, the last stop in Illinois. It is the home of past grandeurs and a sense of deja vu *stalks its streets.*

Cherry Sauce

Yield: 2 cups

1 16-ounce can pitted sweet cherries
2 tablespoons cornstarch
1 tablespoon prepared mustard
1 tablespoon cherry jam

Few drops hot sauce
⅛ teaspoon salt
3 tablespoons lemon juice

109

Drain syrup from cherries. Add enough water to make 1½ cups liquid. In a small saucepan, blend a few tablespoons cherry liquid into cornstarch until smooth. Stir in remaining liquid, mustard, jam, hot sauce, and salt. Cook over low heat, stirring until mixture thickens and boils 4 minutes. Stir in cherries and lemon juice. Heat just until bubbly. Serve hot on rock cornish hens or duck.

Carbondale is the most sophisticated city in Little Egypt. It is the home of the bustling Southern Illinois University whose influence is felt throughout the area.

Sherry Marinade

Yield: 1½ cups

⅔ cup sherry wine
¼ cup mild flavored honey
2 tablespoons grated onion

⅔ cup soy sauce
2 garlic cloves, crushed

Combine all ingredients into pint jar; cover tightly. Shake until blended. Let stand overnight in refrigerator. Use to marinate cuts of lamb, beef, pork, or chicken.

> *Fort Chilton was built in 1812 at what is now St. Jacob to protect pioneer families from Indian attacks.*

Plum Marinade

Yield: 2 cups

1 12-ounce jar plum preserves
4 teaspoons lemon juice
1½ tablespoons soy sauce

⅓ teaspoons ground ginger
2 teaspoons grated onion
⅓ teaspoon salt

Mix ingredients well. Pour over fowl and refrigerate.

> *Ashley, at an altitude of 559 feet, was named after John Ashley, an early settler.*

Dandelion Wine

Mrs. Rademaker of Freeport in Rolling Northwest says, "I remember our uncle and aunt always served this yellow sparkling wine for company and special occasions. We only got a small glass and it tasted so good."

Yield: 5 gallons

2½ gallons boiling water
2½ gallons dandelion blossoms

15 pounds sugar
Juice of 9 lemons

Add boiling water to dandelion blossoms. Let stand 24 hours. Press out all juice. Add sugar and lemon juice to liquid. Add enough water to make 5 gallons. Let stand 14 days. Strain and put into jugs and cork.

—*Agnes Rademaker*

A Little Egypt Scrapbook

Land Between the Rivers

Illinois is one of the few states whose boundaries are almost entirely formed by waterways. The buoyant waters of Lake Michigan, descendant of a prehistoric inland sea, lap at the northeastern boundary of the state. The mighty Mississippi flows for 518 miles from the northwestern tip of the state to form its western boundary before merging with the Ohio River at Cairo. Long before this union, the Ohio has received the waters of the Wabash River which molds the southeastern boundary of the state. But, it is Illinois's internal river network which is its unique drainage system. Almost half of the moisture which falls in Illinois is drained by its rivers. The chief conduit in this network is the Illinois River which begins at the junction of the Kankakee and Des Plaines Rivers southwest of Joliet. The Illinois travels for 273 miles before it joins the Mississippi River a short distance north of Alton. On its journey southwest the Illinois River carries with it the waters of many smaller rivers such as the Sangamon, the Spoon, the Vermillion, the Fox, the DuPage, and others.

The Illinois River widens to form Lake Peoria at the town bearing the same name. Located in the heartland of the early Illinois Territory, this region was selected in 1680 by French travelers to serve as an early although short-lived outpost, Fort Crève Coeur. Several other forts under both French and American flags preceded Fort Crève Coeur until the settlement of Peoria was granted town status in 1835. Soon afterwards one of the first institutions of higher learning, Jubilee College, was awarded a state charter. Rugged ochre stone, quarried from nearby Kickapoo Creek, was used for the construction of its Gothic buildings. Of the original buildings only the chapel remains today, rising above the well-cared-for green lawns of the state park which spread around it. Modern-day Peoria is also the home of Bradley University, originally chartered by the state as Bradley Polytechnic Institute in 1876. Peoria is one of the largest cities in Illinois and owes much of its prosperity to two dissimilar industries. The Caterpillar Tractor Company and other farm implement industries have long been identified with Peoria's economic progress. Equally important is the production of "spirit-ous liquors" which developed because of Peoria's proximity to the vast cornfields surrounding it, the abundance of crystal clear spring water, and the accessibility of coal. Several distilleries had their beginnings in Peoria and have prospered there.

Galesburg is located midway between the Illinois and Missis-sippi Rivers in Knox County and is one of the few towns in Illinois which was planned before it was settled. Developers from the East had persistently searched out the lands of the western Illinois Territory to find a suitable location for a college to educate ministers for the Middle Border. The land was chosen, the town was platted, and Knox College opened its doors in 1838.

In the mid-nineteenth century, immigrants from Sweden began arriving in Galesburg. Among them were the parents of Carl Sandberg, Illinois poet and Lincoln biographer. The humble immigrant home of his parents has been preserved and restored to its original state. A museum houses many artifacts and the poet is buried in the park which surrounds it. Galesburg boasts of another "famous son," Olmstead Ferris. His Ferris Wheel represented one of the wonders of the Columbian Exposition held in Chicago in 1893. Ferris became famous on two continents although historians are divided as to whether Ferris's fame derived from his invention of the much touted amusement park item or his "command perfor-mance" at the Court of St. James where he demonstrated his new "discovery," popping corn, before an amazed Queen Victoria.

Farther west on the sloping skirt of the Mississippi lies the little town of Oquawka, named after the ochre-colored banks of the river which were known as Ozaukee to Indian hunters who had forded the river there. The town later became the seat of Henderson County, and the grain milling center for the locale. A lovely old covered bridge encased the roadway over Henderson Creek where the mill once stood. It bore the inscription:

> Five dollars fine, for leading or driving any beast
> faster than a walk, or driving more than thirty
> head of cattle, mules, or horses at a time on or
> across the bridge.

Nauvoo is perched on a projection of land extending into the waters of the Mississippi. The muffled sound of the mighty river is a softly murmuring background music to the idyllic, picturesque town which is present-day Nauvoo. Grim echoes of the past persist in the remains of the Mormon houses built by the members of Joseph Smith's settlement in the mid-nineteenth century. Religious persecution and hostility had dogged the Mormons until in 1839 they finally found a haven on the promontory jutting out into the river. The settlement soon grew to twenty thousand inhabitants, making it the largest city in Illinois. But contention and ugly violence emerged again as antagonism flared up against the members of the prosperous Mormon settlement. The strife visited upon its inhabitants culminated in the imprisonment of Joseph Smith and his ultimate assassination in the prison at Carthage. Not long afterwards in the midst of open battle and fierce animosity, the Mormons, under the leadership of Brigham Young, hastily left Nauvoo and began their exodus from Illinois to Utah. The construction of a magnificent temple was never finished although the Sunstone, the symbol of Nauvoo, is one of the few vestiges of the temple to remain. The town of Nauvoo remained a ghost town until a group of French settlers attempted to start a communal village in 1849. This, too, was doomed to failure and Nauvoo was once again deserted. German immigrants began arriving in the 1850s and began the permanent settlement that is present-day Nauvoo.

A Sauk Indian village once occupied the steep bluffs which provide the site of Quincy. Quincy is the seat of Adams County, and both city and county were named after the sixth President of the United States who was in office at the time of their founding. The houses of the original town were perched high on the craggy bluffs overlooking the bustling river below. As the town grew, houses and developments began to spill over into the flatlands and heavily forested sections to the east. Early Quincy was a refuge for many abolitionists and other expatriots who escaped from bordering slave states prior to the Civil War via the accommodating Mississippi. Its rise to prominence as a shipping capital declined with the dwindling of heavy steamboat traffic on the river and the replacement of river trade by the railroads. However, Quincy rose with the tide and by the turn of the century both industry and railroads were instrumental in stabilizing its economy.

As the great Mississippi and Illinois rivers flow southward, the tongue of land enclosed by them forms Calhoun County. Much of the land, like that of northwestern Illinois and the southern section of the state, was untouched by the glacial shift which formed most of Illinois's land character. Calhoun County, like its northern and southern counterparts, has a landscape that is rugged with sharp crevices and lofty ridges. The many orchards which cover the irregular terrain have made Calhoun County famous in the Midwest for its apple production. Travel through the main or back roads in this rugged county in spring, when the landscape is snowy with the blossoms which will produce the fruit of autumn, is almost intoxicating with the heady fragrance produced by the plump white flowers. There are few towns and villages here, but Hardin, the county seat, is rooted in the cliffs overlooking the Illinois River.

Not far from the Illinois River, in Shuyler County, lies the town of Rushville, settled in the early nineteenth century. Scripps Park in Rushville is a memorial to a former resident, Edward Wyllis Scripps, founder of the Scripps-Howard newspaper syndicate. The park encompasses the eighty-acre farm of the Scripps family and was donated with other endowments by the Scripps family to the town in the 1920s.

The Spoon River, immortalized by Edgar Lee Masters in his *Spoon River Anthology*, ambles lazily through Fulton County before emptying into the Illinois River. In its wake are vast stretches of rich black soil which provide some of the finest corn growing land in Illinois. Coal deposits, too, reflect the philanthropy of the land. Fulton County at one time encompassed the whole northern part of the state. Taxes and marriage and commercial licenses from as far away as Chicago had to be registered at Lewistown, the county seat. Before he went to Chicago to study law, Edgar Lee Masters spent his boyhood in Lewistown, and many of its environs and inhabitants found their way into Masters' colloquial masterpiece, including Oakhill Cemetery. The *Spoon River Anthology* captures the feeling of midwestern America in its chronicling of local anecdotes, its unabashed reverence for nature, and its both bitter and sweet portraits of the beings who peopled the Spoon River country. In his "Calvin Campbell" from the *Anthology*, Masters dwells on the ironies of nature in this land that was barely removed from its primitive pioneer wilderness state.

> Ye who are kicking against Fate,
> Tell me how it is that on this hill-side,
> Running down the river,
> Which fronts the sun and the south-wind,
> This plant draws from the air and soil
> Poison and becomes poison ivy?
> And this plant draws from the same air and soil
> Sweet elixirs and colors and becomes arbutus?
> And both flourish?
> You may blame Spoon River for what it is,
> But whom do you blame for the will in you
> That feeds itself and makes you dock-weed,
> Jimpson, dandelion and mullen
> And which can never use any soil or air
> So as to make you jessamine or wisteria?

As the Spoon River ambles to its meeting with the Illinois, it passes at a distance one of the most important archeological finds in Illinois. Dickson Mounds represents the remains of an Indian culture spanning several thousand years. Its location was accidentally discovered by a farmer late in the nineteenth century, but serious investigation of the site did not take place until well into this century. Excavation of the earth work has yielded hundreds of skeletal remains and numerous funerary artifacts together with traces of constructional elements from several Indian villages extending from the Archaic to the Mississippian period. A museum has been built by a state agency in the excavation complex, and visitors may view parts of the earth works in a sheltered area. Like the other sections of Illinois which have given testimony to its prehistoric habitation, the sensations evoked as one approaches the Dickson complex seem to draw deeply from the collective human unconscious. A tangible presence can be felt, but as one looks about seeking to realize that presence he is reluctantly brought back to the present by the rustling sound of the whooshing wands of corn in the stillness and amplitude of the surrounding fields.

The land between the rivers is exotic. Ghosts of Indian settlements and of lost searchers for Utopia wander through it. Spring rains are more bountiful here, and snow whishes through it on the wings of memory as if the land were still untouched and pristine, as if no sorrow were ever here, no grand elation: only the gurgling of the streams, the soft call of marsh birds, and the gentle Indians living in peace with it all.

Soups, Salads and Dressings

Migrant Conestoga Soup

Yield: 3 to 4 servings
3 tablespoons butter
3 cups milk, scalded
¾ cup flour

1 teaspoon salt
1 large egg

Melt the butter in the hot milk. In a mixing bowl, mix flour, salt, and egg until lumpy. Drop dough by rounded spoonfuls into the milk mixture and simmer until they are cooked through.

New Canton's first post office was established in 1872 and serves Cincinnati Landing and Brewster. The town was incorporated in 1869.

Settler's Soup

Yield: 8 servings
1 4-pound pot roast
3 quarts water
1 tablespoon salt

4 eggs
1 teaspoon salt
½ cup flour

Place pot roast in a gallon soup pot. Cover with water and one tablespoon of salt. Boil gently for 5 hours until meat falls away from the bone. Remove meat to a platter and cut into chunks. Bring broth to a boil. Add more salt if needed. Beat four eggs, a teaspoon of salt, and flour together in a small bowl. Pour this mixture into the pan of boiling broth, beating lightly with a wire whisk until smooth. Stir slightly once or twice and cook for about three to five minutes. Place meat chunks in broth and serve on mashed potatoes.

Hearty Ground Beef Soup

Yield: 4 quarts

1½ pounds ground beef
2 tablespoons butter
2 tablespoons salt
1 teaspoon Worcestershire sauce
½ teaspoon pepper
6 cups beef broth
1 medium onion, minced

6 carrots, thinly sliced
2 cups chopped celery
¼ cup raw rice
2 10-ounce packages frozen mixed
  vegetables
1 1-pound can tomatoes
1 8-ounce can tomato sauce

Brown beef in butter. Drain. Add all ingredients, except frozen vegetables, tomatoes, and sauce. Simmer 1 hour. Stir in frozen vegetables, tomatoes, and sauce. Simmer 10 minutes.

118

Vegetable Beef Soup

Yield: 10 servings

2 pounds ground chuck beef
2 tablespoons butter
1½ tablespoons vinegar
½ teaspoon soy sauce
1 teaspoon molasses
1 teaspoon sugar
½ teaspoon pepper
1 cup chopped onion
2½ cups sliced carrots
1 cup sliced parsnips
1 cup chopped rutabaga
1½ cups coarsely chopped celery

½ teaspoon dried tarragon
1 tablespoon dried parsley
⅓ cup raw barley
6 cups beef bouillon
½ 10-ounce package frozen corn
½ 10-ounce package frozen green
  beans
½ 10-ounce package frozen peas
½ 10-ounce package frozen chopped
  broccoli
1 8-ounce can tomato sauce
1 16-ounce can tomatoes

Brown ground chuck in butter in a 4-quart pot. Drain. Add the next 14 ingredients. Bring to a rolling boil. Reduce heat, cover, and simmer over low heat for an hour. Add frozen vegetables, tomato sauce, and tomatoes. Stir thoroughly and allow to cook, covered, for 20 to 25 minutes. Adjust seasoning to taste.

> *Mercer County was named after General Hugh Mercer who was killed at the Battle of Princeton during the Revolutionary War. It was established in 1825 and is 556 square miles in size.*

Autumn Soup

Yield: 6 servings
1 pound ground beef
1 cup chopped onion
3 cups water
1 cup chopped carrots
1 cup chopped celery
1 cup chopped potatoes

1½ teaspoons Worcestershire sauce
¼ teaspoon pepper
1 bay leaf
¼ teaspoon sweet basil
1 quart canned tomatoes

In a 3-quart saucepan, cook and stir meat until brown. Drain off fat. Stir in onions with meat and cook 5 minutes until onions are tender. Stir in remaining ingredients except tomatoes. Heat to boiling. Reduce heat, cover, and simmer 20 minutes. Add tomatoes. Cover and simmer 10 minutes longer or until vegetables are tender.

119

> *Niota was known as Appanoose and is called today, like the railroad that passes through it, East Fort Madison. The post office which was established in 1887 served Old Niota and Powellton.*

Barley Soup

Yield: 6 to 8 servings
1 tablespoon butter
½ pound ground beef
½ cup chopped onions
2 quarts cold water
2 beef bouillon cubes
2 teaspoons salt

Dash pepper
½ cup pearled barley
1 cup chopped raw potatoes
1 10-ounce package frozen mixed
  vegetables (optional)

Melt butter in a kettle. Add beef and onions, breaking up beef with fork. Brown meat and onions, stirring often. Add remaining ingredients, except frozen vegetables. Heat to boiling; add frozen vegetables; cover and cook for 30 minutes longer.

Brain Soup

Yield: 6 servings

2 calf's brains, washed and skinned
Water
Juice of 2 lemons, divided
½ teaspoon salt
2 tablespoons butter
4 slices cooked bacon, cut into bits

3 cups milk
1 cup light cream
Salt and pepper to taste
½-inch slices of French bread,
   buttered and toasted

Barely cover brains with cold water to which half the lemon juice has been added. Soak for 2 hours. Drain brains and place in 2-quart saucepan. Cover with 4 cups boiling water. Add remaining lemon juice and salt; simmer for 40 minutes. Melt butter in a 2-quart saucepan. Add bacon, milk, and cream; heat the mixture thoroughly, but do not boil. Drain brains, reserving cooking liquid. Chop brains and return to cooking liquid. Blend in milk, and cream mixture, salt and pepper. Bring to a boil and remove from heat. Place one French bread slice in each soup plate. Ladle mixture over bread and serve.

Oxtail Soup

Yield: 8 servings

2½ pounds oxtails, cracked and cut in
   1½-to 2-inch pieces
1 teaspoon salt
½ teaspoon pepper
2 tablespoons flour
2½ tablespoons butter
3 cups chopped turnips

1½ cups sliced carrots
1½ cups chopped onions
1½ tablespoons dried parsley
Salt to taste
Pepper to taste
2 tablespoons flour

Sprinkle oxtails with a mixture of salt, pepper, and flour. Brown lightly in butter in a 6-quart saucepan. Add turnips, carrots, onion, and parsley. Cover with 4 quarts of water. Salt and pepper to taste.

120

Bring mixture to a boil, reduce heat, and let cook over low heat for 1½ hours. Remove ¼ cup of hot mixture to a small dish and blend with 2 tablespoons of flour. Add to soup mixture, blending thoroughly. Cook over moderately high heat for 15 minutes. Serve hot.

> *Pontoosuc has had an active post office since 1849 when it was known as East Bend. Prior to that time it was called Spillman's Landing after its first settler.*

Scotch Broth

Yield: 8 servings

½ cup raw barley
1 teaspoon salt
4 quarts water
1½ pounds lamb shoulder, cut into
  1-inch cubes
1 large onion, chopped

1 small head cabbage, chopped
1 stalk celery, chopped
2 carrots, chopped
2 tablespoons dried parsley
Salt and pepper and taste

Place barley in a 6-quart saucepan. Add salt and 4 quarts water and bring to a boil. Add lamb and boil for 30 minutes, skimming residue from surface. Add vegetables, salt, and pepper to taste. Cook over low heat for an hour and 15 minutes.

121

> *Peoria Lake was named Pimiteoui by the Indians. The word means "Fat Lake." There were six different forts on its shores before statehood in 1818.*

Salmon Bisque

Yield: 4 cups

1 16-ounce can salmon, oil included
2 large tomatoes, skinned and
  chopped
½ cup chopped onion
3 tablespoons chopped celery leaves
2 cups chicken stock

4 tablespoons butter
4 tablespoons flour
3 cups heavy cream
1½ teaspoons salt
½ teaspoon white pepper

Place salmon in a saucepan. Add tomatoes, onion, celery leaves, and chicken stock. Simmer for 20 minutes. Melt butter in a 2-quart saucepan. Blend in flour. Stir in cream. Add salt and pepper. When the sauce is smooth and boiling, fold in the salmon mixture. Do not boil; serve it at once.

> *Hardin is the seat of Calhoun County and was first called Childs' Landing. The only bridge over the Illinois River in the county is here, and, like the great river passing by, time travels slowly. The air is lush with the scent of apple blossoms in the spring.*

Crab Soup

Yield: 6 servings

4 tablespoons butter
3½ tablespoons flour
1 scallion, chopped, greens and all
3 cups hot milk
½ teaspoon pepper
1 10-ounce package frozen peas
2 cups chicken bouillon or broth

1 10-ounce package frozen cooked crab
1 cup grated Swiss cheese
Juice of 1 lemon
½ teaspoon dried tarragon
1 tablespoon sherry
Salt and pepper to taste
½ cup heavy cream

In a 3-quart saucepan make a roux of the butter and flour. Add scallion. Blend in hot milk to make a medium white sauce. Add pepper. Boil frozen peas in chicken bouillon until tender, 5 minutes. Blend bouillon and peas into white sauce. Over low heat carefully blend in all ingredients except heavy cream. Cook gently until cheese is melted. Do not boil. Remove from heat and swirl in heavy cream.

> *Preemption was named for the preemption laws after being called Fairfield and Madura. Its post office was established in 1843 and also serves Southern Junction.*

Spicy Oyster Soup

Yield: 6 to 8 servings

5 tablespoons butter
5 shallots, minced
½ cup dry white wine
1 pint raw oysters, finely chopped
1 teaspoon salt
¼ teaspoon white pepper
⅛ teaspoon nutmeg
½ 5-ounce package frozen chopped

spinach
2 cups chicken broth
4 cups light cream
2 tablespoons cornstarch
1 teaspoon Worcestershire sauce
2 drops hot pepper sauce
½ cup heavy cream, whipped
Lemon rind

Melt butter in a 4-quart kettle; add shallots and simmer. Stir in wine and bring to a boil. Cook until liquid is reduced. Add oysters and their liquid to wine mixture. Stir in salt, pepper, and nutmeg. Cook and stir over moderate heat for 5 minutes. Remove from heat. In a saucepan, combine spinach and chicken broth. Boil. Reduce heat and cook until spinach is soft. Add the cream and heat gently. Do not boil. Combine the two mixtures and let stand until cooled. Dissolve cornstarch in a little cold water. Stir into soup. Continue stirring until soup is thickened and blended. Add remaining ingredients. Serve hot with a dollop of whipped cream and grating of lemon rind.

Utah was once named Tylerville and has been off and on the map since 1850. Now only the wind rustles its tall grasses, sighing its almost forgotten name.

123

The Sunstone—Architectural Detail from the Mormon Temple—Nauvoo

Bean Soup

Yield: 6 servings

1 pound (2⅓ cups) dried navy beans
2 quarts cold water
1½ pounds meaty ham bone or
   1½ pounds smoked hocks
1 potato, peeled and chopped

1 turnip, peeled and chopped
½ teaspoon salt
6 whole black peppers
1 bay leaf
1 medium onion, sliced

Thoroughly wash beans. Place in a 3-quart saucepan. Cover with 2 quarts cold water. Add ham bone, potato, turnip, and seasonings. Cover and heat to boiling. Boil gently until beans are tender, about 3 to 3½ hours. Add onion during the last half hour. Remove ham bone; cut ham off bone; return meat to soup.

> *Pike County was established January 31, 1821, and was named for General Zebulon Pike, an explorer of the Louisiana Purchase. Pike County once encompassed all of the state north and west of the Illinois River.*

Black Bean Soup

Yield: 8 servings

1 cup black beans, dried
3 shallots, minced
½ cup finely minced celery
½ cup chopped carrot
2 tablespoons butter
¾ teaspoon salt

½ teaspoon pepper
½ teaspoon dry mustard
½ teaspoon nutmeg
2 tablespoons cognac
½ cup heavy cream
1 tablespoon dried parsley

Soak beans in water to cover in covered container overnight. Drain and place in a 3-quart saucepan. Add 5 cups water. Bring to a boil. Sauté shallots, celery, and carrots in butter until soft but not brown. Blend into bean mixture. Add salt, pepper, mustard, nutmeg, and cognac. Let mixture simmer for 1½ hours until beans and vegetables are soft. Puree mixture in blender or food processor. Return mixture to heat and cook gently over low heat for 15 minutes. Fold in heavy cream. Garnish with parsley.

> *Monmouth is the seat of Warren County and the home of Monmouth College. Established in 1831, Monmouth was one of the first towns in Illinois to have paved Streets.*

Cucumber Soup

Yield: 8 servings

1 large onion, chopped
2 large green peppers, chopped
3 large ripe tomatoes, chopped
1 garlic clove, crushed
¼ teaspoon pepper

1 teaspoon salt
3 tablespoons Lucca olive oil
3 tablespoons red wine vinegar
¾ cup water
1 cucumber, thinly sliced

Combine onions, peppers, and tomatoes with garlic and blend or strain through small mesh sieve. Stir in pepper and salt. Add olive oil, beating constantly. Add vinegar and water. Blend well. Chill 2 to 4 hours. Stir in ¾ of the cucumber slices. Spoon into small soup cups. Garnish each serving with remaining cucumber slices. Serve with French bread.

> *La Prairie was first incorporated as a town in 1869. The CB and Q Railroad clackety-clacks through as it did when the town was called Gibbstown and Pitman.*

Corn Soup

Yield: 6 servings

1 scallion, minced, green and all
½ cup celery, chopped fine
3½ tablespoons butter
3 tablespoons flour

3 cups hot milk
1½ cups cooked corn
½ teaspoon salt
¼ teaspoon pepper

Sauté scallion and celery in butter until soft but not brown. Blend in flour and gradually add hot milk, stirring constantly until thick and smooth. Add corn, salt, and pepper and cook over low heat for 20 minutes, stirring constantly.

> *Fraker's Grove was a Potowatomi village when Michael Fraker, the first settler in northeastern Knox County, arrived. He made peace with the Indians of the area through kindness and understanding.*

Prairie Corn Chowder

Yield: 6 servings

3 tablespoons chopped bacon
1 medium onion, chopped (½ cup)
2 cups cubed potatoes
2 cups boiling water
2 16-ounce cans corn
1½ quarts heavy cream

2 teaspoons salt
¼ teaspoon pepper
¼ teaspoon rosemary
¼ cup chopped pimiento
½ cup shredded Cheddar cheese
2 tablespoons minced parsley

Brown bacon in a heavy 2-quart pot. Remove bacon bits. Add onion; sauté until soft. Add potatoes and water; simmer about 20 minutes or until potatoes are cooked. Add corn, cream, salt, pepper, rosemary, pimiento, and bacon. Heat; add cheese and parsley.

> *Adams County was named for John Quincy Adams, sixth President of the United States, and was established in 1825. Its size is 866 square miles.*

Onion Soup with Toasted Bread and Cheese

126

Yield: 6 servings

5 tablespoons butter
2½ tablespoons vegetable oil
2½ pounds onions, thinly sliced
1 teaspoon salt
3½ tablespoons flour

2 quarts beef stock
12 1-inch thick slices of French bread
2½ teaspoons Lucca olive oil
2 garlic cloves, cut in halves
1½ cups grated Swiss cheese

In a 5-quart soup kettle, melt the butter with the oil over moderate heat. Stir in the onions and salt. Cook uncovered over low heat, stirring occasionally, for 20 minutes or until the onions are nicely browned. Sprinkle flour over the onions and cook, stirring for 2 to 3 minutes. Remove from the heat. In a separate saucepan, bring the stock to a boil. Stir the hot stock into the onions. Return the soup to low heat and simmer for another 30 minutes. Skim off the fat. Taste for seasoning.

Preheat oven to 325 degrees F. Place the slices of bread side by side on a buttered cookie sheet and bake for 10 minutes. Spread both sides of each slice with a thin coat of olive oil. Turn the slices over and bake for another 10 minutes or until lightly browned. Rub each slice with cut side of garlic clove. Place one slice of bread into each individual soup bowl and ladle the soup over. Sprinkle with the grated cheese.

Cream of Onion Soup

Yield: 6 to 8 servings
3 cups sliced onions
3 tablespoons butter
2½ tablespoons flour
1 cup chicken bouillon or broth
4 cups hot milk

½ teaspoon nutmeg
½ teaspoon pepper
½ cup heavy cream
½ cup grated Swiss or Gruyere
cheese

Sauté onions in butter in 3-quart saucepan. When onions are soft but not browned, blend in flour. Blend in chicken bouillon or broth. Gradually add hot milk, stirring constantly until thick and smooth. Add nutmeg and pepper and cook for 10 to 12 minutes, stirring constantly. While still over heat, blend in cream. Ladle into soup plates and sprinkle generously with grated cheese.

127

Split Pea Soup

Yield: 6 to 8 servings
1 cup dried peas
1 cup onions, minced
6 slices bacon, cut into small pieces
3 tablespoons butter

2½ tablespoons flour
2 cups hot milk
1 teaspoon salt
½ teaspoon pepper

Soak peas in water to cover in covered earthenware container. Drain and place in a 3-quart saucepan. Add 2 quarts water, onions, and bacon. Simmer for 1½ hours or until peas are very tender. Put into blender or food processor and purée peas. Make a roux of the butter and flour. Stir in hot milk until smooth and thickened. Blend in pea mixture, salt, and pepper. Simmer for 15 minutes.

Creamy Pea Soup

Yield: 4 servings
2 scallions, chopped, greens and all
1 10–ounce package frozen peas
½ teaspoon salt
2½ tablespoons butter
2 tablespoons flour

3 cups chicken bouillon or broth
½ teaspoon pepper
½ cup heavy cream
Few sprigs fresh dill or 1 teaspoon
    dried dill weed

Place scallions and peas in 2-quart saucepan. Add salt and water to barely cover. Cook vegetables until tender, about 12 to 15 minutes. Drain and purée in blender or food mill. Make a roux of the butter and flour. Gradually add hot chicken bouillon and beat with whisk until smooth and thickened. Add pepper. Blend in vegetable mixture and bring to a boil, stirring constantly. Remove from heat and blend in heavy cream. Ladle into soup plates and garnish with a sprig of fresh dill.

128

Potato Soup

Yield: 8 servings
2 cups chopped scallions
4 tablespoons butter
2 quarts milk
4 cups cooked and mashed potatoes

Salt and pepper to taste
½ cup heavy cream
1½ teaspoons parsley

Sauté scallions in butter in 4-quart saucepan until soft but not browned. Add milk and bring to a simmer. Gradually add a little of the milk mixture to the potatoes and blend thoroughly. Continue adding milk mixture to potatoes until potatoes resemble a puree in texture. Combine potatoes with remaining milk mixture and beat with a whisk until smooth. Bring to a boil, stirring constantly and add salt and pepper to taste. Remove from heat and swirl in heavy cream. Serve hot and sprinkle each serving with parsley.

> *Calhoun County was named after John C. Calhoun, the "Father of Nullification" and Vice President of the United States. The county was established in 1825.*

Hot Vichyssoise

Yield: 6 servings
5 tablespoons butter
6 onions, sliced
12 large leeks, chopped
5 potatoes, chopped
6 cups chicken stock

1 teaspoon salt
White pepper to taste
2 cups heavy cream
2 tablespoons minced chives

Melt butter in a 2-quart kettle. Add onion and leeks; simmer for 12 minutes. Add potatoes, chicken stock, and seasonings. Boil. Reduce heat and simmer 1 hour. Strain through sieve and blend in cream. Reheat gently. Serve hot with chives sprinkled over.

129

> *Alexis sits astride the boundary line of Mercer and Warren Counties. Once known as Alexandria, it was incorporated as a village in 1873.*

Cream of Tomato Soup

Yield: 6 servings
2 tablespoons butter
1½ tablespoons flour
2 tablespoons chopped scallions
2 cups scalded milk
1 cup chopped fresh tomatoes or

1 8-ounce can tomatoes
½ teaspoon sugar
½ teaspoon salt
⅛ teaspoon pepper
⅛ teaspoon baking soda

Make a roux of the butter and flour in a 3-quart saucepan. Add scallions. Mix with scalded milk until a light sauce is achieved. Remove from heat. Cook tomatoes over medium heat for 25 minutes. Strain tomatoes. Add sugar, salt, pepper, and soda to tomatoes. Blend tomato mixture into bechamel. Serve hot.

Cold Tomato Soup

Yield: 6 servings

6 large tomatoes, chopped
1 onion, chopped
¼ cup water
Salt to taste
Freshly ground black pepper to taste
1 teaspoon tarragon

2 tablespoons tomato paste
2 tablespoons flour
2 cups hot chicken stock
1 cup heavy cream
6 lemon slices

Place tomatoes in a 2-quart pot with onion, water, salt, pepper, and tarragon. Bring to a boil and cook 7 minutes. Stir in tomato paste. Blend well. Mix flour with a small amount of cold water and add to tomato mixture. Blend. Add hot chicken stock and stir until soup comes to a boil. Remove from heat and sieve, using a wooden spoon to force as much pulp as possible. Stir and cool. When cooled, stir in cream. Serve topped with lemon slices.

130

Zucchini Soup

Yield: 8 servings

3 cups sliced zucchini
1 small garlic toe, minced
1 cup chopped onion
½ cup (1 stick) butter
1 cup sliced celery hearts
1 10-ounce package frozen mixed vegetables

1 9½-ounce can green beans
2 tablespoons sugar
½ cup uncooked rice
1 cup water
½ cup milk
Salt and pepper to taste

Sauté zucchini, garlic, and onions in butter until soft but not browned in 3-quart pot. Add next 6 ingredients and let cook over low heat for 20 minutes covered. Uncover and blend milk into mixture. Add salt and pepper to taste.

Kirkwood, whose name means church in the forest, was incorporated as a village in 1874. It was formerly known as Center Grove, Linden, and Young America.

131

Native Birds

Cabbage Soup

Yield: 6 servings

2 cups finely shredded cooked beets
2 cups chopped cabbage
1½ cups chopped onions
2-pound blade bone pot roast
1 garlic clove, crushed
1 carrot, chopped
1 celery stalk, chopped

½ cup vinegar
⅓ cup sugar
⅔ cup raisins
¾ teaspoon salt
½ teaspoon pepper
½ cup sour cream
1 teaspoon dried dill weed

Place beets, cabbage, onions, pot roast, garlic, carrot, and celery in a 4-quart saucepan. Cover with 2 quarts of water. Cook covered for 1½ hours, until meat and vegetables are soft. Add vinegar, sugar, and raisins. Add salt and pepper. Continue cooking for 30 minutes. Remove pot roast to a separate dish. Cut in serving pieces and place a piece of meat in each soup bowl. Ladle soup into soup bowls. Garnish with a dollop of sour cream sprinkled with dill weed.

> *Gulfport sits in the low land of the Mississippi. It was originally named East Burlington and was platted in 1855 as a ferry port.*

Cream of Lettuce Soup

Yield: 4 to 6 servings

½ pound bacon
3 cups cold water
¾ cup flour
½ pint sour cream

2 cups heavy cream
2 teaspoons salt
1 medium head of lettuce, shredded

Cut bacon into 1-inch pieces, place in a 3-quart pan, and fry until golden brown. Add 3 cups cold water, bring to a boil and simmer 10 minutes. Gradually add flour to sour cream. Beat with a whisk until smooth. Add cream, stirring well. Add a ladle or so of bacon broth to sour cream mixture slowly to warm it. Pour sour cream mixture through wire sieve into broth and stir until it simmers. Add salt and shredded lettuce. Simmer for 5 minutes.

> *Pittsfield is the seat of Pike County. John Hay, secretary to President Lincoln, described the town as a center of "light and learning." Pittsfield's court house is an architectural landmark designed by Henry Elliot and constructed in 1894.*

Creamed Spinach Soup

Yield: 6 servings

1 10-ounce package frozen chopped
   spinach
2 cups chicken broth
1 onion, chopped
4 tablespoons butter

4 tablespoons flour
1 cup light cream
¼ teaspoon mace
Salt and pepper to taste
½ cup heavy cream

Cook spinach in chicken broth in a 2-quart saucepan according to package directions. Sauté onion in butter until soft. Stir in flour. Add cream, stirring until smooth. Pour into spinach-broth mixture. Add seasonings and boil, stirring mixture. Add heavy cream and serve.

> *Aledo is the seat of Mercer County and was established in 1855. Aledo got its name by early settlers drawing letters from a hat until a pronounceable combination turned up.*

Escarole Soup

Yield: 6 servings

2 soup bones
1 teaspoon salt
2 tablespoons tomato paste
1 carrot, chopped
1 potato, peeled and chopped
1½ quarts water
1 tablespoon minced parsley
¾ pound ground beef
2 garlic cloves, minced

1 egg
Salt to taste
Pepper to taste
3½ tablespoons grated Parmesan
   cheese
1½ pounds escarole, chopped
1 onion, chopped
½ cup chopped celery

In a 3-quart saucepan simmer bones, salt, tomato paste, carrots, potatoes, and water for ½ hour. Mix together parsley, ground beef, garlic, egg, salt, pepper, and cheese. Form into small meatballs and add to soup. Simmer 10 minutes; add escarole and remaining vegetables. Simmer 30 minutes. Serve with grated Romano cheese.

> *Astoria was named for John Jacob Astor who owned land in the area. It was a station on the four-horse stagecoach line between Peoria and Quincy.*

Cream of Avocado Soup

Yield: 6 servings

2 large avocados, chopped
4 cups chicken stock
1 cup powdered non-dairy creamer
2 teaspoons lemon juice

¾ teaspoon salt
¼ teaspoon Worcestershire sauce
¼ teaspoon white pepper
½ teaspoon dry mustard

Combine avocado and 2 cups chicken stock in the blender until smooth. Combine all ingredients in a 2-quart saucepan and beat with a wire whisk. Bring to a boil, stirring constantly. Serve garnished with slices of avocado.

> *Seaton, known in the past as Pope's River and Sully, was named for John L. Seaton. It has had an active post office since 1883 and was incorporated as a village in 1907.*

Mushroom Soup

Yield: 6 to 8 servings

4 tablespoons butter
2 pounds mushrooms, chopped
1½ quarts water

1 cup beef bouillon
½ teaspoon pepper
1 tablespoon cognac

Sauté mushrooms in butter until soft in a 4-quart saucepan. Add 1½ quarts water. Cover and simmer for 1½ hours. Drain mushroom pieces, reserving liquid, and purée in blender or food processor. Return to liquid, blending thoroughly. Add bouillon, black pepper, and cognac. Mix thoroughly and let simmer for 10 to 15 minutes.

> *Brown County was named for Jacob Brown who was a Major General during the War of 1812. It was established in 1839 and is 307 square miles in size.*

Peanut Soup

Yield: 4 to 6 servings

4 or 5 scallions, sliced
2 celery stalks, minced
2 tablespoons butter
3 tablespoons flour
1 10¾-ounce can chicken broth
2 cups heavy cream

½ cup creamy peanut butter
1½ teaspoons lemon juice
3 tablespoons roasted peanuts, chopped
2 tablespoons minced chives

In a 2-quart saucepan sauté onions and celery in butter until tender. Blend in flour. Gradually add chicken broth and cream. Add peanut butter and lemon juice. Heat for 15 minutes. *Do not boil.* Just before serving, purée soup in blender or food processor. Top servings with chopped peanuts and minced chives.

> *Kampsville is near the site of the Koster Farm, the archaeological dig which has brought forth Indian remains from more than 10,000 years ago when the last glacier receded.*

Cheese Soup

Yield: 6 servings

½ cup chopped carrots
½ cup chopped green pepper
½ cup chopped onion
½ cup chopped celery
4½ tablespoons butter

⅓ cup flour
1 quart seasoned chicken stock
12 ounces Cheddar cheese, grated
4 cups light cream
Salt and white pepper to taste

Sauté vegetables in butter until tender in a 3-quart saucepan. Blend in flour. Cook one minute, stirring constantly. Add stock and cook until thickened, stirring. Stir in cheese. Add cream. Season to taste.

> *Henderson County was named by early immigrants from Henderson County in Kentucky. The county was established in 1841 and is 381 square miles in size.*

Fruit Soup

Yield: 10 cups

4 cups rhubarb, fresh or frozen
1¼ cups water
⅛ teaspoon salt
1 teaspoon lemon juice
2½ tablespoons tapioca
Sugar to taste

1 12-ounce can tart cherries, drained
1 10-ounce package frozen strawberries
1 10-ounce package frozen raspberries

Combine rhubarb, water, salt, lemon juice, tapioca, and sugar in a 3-quart saucepan. Cook until tender. Remove from heat and add the cherries, strawberries, and raspberries. Serve warm.

136

Oak Hill Cemetery—Lewistown

Layered Salad

Yield: 8 servings

1 head iceberg lettuce, broken into small pieces
1 cup chopped celery
2 red onions, chopped
1 green pepper, chopped
¾ pound fresh mushrooms, thinly sliced
1 10-ounce package frozen green

peas, thawed
1 cup mayonnaise
2 tablespoons sugar
1 tablespoon water
Salt and pepper to taste
1 cup grated Cheddar cheese
½ pound bacon, fried crisp

Layer first 6 ingredients in order listed. Combine mayonnaise, sugar, water, salt, and pepper. Mix well. Spread mayonnaise mixture over top layer. Sprinkle with cheese. Refrigerate covered overnight. Use bacon as garnish when served.

> *Liverpool's first post office was set up in 1849. Once an important river town as a depot for products transported by boats, its glory is now only mist-shrouded memory.*

Tomatoes with Dill Dressing

Yield: 6 servings

½ cup sour cream
1 tablespoon mayonnaise
Pinch cayenne
Pinch salt

⅛ teaspoon dry mustard
¼ teaspoon dill weed
1½ teaspoons lemon juice
3 large tomatoes

Combine sour cream, mayonnaise, cayenne, salt, dry mustard, dill, and lemon juice. Chill. Slice tomatoes; place in a shallow bowl. Pour dressing over tomatoes to serve.

137

> *Roseville was originally called Hat Grove because a grove of trees nearby looked like a hat. The first settler was Truman Eldridge who built a mill here in 1836. Today Roseville is known for its superior beef, produced from the herds of Black Angus cattle which are raised in the countryside around the town.*

Broccoli Salad

Yield: 4 to 6 servings

2 10-ounce packages frozen broccoli, thawed and cut up
1 cup chopped celery
½ cup chopped onion
2 hard-cooked eggs, chopped

1 2-ounce jar pimientoes
1 tablespoon seasoned salt
1 teaspoon tarragon
½ teaspoon pepper
¾ cup mayonnaise

In a large bowl, combine all ingredients. Toss together until evenly coated. Refrigerate. Stir before serving.

Cashew Pea Salad

Yield: 5 to 6 servings

1 10-ounce package frozen peas, thawed
¾ cup cashews
6 slices crisp fried bacon, crumbled

2 scallions, thinly sliced
1½ cups sour cream
⅛ teaspoon nutmeg
⅛ teaspoon allspice

Mix all ingredients gently.

138

Caviar Potato Salad

Yield: 8 to 10 servings

2 pounds potatoes, cooked, skinned, and cubed
2 cups sour cream

Pepper
2 2-ounce jars red caviar

Place potatoes in a serving bowl. Mix with sour cream and pepper to taste. Stir in caviar. Chill.

Spinach and Onions in Yogurt

Yield: 8 servings

1 cup chopped onions
3 tablespoons butter
2 10-ounce packages frozen
  chopped spinach, thawed
2 8-ounce cartons unflavored yogurt

1 teaspoon salt
¼ teaspoon freshly ground black
  pepper
⅛ teaspoon nutmeg

Sauté onions in butter until browned. Add drained spinach. Cook over moderate heat for 5 to 7 minutes. Cool. Stir in yogurt and seasonings.

> *Canton was founded in 1825 by Isaac Swan. The town got its name because it was thought to be directly opposite to Canton, China. The area around Canton contains the largest source of soft coal in the United States.*

Mushroom Cream Salad

Yield: 4 servings

1 pound fresh mushrooms, coarsely
  chopped
3 tablespoons grated onion
2 tablespoons lemon juice
2 teaspoons sugar
1 teaspoon salt

⅛ teaspoon dry mustard
½ teaspoon pepper
½ cup heavy cream
¼ cup sour cream
Romaine, tomato wedges, and
  parsley sprigs for serving

139

Toss mushrooms, onion, lemon juice, sugar, salt, mustard, and pepper in bowl. Cover and refrigerate 30 minutes. Beat cream in a chilled bowl until thick; fold in sour cream. Stir in mushroom mixture. Line serving bowl with romaine; mound mushroom mixture in center. Garnish with parsley and tomato wedges.

> *Oquawka means "yellow-banks" in Sauk. It is the seat of Henderson County. Founded by Alexis and Stephen Phelps in 1827 as an Indian trading post, the town is a summer resort for residents of larger nearby communities.*

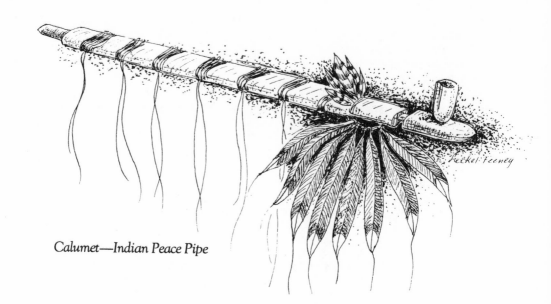

Calumet—Indian Peace Pipe

Pickled Eggs

Yield: 12 servings
2 tablespoons mild dry mustard
2 cups white vinegar
½ cup water
1 cup sugar
1 tablespoon celery seed

1 tablespoon salt
1 tablespoon mustard seed
6 whole cloves
2 medium onions, sliced
12 hard-cooked eggs

In saucepan blend mustard with a little vinegar; add remaining vinegar and next 6 ingredients. Cover. Heat to boiling. Simmer 10 minutes. Cool. Pour over onions and eggs; cover and refrigerate overnight.

> *Rome was founded in 1835. It has been variously known as LaSalle, Rome Farms, Rome Station, and Cottage Beach. It is a resort town and is just across the river from the Woodford County Public Hunting Area.*

Syboy Salad

Yield: 6 servings

¼ cup Lucca olive oil
1 tablespoon lemon juice
½ teaspoon sugar
1 small garlic clove, minced
1 teaspoon oregano
Salt and pepper to taste
5 tomatoes, sliced
2 red onions, thinly sliced

Combine oil, lemon juice, sugar, garlic, oregano, salt, and pepper. Pour over tomatoes and onions. Marinate 4 hours in refrigerator.

Chillicothe, named by its first settlers for Chillicothe, Ohio, was established in 1836 when the Indians of the area moved west after the Black Hawk War.

Spinach Salad with Hot Dressing

Yield: 6 servings

1 pound fresh spinach, washed and
  trimmed
1 tablespoon bacon drippings
1 tablespoon flour
1 tablespoon sugar
½ teaspoon salt
⅛ teaspoon pepper
¼ cup mayonnaise
3 tablespoons vinegar
½ cup water
6 slices bacon, fried and chopped
2 tablespoons minced onion

Tear spinach into bite-size pieces and place in a large bowl. Blend flour, sugar, salt, and pepper into drippings. Add mayonnaise; blend carefully. Combine vinegar and water and add slowly to flour mixture. Stir until smooth. Heat sauce just until it begins to bubble. Pour sauce over spinach and sprinkle with bacon and onion. Toss until coated.

The Wabash Railroad clatters through Mound Station whose first post office was established in 1860. It is also known as Timewell.

Sauerkraut Salad

Yield: 4 servings

1 cup Lucca olive oil
½ cup vinegar
1¼ cup sugar
1 teaspoon tarragon
1 34-ounce can sauerkraut, drained
  and washed
1 cup chopped celery
1 carrot, grated
1 cup chopped green peppers
1 small onion, chopped

Blend the oil, vinegar, sugar, and tarragon. Add all other ingredients. Mix well. Refrigerate for 24 hours.

Hanna City, once known as Leo, Logan, and Summerville, was platted in 1883 and was incorporated as a village in 1903. Once a mining town, it is now a "bedroom community" for the industries in Peoria.

Kidney Bean Salad

Yield: 6 servings
2 16-ounce cans red kidney beans, drained
1 cup chopped celery
½ cup chopped sweet pickles
½ cup chopped onion
3 hard-cooked eggs, chopped

¼ cup mayonnaise
1 tablespoon pickle liquid
2 teaspoons prepared mustard
1 teaspoon salt
¼ teaspoon pepper

To beans, add celery, pickles, onion, and eggs. Mix together mayonnaise, pickle liquid, mustard, salt, and pepper. Toss lightly with bean mixture.

142

Browning was named for Orville O. Browning, a U. S. Senator during Lincoln's presidency. Its first post office was established in 1850 and serves Bluff City, Bluff Springs, and Sheldon's Grove.

Downtown Salad

Yield: 8 servings
⅔ cup vinegar
⅔ cup sugar
⅓ cup vegetable oil
1 teaspoon salt
½ teaspoon pepper

1 head cabbage, shredded
1 pound carrots, thinly sliced
3 cucumbers, thinly sliced
1 cauliflower, divided into flowerettes
10 scallions, sliced

Mix vinegar, sugar, oil, salt, and pepper. Pour over vegetables in large bowl. Mix. Refrigerate.

Warren County was named for Joseph Warren, a physician who served at Lexington, and a Major General of the Massachusetts militia. The county was established in 1825 and is 542 square miles in size.

Carrot Slaw

Yield: 6 servings
¼ teaspoon paprika
½ teaspoon salt
¼ teaspoon celery seed
½ cup mayonnaise

1 cup shredded carrots
3 cups shredded cabbage, chilled
2 tablespoons minced green pepper

Mix together seasonings and mayonnaise. Toss with remaining ingredients.

> *Disco was not named after a dance; no one is sure how it got its name. Its post office fled in 1920 after almost fifty years of operation, and now it is an adjunct of Dallas City.*

Mexicali Slaw

Yield: 6 servings
1 quart shredded cabbage, chilled

1 green pepper, coarsely chopped

Dressing

¼ cup mayonnaise
¼ cup sour cream
3 tablespoons wine vinegar
3 tablespoons sugar

½ teaspoon chili powder
½ teaspoon celery seed
½ teaspoon salt

Combine dressing ingredients. Chill. Toss together vegetables and dressing.

> *Cuba was once two villages named Centerville and Middleton. When the towns merged, neither would accept the name of the other. Since Havana sixteen miles away was thriving, Cuba was a logical choice.*

German Slaw

Yield: 6 servings
4 cups shredded cabbage, chilled
¼ cup chopped green pepper

2 tablespoons minced parsley
1 tablespoon minced onion

Dressing

¾ cup chopped bacon
2 tablespoons lemon juice
1 teaspoon salt

½ teaspoon dry mustard
½ cup mayonnaise

Fry bacon to golden brown. Add lemon juice and seasonings. Stir well; mix with mayonnaise. Toss together vegetables and dressing.

> *Toulon was founded in 1841 and is the seat of Stark County. It was originally called Miller's Point. Today Toulon manufactures superior Swiss cheese.*

Hot Slaw

Mrs. White of Smithshire in Land Between the Rivers says, "My great-grandmother, Mary Ellen Starkey, served this when we were tired of fresh slaw."

Yield: 6 servings
5 cups cabbage, shredded
4 slices bacon, chopped
2 tablespoons brown sugar
2 tablespoons flour
½ cup water
⅓ cup vinegar
Salt and pepper to taste

144   Cook cabbage in boiling water 5 minutes. Drain completely. Fry bacon in large skillet until crisp. Remove bacon. Add sugar and flour to bacon fat. Blend well. Add water, vinegar, salt, and pepper. Cook until thickened. Add cabbage. Heat thoroughly and serve.

—*Carolyn White*

> *Hamilton is situated on Lake Cooper which is formed by a dam on the Mississippi. The town was founded by Artois Hamilton in 1852 and is now the home of "the world's largest manufacturer of Bee products," D. Dadant & Sons.*

Cole Slaw with Mustard Dressing

Yield: 6 servings
4 cups shredded cabbage, chilled
1 onion, thinly sliced
¼ cup minced parsley

Dressing

1 teaspoon salt
½ teaspoon white pepper
2 tablespoons chili sauce
1 teaspoon dry mustard
1 tablespoon sugar
¼ cup vegetable oil
2 tablespoons vinegar or lemon juice

Combine all dressing ingredients. Stir until thickened. Chill. Toss together vegetables and dressing.

Galesburg is the birthplace of Carl Sandburg and the home of Knox College. The town was founded by Reverend George Washington Gale immediately after the end of the 1832 Black Hawk War.

Red and Green Cabbage Slaw

Yield: 6 servings
1 medium onion, chopped
2 cups shredded red cabbage, chilled

2 cups shredded green cabbage, chilled

Dressing

¼ cup vegetable oil
2 tablespoons vinegar
½ teaspoon celery seed

1 teaspoon salt
½ teaspoon sugar
¼ teaspoon pepper

Combine dressing ingredients and chill. Shake before using. Toss together vegetables and dressing.

Henry's slogan is "Best town in Illinois by a dam site." It was settled in 1833 and named after General James D. Henry, who was known for his exploits during the Black Hawk War.

Slaw with Cooked Dressing

Yield: 6 servings
1 quart shredded cabbage, chilled
⅓ cup chopped green pepper
⅓ cup grated onion

Dressing

3 tablespoons butter, at room
   temperature
3 tablespoons sugar
1½ teaspoons dry mustard
¼ teaspoon celery seed

½ teaspoon salt
Dash pepper
1 egg
¼ cup vinegar
¼ cup water

Cream butter and sugar; add remaining dry ingredients. Stir in egg. Combine vinegar with water and add to mixture. Cook over a low flame; stir constantly until thickened. Chill. Toss together vegetables and dressing.

> *Knoxville's first post office was established in 1844 when it was known as Henderson and earlier Knox Courthouse. The courthouse was built in 1839 and still stands as a remainder of the days when the town was the seat of Knox County.*

Cabbage-Sour Cream Slaw

Yield: 6 servings
4 cups shredded cabbage, chilled

Dressing

2 tablespoons sugar
¼ teaspoon salt
Dash pepper

¼ teaspoon dry mustard
3 tablespoons lemon juice
½ cup sour cream

Combine all dressing ingredients. Toss together cabbage and dressing.

> *Elmwood was founded in 1864 by William J. Phelps and is the birthplace of the American sculptor Lorado Taft whose bronze statue "Pioneers of the Prairie" stands in Central Park here.*

Cabbage, Carrot, and Onion Slaw

Yield: 6 servings
3 cups shredded cabbage, chilled
1 large carrot, grated
1 medium onion, thinly sliced

½ teaspoon salt
¼ teaspoon celery seed
⅓ cup French dressing

Toss together all ingredients

> *Payson's first post office was established in 1837. It serves Bluff Hall and Fall Creeks. Payson was incorporated as a village in 1869.*

Burial Mounds—Dickson

Salmon Salad Mold

Yield: 8 servings

2 envelopes unflavored gelatin
½ cup cold water
¼ cup lemon juice
2 cups sour cream
½ cup mayonnaise
½ teaspoon salt

1 16–ounce can salmon, drained,
   boned, and flaked
1 cup pared and chopped cucumber
1 cup finely minced chopped celery
½ cup shredded Cheddar cheese

Soften gelatin in cold water. Dissolve over low heat. Combine with lemon juice and add to sour cream, mayonnaise, and salt. Stir. Add salmon, cucumber, and celery. Stir. Pour into an oiled 1½-quart casserole. Sprinkle with cheese. Chill until firm. Cut in squares. Serve on salad greens.

Avocado Mold

Yield: 4 servings

1½ envelopes unflavored gelatin
½ cup cold water
2 ripe avocados, peeled
1½ cups sour cream

1½ tablespoons lemon juice
1 teaspoon salt
½ teaspoon white pepper

In a small saucepan soften gelatin in water. Place pan over hot water and stir until gelatin is dissolved. Mash the avocados and stir in the sour cream, gelatin, lemon juice, salt, and pepper. Pour mixture into an oiled 1-quart mold. Cover. Chill until firm. Unmold.

Perfect Salad

Yield: 6 servings

1 envelope (1 tablespoon) plus 1
   teaspoon unflavored gelatin
¼ cup cold water
1¼ cups boiling water
1 8-ounce jar pimiento-stuffed olives
1 teaspoon salt
½ cup sugar
¼ cup lemon juice
2 tablespoons white vinegar

1 tablespoon grated onion
¾ cup shredded cabbage
¼ cup chopped green pepper
½ cup shredded carrots
½ cup chopped celery
⅓ cup pecans, chopped
Lettuce
6 tablespoons mayonnaise

Soften gelatin in cold water. Add boiling water; stir to dissolve gelatin. Reserving liquid, drain olives. Add salt, sugar, lemon juice, vinegar, and 1 tablespoon olive liquid; stir until sugar is dissolved. Chill until thickened. Chop ¼ cup olives. Add onion, cabbage, pepper, carrots, celery, olives, and nuts. Pour into 6 buttered individual ½-cup molds. Chill until firm. Unmold. Serve on lettuce with a tablespoon of mayonnaise.

Roquefort Salad Mold

Yield: 8 servings

¾ cup Bleu cheese, crushed
2 3-ounce packages cream cheese, at room temperature
1½ teaspoons heavy cream
1 tablespoon unflavored gelatin
1 tablespoon lemon juice
1 pint heavy cream, whipped
½ teaspoon salt
½ teaspoon white pepper

Mix Bleu cheese, cream cheese, and cream together. Soften gelatin in lemon juice and stir over hot water until dissolved. Cool. Fold whipped cream into cheese and gelatin mixture. Add salt and pepper. Place in a 1-quart oiled ring mold and refrigerate until set. Unmold and fill center with fresh fruit.

149

Pineapple-Rum Mold

Yield: 6 servings

2 tablespoons or envelopes unflavored gelatin
½ cup fresh or frozen lime juice
1 14-ounce can pineapple bits
1½ teaspoons grated lime or lemon peel
½ cup sugar
¼ teaspoon salt
1 cup orange juice
½ cup light rum
1 avocado

Soften gelatin in lime juice. Drain syrup from pineapple into pint measure; add water to make 2 cups liquid. Combine with lime peel, sugar, and salt. Heat, stirring to dissolve sugar. Add softened gelatin; heat and stir until dissolved. Cool and stir in orange juice and rum. Chill until mixture thickens and begins to jell. Cut avocado in half, remove seed, and dice meat. Fold avocado and pineapple into thickened gelatin. Turn into a 1½-quart mold and chill until firm. Turn out on a chilled serving dish. Garnish with lettuce.

Molded Salad

Yield: 6 servings

1 2-ounce package lime-flavored gelatin
1 cup boiling water
1 cup sour cream
1 4-ounce jar maraschino cherries, sliced
1 8-ounce can crushed pineapple, drained
¾ cup chopped pecans

Dissolve gelatin in boiling water. Cool. Stir in remaining ingredients. Pour into a 1½ quart mold, and chill until firm.

Egg Nog Molded Salad

Yield: 8 servings

2 cups crushed pineapple with juice
1 tablespoon unflavored gelatin
3 tablespoons fresh lime juice
1½ cups egg nog
¾ cup chopped celery
1 3-ounce package raspberry-flavored gelatin
2 cups boiling water
1 10-ounce package frozen cranberry relish, thawed
½ cup chopped pecans

Drain juice from pineapple into saucepan; heat to boiling. Soften gelatin in lime juice. Add pineapple juice. Cool. Add egg nog and chill until partially set. Fold in drained pineapple and celery. Pour into a 2-quart mold and chill. Dissolve raspberry gelatin in boiling water. Add cranberry relish and nuts. Chill until mixture begins to thicken. When egg nog layer is almost set, pour raspberry mixture on top and chill until firm. Unmold on bed of lettuce.

Blueberry Salad

Yield: 8 servings
2 packages orange-flavored gelatin
2 cups hot water
1 3-ounce package cream cheese
1 cup sour cream
½ teaspoon salt

¼ cup sugar
2 egg yolks
Grated rind and juice of 1 lemon
2 egg whites, beaten stiff
1½ cups fresh blueberries

Dissolve gelatin in hot water; chill until partially thickened. Beat cheese, sour cream, salt, sugar, and egg yolks with electric mixer until light and fluffy. Add rind and juice of lemon. Fold in egg whites. Fold into gelatin mixture with blueberries. Pour into a 2-quart mold and chill until firm.

Fandon is unincorporated. It has also been known as Middletown and Young. Its first post office opened in 1871 and is still active for the one hundred inhabitants of the settlement.

Orange Sherbet Salad

Yield: 6 servings
1 6-ounce package orange gelatin
1 cup boiling water
1 pint orange sherbet

1 cup mandarin oranges
1 cup crushed pineapple
1 cup heavy cream, whipped

Add gelatin to boiling water and dissolve. Then add sherbet and fruit. Fold in cream. Pour into mold and freeze.

Versailles was first known as Sugar Grove when its post office was established in 1837. Incorporated in 1861 as a village, it was named after Versailles, Kentucky.

Ambrosia Salad

Yield: 6 servings
1 cup shredded coconut
1 cup mandarin orange sections
1 cup pineapple chunks

1 cup miniature marshmallows
1 cup sour cream

Mix all ingredients well and chill overnight.

Twenty-Four Hour Salad

Yield: 8 servings

2 eggs
¼ cup sugar
Juice of 1 lemon
1 cup heavy cream, whipped
24 marshmallows, quartered
1 pound white grapes, seeded and

halved
1 8-ounce can crushed pineapple, drained
¾ cup slivered almonds
Lettuce leaves

Combine eggs, sugar, and lemon juice in top of double boiler. Cook until thickened. Fold mixture into cream. Fold in marshmallows, fruit, and nuts. Chill overnight. Serve on lettuce.

152

Orange-Cream Fruit Salad

Yield: 8 servings

2 10-ounce cans pineapple tidbits, drained
2 8-ounce cans peach slices, drained
2 5½-ounce cans mandarin oranges, drained
3 medium bananas, sliced

2 medium apples, cored and chopped
1 3¾-ounce package instant vanilla pudding
1½ cups light cream
⅓ cup orange juice, concentrated
¾ cup sour cream

Combine and mix fruits. Combine pudding mix, cream, and orange juice; beat with a rotary beater until blended, 2 minutes. Beat in sour cream. Fold into fruit mixture. Cover and chill.

Frosted Fruit Salad

12 servings

1 3-ounce package lemon-flavored
gelatin
1 3-ounce package orange-flavored
gelatin
2 cups boiling water

1½ cups cold water
1 1-pound 4-ounce can (2½ cups)
crushed pineapple, drained
2 bananas, chopped
30 small marshmallows

Frosting

1 egg, beaten
2 tablespoons flour
2 tablespoons butter
½ cup sugar

1 cup pineapple juice
1 cup heavy cream, whipped
¾ cup shredded sharp cheese

Dissolve gelatins in boiling water. Add cold water. Chill until thickened. Fold in fruit and marshmallows. Pour into oiled 9-by-13-inch pan.

Frosting

153

Combine egg, flour, butter, sugar, and juice. Cook slowly until thickened; stir constantly. Cool. Fold mixture into cream. Spread over gelatin mixture; sprinkle with cheese. Chill until firm.

> Abingdon was named by Abraham Swartz for his hometown in Missouri. Its first post office was established in 1857. Abingdon is the home of the Animal Trap Company which designed and built the best mousetrap in the world.

Violets—Native Wildflower

Clover—Native wildflower

154

Egg Salad

Yield: 6 servings

¼ cup green pepper, chopped
2 tablespoons pimiento
¼ cup chopped celery
1 tablespoon chopped parsley
2 tablespoons minced onion
1½ teaspoons salt
¼ teaspoon pepper

9 hard-cooked eggs, chopped
1 3-ounce package cream cheese, at
    room temperature
¼ cup mayonnaise
Black olives, for garnish
Watercress, for garnish

Mix together green pepper, pimiento, celery, parsley, onion, salt, and pepper. Add eggs; mix lightly. Blend cream cheese with mayonnaise. Add to eggs. Serve on lettuce. Garnish with olives and watercress.

> *Mount Sterling is the seat of Brown County and was settled by Robert Curry in 1830. The town was named by him because of the "sterling" soil in the vicinity.*

Chicken Liver Salad

Yield: 8 servings

¼ cup Lucca olive oil
4 tablespoons lemon juice
½ teaspoon salt
½ teaspoon sugar
¼ teaspoon chervil
¼ teaspoon tarragon
⅓ teaspoon dry mustard
⅛ teaspoon white pepper

2 quarts lightly packed curly endive
1 large red onion, thinly sliced
1 cup chopped celery
¼ cup chopped parsley
1 pound chicken livers
1 tablespoon Lucca olive oil
1 tablespoon butter

Stir together the ¼ cup olive oil, lemon juice, salt, sugar, chervil, tarragon, mustard, and pepper; cover and set aside.

In a large bowl, combine the endive, onion, celery, and parsley. Cover and chill 4 hours. Before serving, sauté the chicken livers in butter and olive oil. Cook until browned but still pink in the center. Remove the livers and slice thinly, then return to pan and stir to coat with drippings. Pour into the salad mixture. Stir dressing and pour over. Toss to mix well.

Peoria was first settled in 1692 by Henri de Tonti and Francois de la Forest and named after an Indian Tribe. The city has all the attributes of a metropolitan area and owes its prominence to its strategic location on the Illinois River.

155

Chicken Salad

Yield: 12 servings

5 pounds chicken legs and breasts
3 garlic cloves, crushed
1 carrot, sliced
2 stalks celery, sliced
1 tablespoon parsley
1 tablespoon dill weed
1 tablespoon pepper
1 tablespoon salt
1 9½-ounce can pitted black olives,

sliced in half
2 tablespoons lemon juice
2 teaspoons dill seed
6 tablespoons Lucca olive oil
½ pound raw mushrooms, sliced
½ cup mayonnaise
10 ounces slivered almonds
1 tablespoon butter

Place chicken pieces in a large kettle with garlic, carrot, celery, parsley, dill weed, pepper, and salt. Simmer for 1½ hours or until chicken is tender but not falling from bone. Skin and bone chicken. Cut meat into large bite-size pieces. Place chicken in a large bowl. Add salt and pepper to taste, olives, lemon juice, dill seed, olive oil, and mushrooms. Toss and refrigerate for at least 2 hours (may be

 held overnight). When ready to serve, stir in the mayonnaise. Brown the almonds in the butter until golden and scatter them on top of the salad.

> *Dickson Mounds is an Illinois state museum outside Lewistown which has a display of 230 Indian skeletons lying in the exact positions in which they were buried. Here, on the banks of the Spoon, Illinois is palpably linked with its legendary past.*

Chicken Fruit Salad

Yield: 6 servings

3 cups chopped cooked chicken
1 cup celery, minced
2 tablespoons minced parsley
1 teaspoon salt
2 tablespoons lemon juice
1 11-ounce can mandarin oranges,
drained
1 9-ounce can pineapple tidbits,
drained
2 cantaloupes, cut into balls
½ pint heavy cream, whipped
1 cup mayonnaise

Combine all ingredients. Garnish with sprigs of parsley.

156

> *Jubilee College State Park is named after the college founded here in 1839 by Reverend Philander Chase who was the first Bishop of the American Protestant Episcopal Church. On the day the cornerstone was laid the Bishop said, "The day fine, the sky serene, and just enough wind to remind us of the breath of God."*

Tuna Salad Mold

Yield: 6 to 8 servings

2 2-ounce packages lime-flavored
gelatin
1 6-½ ounce can tuna, drained
1 cup cottage cheese
1 8-ounce can pineapple chunks,
drained.
½ cup sliced pimiento-stuffed olives

Fix gelatin according to directions. When it starts to jell, whip in tuna, cottage cheese, pineapple, and olives. Return to refrigerator to set. Serve on beds of lettuce.

> *Farmington was platted in 1834. In 1856, anticipating the techniques of Carrie Nation, a group of crusading townswomen swooped down upon the local saloons, smashing glasses, mirrors, and bottles of the demon rum.*

Calico Salad

Yield: 4 to 6 servings

2 cups small macaroni shells, cooked and chilled
1 6½-ounce can flaked tuna
1 tablespoon lemon juice
2 pimientos, chopped
⅓ cup chopped green pepper
¼ cup chopped purple onion

1 teaspoon salt
Pepper to taste
1 garlic clove, crushed
Dash thyme
1 9½-ounce can peas, drained
½ cup Russian dressing

Blend all ingredients except for Russian dressing. Just before serving add Russian salad dressing. Mix again. Serve with crisp crackers.

> *Coatsburg was first surveyed by R. P. Coates in 1855. Coatsburg vied with Quincy as the seat of Adams County when the Quincy Courthouse burned. Quincy won.*

Shrimp and Lima Bean Salad

Yield: 4 to 6 servings

2 cups canned lima beans, drained
¾ pound cooked shrimp, shelled and deveined
1 cup thinly sliced celery
1 tablespoon chopped onions
1 tablespoon chopped pimiento

¼ teaspoon salad herbs
½ teaspoon paprika
¼ teaspoon pepper
¼ cup white wine vinegar
½ cup vegetable oil

Combine beans, shrimp, celery, onions, and pimiento. Crush salad herbs and sprinkle over salad. Combine paprika, pepper, and vinegar in jar. Shake. Add oil and shake again. Pour just enough dressing over salad to moisten it well. Toss. Chill.

> *Princeville was named after Daniel Prince who settled here on the Prairie Trail. Legend has it that he arrived in 1821 and stayed with an Indian friend during the Black Hawk War instead of seeking shelter at a frontier stockade.*

A Land Between the Rivers Scrapbook

Basic Mayonnaise

Yield: 1 cup
1 egg yolk
½ teaspoon salt
⅛ teaspoon pepper
⅛ teaspoon dry mustard

1 tablespoon lemon juice
¾ cup vegetable oil
1 tablespoon heavy cream

Place yolk, salt, pepper, mustard, and ½ tablespoon lemon juice in a bowl and blend carefully. Beat in the oil *very* slowly, ½ teaspoon at a time. When half the oil is in the egg mixture and it is thickening, the oil may be added more rapidly. Add ½ tablespoon lemon juice. When thick and fluffy, add cream.

> *Warsaw was named after a novel,* Thaddeus of Warsaw, *because its original name, Spunky Point, was thought to be indelicate. Warsaw was the location of Fort Edwards which was built in 1814 by General Zachary Taylor.*

Salad Dressing

Mrs. Drake of Freeport in Rolling Northwest says that milk may be substituted for the water. She also says that this recipe is one which "my mother used in 1890."

Yield: 1 pint
2 eggs, beaten
⅓ cup sugar
2 tablespoons flour
½ teaspoon salt

½ teaspoon mustard
⅓ cup vinegar
⅔ cup water

Mix all ingredients and boil until thickened stirring constantly.
—*Fannie Drake*

159

> *McDonough County was named for Thomas McDonough, a commodore in the United States Navy, who commanded the fleet near Plattsburg in 1814. The county was established in 1826 and is 582 square miles in size.*

Cream Garlic Dressing

Yield: 2 cups
2 cups mayonnaise
½ cup grated onions
2 tablespoons vinegar

1 cup sour cream
¼ cup sugar
2 teaspoons garlic powder

Blend all ingredients until creamy, about 3 minutes. Refrigerate.

> *Industry's first settler was William Carter who raised his cabin here in 1826. John M. Price opened a blacksmith shop and it became the area's first industry; thus the village's name.*

Curry Dressing

Yield: 1 cup

¼ cup lemon juice
1 tablespoon sugar
¾ teaspoon salt
¼ teaspoon dry mustard

¼ teaspoon paprika
¼ teaspoon pepper
¾ cup Lucca olive oil
¼ teaspoon curry powder

Combine all ingredients in a screw-top jar and shake well. Chill and serve.

> *Macomb was called Washington in 1830 but changed its name to honor Alexander Macomb who was commander in chief of the United States Army from 1828-1841. Macomb is the site of Western Illinois University which was established in 1899 as a teachers' college.*

Snowy Dressing

Yield: 1 cup

¾ cup Lucca olive oil
¼ cup white vinegar
3 tablespoons sugar
1 tablespoon salt

1 teaspoon dry mustard
½ teaspoon white pepper
½ teaspoon onion juice
¼ cup crumbled Bleu cheese

160

Combine ingredients in jar. Cover and shake. Chill.

> *Carthage is the seat of Hancock County. The old jail is kept up by the Mormon Church as a monument to Joseph Smith, the founder of the church. Smith was killed while imprisoned by a mob who wanted the Mormons out of Illinois.*

Bleu Cheese Mayonnaise

Yield: ¾ cup

¼ cup mayonnaise
¼ cup sour cream

2 tablespoons crumbled Bleu cheese
Few drops hot pepper sauce

Mix together ingredients. Chill.

> *Fulton County was named for Robert Fulton, the first builder of steamboats for American waters. The county was established in 1823 and is 874 square miles in size.*

Bleu Cheese Dressing

Yield: 2 quarts

4 cups mayonnaise
¼ cup barbecue sauce
4 teaspoons vinegar
½ pint sour cream

4 teaspoons grated onion
¼ cup ketchup
4 teaspoons lemon juice
8 ounces Bleu cheese, crumbled

Blend all ingredients. Chill before serving.

Bellevue, high on a bluff just west of Peoria, was incorporated as a village in 1941. The Kickapoo River Valley spreads out below this village, justifying its founders' use of the French name.

Russian Salad Dressing

Yield: 2½ cups

¾ cup sugar
1 teaspoon salt
½ teaspoon pepper
½ teaspoon paprika

1 cup vinegar
14 ounces ketchup
¾ cup Lucca olive oil
2 garlic cloves, optional

161

Boil sugar, salt, pepper, paprika, and vinegar, stirring constantly for 5 minutes. Cool; add ketchup, oil, and garlic. Beat with rotary beater for 5 minutes. Refrigerate.

Wyoming was named after Wyoming Valley, Pennsylvania by General Samuel Thomas who first settled the town in 1834. It was originally known as Spoon River.

Thousand Island Dressing

Yield: 1 cup

½ cup mayonnaise
¼ cup chili sauce
¼ teaspoon Worcestershire sauce
¼ teaspoon salt
Dash paprika

1 hard-cooked egg, minced
1 teaspoon minced green pepper
2 teaspoons minced pimiento
½ teaspoon onion juice

Mix together ingredients. Chill.

Nauvoo in 1845 was the largest city in Illinois with a population of 20,000. Here was the first large settlement of Mormons in the United States. The town is being restored to its original charm and is a Mecca for thousands of tourists annually.

Green Goddess Salad Dressing

Yield: 1 cup

½ cup mayonnaise
½ cup sour cream
¼ cup chopped parsley
2 teaspoons lemon juice

4 teaspoons anchovy paste
1 garlic clove, crushed
3 tablespoons tarragon vinegar

Mix thoroughly and serve over lettuce salad.

Kingston Mines is located on the site of a long forgotten Indian village. Established in 1850, it was also known as Kingston and Palmyra.

Fruit Salad Dressing

Yield: 1½ cups

2 tablespoons cornstarch
⅓ cup sugar
¼ cup lemon juice
2 tablespoons orange juice

⅓ cup pineapple juice
¼ cup water
2 eggs, slightly beaten

Mix together cornstarch and sugar. Combine liquid ingredients in saucepan. Gradually add cornstarch mixture, stirring continually. Cook, stirring constantly, until thick. Add some hot mixture to slightly beaten eggs; blend eggs into mixture in saucepan. Cook 2 minutes longer. Cool before chilling.

Hancock County was named for John Hancock, President of the Continental Congress and the first signer of the Declaration of Independence. The county was established in 1825 and is 797 square miles in size.

Sunshine Fruit Dressing

Yield: 2 cups

⅔ cup sugar
2 tablespoons flour
2 eggs, beaten
2 tablespoons butter

3 tablespoons lemon juice
4 tablespoons orange juice
1 cup pineapple juice
½ cup heavy cream

Mix sugar and flour in a saucepan; add remaining ingredients except cream and cook over low heat, stirring constantly, until thickened. Cool. Whip cream in a chilled container then fold into cooled, cooked dressing.

> *Ellisville's first post office opened its doors in 1838 and was one of the first in Fulton County. However, the village was not incorporated until 1872.*

Breadbasket Flatlands

The breathless heat of Illinois summers together with the rich residual soil left by glacial shifts have provided the phenomenon which has made the Breadbasket Flatlands one of the most luxuriant places for corn production in the United States. Shimmering green seas of nodding corn stalks wait impatiently to deliver their burdens in the throbbing heat of the endless flat prairie plain that stretches from horizon to horizon.

Earlier Illinois settlers had avoided this region of the state in favor of the areas to the south and near the rivers, fearing that the stretching flat plain would not support any growth save the tall prairie grass which tangled and clotted the earth. But it was here in the mid-nineteenth century that John Deere's "plow that broke the plains" parted the matted, waist-high grasses and turned the rich black soil into the food that would feed the nation. With the invention of this remarkable implement, immigrants and farmers from other parts of the populated United States began to make their way into this heartland of Illinois. The Cumberland Trail provided their passage.

The Cumberland Trail, or National Road, was the first and longest highway in the United States. Beginning at Cumberland, Maryland, the road stretched almost 600 miles when first connected to Vandalia in the mid-nineteenth century. To travel over this road is to have the fulfillment of the American Dream pass before one. The whole gamut of life on the developing frontier surged over this thoroughfare. Congestion of vehicles, livestock, and pedestrians on this historic throughway in pioneer days would have rivaled the immobilizing glut of traffic which paralyzes a modern day highway at the rush hour. Steady streams of intrepid immigrants traversed the route hoping to find "The Promised Land" for themselves and their families just beyond the crest of the horizon. Farm goods and manufactured products passed each other going in opposite directions. Adventurers and entrepreneurs rode the stage coaches, stopping at the infrequent inns along the way where the bed linens might be changed only once a season but where the food was good and hearty.

At Vandalia a "Madonna of the Trail" monument stands eighteen feet tall overlooking the capitol building as a reminder of the rigors of the journey over the Cumberland Trail for the settlers who passed through on their way west. Vandalia was the second capital of Illinois, from 1819 to 1937. The two-story white, brick State House still stands, its simple but classical Greek Revival design demonstrating a lovely example of the best architecture of the period. In 1837 the Chicago city charter was issued from this building to that tiny settlement in the swamps to the north.

From miles away the weathered dome of the capitol building in Springfield dramatically dominates the skyline beckoning all who would come to the city which has been the state capital since 1837. The entire city is a kind of monument to Abraham Lincoln, for this is Lincoln country. Plaques mark the sites of most of his activities, and Carl Sandberg and Vachel Lindsay have sung his and Springfield's praises in some of their greatest poetry and prose. Founded by Elisha Kelly in the verdant valley of the Sangamon River, Springfield is a treasure of attractions for the visitor. The State Library, the State Archives, the first capitol building and various museums are but a few. In and around Springfield are constant reminders of Abraham Lincoln's youth and of his development into a great statesman. Not far from Springfield lies the village of New Salem where Lincoln resided before his rise to political prominence. The Rutledge Tavern, the old mill, and other buildings and furnishings have been carefully reproduced to appear exactly as they were in Lincoln's day.

The most recent glaciation left a great morainal deposit at Shelbyville, somewhat wrinkling the vast plain. At this point the glacier stopped its long thrust south and left boulders and rocks from the far north which it had gathered and pushed during its advance. As the great ice sheet melted and poured off its waters, streams were dug, and the land south of Shelbyville still shows the effect of that erosion. Land here that is rock-strewn and rough is used for orchards and grazing and not planted in the ubiquitous corn and wheat as is most of the land around it. Here and there hedge fences of osage oranges are still visible. Before the use of barbed wire to fence in cattle, these hardy shrubs served to keep the animals within their limits.

The giant complex of the University of Illinois sprawls over Champaign-Urbana. One of the most highly rated universities in the country, this land-grant center of education and culture is a testament to the foresightedness of the great legislators of the past who envisioned the need for a future filled with educated citizens to guide the state. Its huge enrollment consists of students from all over the world.

Jacksonville was one of the first towns to be considered for the site of the University of Illinois. The town was also an unsuccessful contender for the honor of being the state capital. Founded in 1825 and named after Andrew Jackson, Jacksonville drew its early settlers from New England, causing it to be considered "the most Yankee" city in the entire state. Illinois College, one of the first institutions of higher learning chartered by the state was founded here in 1829. Ward Beecher, brother of Henry Ward Beecher and Harriet Beecher Stowe, was its first president. Both Stephen A. Douglas and William Jennings Bryan began law practices here.

The coming together point of several important Indian trails used extensively by trappers and traders became the location of present day Bloomington-Normal. Legend has it that the trappers left a cache of liquor here which, when discovered by a passing group of Indians, provided a splendid and hilarious party. Thereafter, the area was known as Keg Grove and that remained its name until 1822 when the settlers changed it to Blooming Grove to rid it of the liquor stigma. In 1857 when Illinois State Normal University was begun, Bloomington's sister town of North Bloomington changed its name to Normal. Bloomington-Normal became a household word in the late nineteenth century when a patent medicine czar published his *Almanac* there. The *Almanac* touted the curative powers of his medicine for cases of malaria and chillblains. One of Bloomington's most prominent families was the Stevenson family, owners of the *Bloomington Herald*. The family contributed two Vice Presidents and one U. S. Senator, all bearing the name of Adlai Stevenson, to national politics.

Pekin, of Everett McKinley Dirksen fame, is located on the Sangamon River and serves as the seat of Macon County. Dubbed the "Soy Bean Capital of the World," Pekin owes as much of its growth and prosperity to agricultural food processing as it does to the actual growing of the products in the surrounding farm lands. The oldest radio station in Illinois, WDZ, began broadcasting from this region in 1921.

The development of the many communities in Breadbasket Flatlands proceeded in tandem with the expansion of the railroad in Illinois. Villages and towns sprang up or actually moved their locations to take advantage of this growing mode of shipping farm produce to distant markets. Often the towns were carefully placed equidistant from one another along the busy railroad beds. Towns like Pontiac, Dwight, and Odell were, for example, precisely planned to be ten or eleven miles apart.

One of the many towns which owes its prosperity to the vast rail network in Illinois is Kankakee in the northern reaches of Breadbasket Flatlands. Several French communities dotted the banks of the Kankakee River before Kankakee's importance as a village shipping center overshadowed them. L'Erable, St. Anne, and Bourbonnais are three communities which resemble French provincial villages and which still cling to some French cultural traditions that go back to the fur trapping days. Kankakee was only a rival to these villages until the Illinois Central Railroad connected it to the giant metropolis to the north insuring its place as a thriving and self-sufficient farming community. Kankakee soon took precedence over the smaller towns around it which had enjoyed supremacy over the river traffic of the Kankakee River.

Aside from the railroads, the tarred country roads, which grid out the Breadbasket Flatlands of Illinois and pass between acres of wheat and corn, over narrow bridges and beside impressive farm houses, take one through all that is America today. Several years ago, when asked why many of the country roads had only one paved lane, C. C. Wiley, professor of highway engineering at the University of Illinois for fifty years said, "Isn't it better to have one lane all the way there, than two lanes only halfway?" That question summarizes the philosophy of the flatlands, the bounteous cornucopia of the state.

167

Main Dishes

Baked Eggs

Yield: 8 servings
2 cups grated Cheddar cheese
4 tablespoons butter
1 dozen eggs

2 cups light cream
1 teaspoon prepared mustard
1 teaspoon each salt and pepper

Preheat oven to 350 degrees F. Spread grated cheese in bottom of a 9-by-13-by-2-inch pan. Dot with butter Lightly whip the eggs; add cream, prepared mustard, and seasonings. Pour over cheese and butter. Bake for 40 minutes.

> *Assumption was first named Tacusah but was renamed in 1856 by Colonel Malhoit from Assumption Parish Louisiana who settled here with thirty-five other families.*

168

Fresh Apple Omelet

Yield: 4 servings
3 tablespoons flour
¼ teaspoon baking powder
Dash salt
2 egg whites
3 tablespoons sugar
4 tablespoons heavy cream

2 egg yolks, well-beaten
1 tablespoon lemon juice
1 large apple, thinly sliced
¼ cup sugar
¼ teaspoon cinnamon

Preheat oven to 375 degrees F. Sift flour with baking powder and salt. In a medium sized bowl, beat egg whites until stiff. Into flour mixture in a small bowl, beat cream and egg yolks until smooth, and gently fold into egg whites along with lemon juice. Slowly heat a buttered 10-inch skillet. Pour batter into the skillet. Arrange apples over the top. Sprinkle with ¼ cup sugar mixed with cinnamon. Bake about 10 minutes or until top is glazed. Serve warm.

> *Lincoln is the seat of Logan County and was named after "Old Abe" who agreed to the naming, but said, "Never knew of anything named Lincoln that ever amounted to much."*

Sauced Omelet

Yield: 6 servings
4 tablespoons butter, divided
¼ cup enriched flour
½ teaspoon salt
Pepper to taste

1 cup milk
4 egg yolks, well-beaten
4 egg whites, stiffly beaten

Sauce

2 tablespoons butter
3 tablespoons chopped onion
¼ cup chopped olives
¼ cup chopped green pepper
2 tablespoons enriched flour

¼ teaspoon salt
Dash pepper
1 teaspoon sugar
2 cups tomatoes

Make a roux of 2 tablespoons butter, flour, salt, and pepper. Add milk gradually. Cook until thick, stirring constantly. Fold in egg yolks. Fold in egg whites. Heat remaining butter in a 10-inch skillet. Pour in egg mixture. Cover and cook over low heat until mixture puffs, about 10 to 12 minutes. Uncover and finish cooking in broiler, about 1 minute. Fold over. Serve on a warm platter with sauce.

169

Melt 2 tablespoons butter. Add onion, olives, green pepper, and cook until green pepper is soft. Add remaining ingredients and simmer until thick, about 40 minutes.

> *Chanute Field was developed as an Air Force Base in 1917. It was named for the French-born civil engineer and aviation expert, Octave Chanute. The flight experimentation of Wilbur and Orville Wright owed some of its success to the information supplied by Chanute.*

Overnight Cheesewiches

Yield: 6 servings
8 slices white bread
⅔ pound Cheddar cheese, cubed
8 eggs, well beaten

4 cups heavy cream
1 teaspoon salt
½ teaspoon dry mustard

Cube bread into a 9-by-12-inch pan. Add cheese. Combine eggs, cream, salt, and mustard. Pour over bread and cheese and refrigerate overnight. Bake 1 hour at 325 degrees F.

Casey was incorporated in 1871 and named after Zadok Casey who was a settler here. Casey was an oil boom town in the 1920s, but the wells have mostly gone dry.

Swiss Cheese Soufflé

Yield: 4 to 6 servings
3 tablespoons butter
¼ cup flour
½ teaspoon salt
Dash pepper
½ cup heavy cream
½ cup dry vermouth

1½ cups coarsely grated Swiss cheese
4 egg yolks, beaten
4 egg whites, slightly beaten
½ teaspoon cream of tartar

Preheat oven to 300 degrees F. Melt butter. Add flour, salt, and pepper. Stir over medium flame until blended. Add cream, stirring constantly, until thickened. Stir in vermouth and cheese; continue stirring to melt cheese. Remove from heat. Add some hot mixture to beaten egg yolks; mix well. Stir into remaining hot mixture. To slightly beaten egg whites, add cream of tartar; beat until stiff. Fold cheese mixture into egg whites. Turn into unbuttered 1½-quart casserole. Bake 1 hour and 25 minutes. Serve immediately

170

Washington was settled in 1825 by William Holland who built a blacksmith shop here to serve Indians. It was originally called Holland's Grove.

Soufflé Roll

Yield: 6 servings
4 tablespoons butter
½ cup flour
1 teaspoon salt
White pepper to taste

2 cups heavy cream
5 egg yolks
5 egg whites

Filling

1 pound mushrooms, chopped
2 tablespoons butter
1 10-ounce package frozen spinach, cooked and drained

1 8-ounce package cream cheese
Salt and pepper to taste
Parsley

Melt 4 tablespoons butter in a saucepan, blend in flour, salt, and pepper. Stir in the cream; bring to a boil and stir until thickened.

Cool. Add the egg yolks. Beat the egg whites until stiff and fold into the cooled mixture. Preheat oven to 400 degrees F. Butter and flour a waxed paper-lined jelly roll pan. Pour in the soufflé mixture, spreading lightly. Bake for 30 minutes or until browned. Turn immediately onto a towel.

Sauté mushrooms in the butter lightly. Add the spinach and heat thoroughly. Add the cream cheese and mix well. Season to taste. Spread warm filling evenly over soufflé, roll with the help of the towel. Garnish with parsley.

> *Pekin was named after Peking, China. It was first settled in 1824 and was the birthplace of Everett McKinley Dirksen. In the 1850s Pekin was a major port on the river and had 1,800 arrivals and departures of steamboats in a single year.*

Dairy Casserole

Yield: 8 servings

1 8-ounce package noodles
2 tablespoons butter
1½ pounds ground beef
1 teaspoon salt
¼ teaspoon pepper
¼ teaspoon garlic salt

1 cup tomato sauce
1 cup grated Swiss cheese
1 cup cottage cheese, drained
1 cup sour cream
8 scallions with stems, chopped
½ cup chopped parsley sprigs

171

Cook noodles according to directions on package. Drain and rinse in cold water. Melt butter in skillet and brown meat, crumbling as it cooks. Preheat oven to 325 degrees F. Add salt, pepper, garlic salt, and tomato sauce to meat. Cover and simmer 5 minutes. Blend ½ cup Swiss cheese, cottage cheese, sour cream, scallions, and parsley. In a buttered 2-quart casserole, layer the meat mixture, cheese mixture, and noodles, ending with noodles. Sprinkle cheese on top and bake 30 minutes or until brown.

> *Litchfield was named for Electus Bachus Litchfield who came here in 1853 from Delphi, New York. It was incorporated as a city in 1859. Litchfield was the site of the first commercial oil production in the state.*

Stuffed Shells

Yield: 6 to 8 servings

1 12-ounce package jumbo pasta shells
2 9-ounce packages frozen creamed spinach
1 pound Ricotta cheese
1 egg, beaten
1 8-ounce package shredded Mozzarella cheese
1 teaspoon salt
¼ teaspoon pepper
1 pound ground beef
1 32-ounce jar spaghetti sauce

Preheat oven to 350 degrees F. Cook macaroni shells; prepare creamed spinach as label directs. Stir in Ricotta, egg, Mozzarella, salt, and pepper. Stuff each shell with a tablespoon of mixture. Arrange shells in one layer in a casserole dish. In a 10-inch skillet cook ground beef until browned. Stir in the spaghetti sauce. Spread over shells. Cover with foil and bake for 45 minutes.

> *Delavan was named after Edward Cornelius Delavan, a teetotaler and land promoter. Many farm machines and new strains of corn were invented here.*

172

Linguine with White Clam Sauce

Mrs. Zichterman of Decatur in Breadbasket Flatlands says that this is a favorite of her husband, and is great with a tossed salad and hot French bread.

Yield: 4 to 6 servings

3 tablespoons Lucca olive oil
3 garlic cloves, peeled
4 8-ounce bottles clam broth
2 8-ounce cans minced clams
1 10-ounce can whole baby clams
¾ cup dry white wine
¼ teaspoon hot red pepper flakes
Pinch salt
1 pound linguine
3 tablespoons butter
3 tablespoons chopped parsley
18 to 24 cherrystone clams (optional)

In a deep saucepan heat the oil. Remove the pan from the heat; force garlic cloves through a garlic press into the hot oil. Reserving liquid, drain clams. Pour clam broth, liquid from canned clams, wine, red pepper flakes, and a gentle shake of salt into saucepan. Cook over medium heat, uncovered, for 10 minutes. Lower the heat and cook, stirring frequently for 25 minutes, or until the sauce has reduced to about one-third of its original volume. Meanwhile cook the pasta until just tender. Drain. Place hot, drained pasta into a large warm bowl. Add the butter and parsley. Toss gently. Stir minced and whole clams into sauce, blending well. Bring to a simmer. Remove from heat. Spoon half of sauce into pasta bowl and toss. Serve pasta in hot plates; spoon remaining sauce on top.

—*Karen Zichterman*

> *Bethany was known as Marrowbone in the 1820s. The local legend says that two trappers stayed the night here and named it for the breakfast they consumed of marrow from the bones of a deer they had killed the day before. The name Bethany was chosen in 1831 by Baptist settlers.*

Fettucini with Cheese and Cream

Yield: 2 servings
½ pound fettucini
½ cup (1 stick) butter
7 garlic cloves, peeled and crushed
½ cup Parmesan cheese
½ cup heavy cream
½ cup parsley

Cook the fettucini in boiling water until just tender. Put the butter in a small pan; place garlic on top of the butter and melt over low heat. When the fettucini is done, drain and place in a bowl. Pour the butter over the fettucini. Add Parmesan cheese. Mix thoroughly and add cream. Add chopped parsley and mix.

173

> *Martinsville was founded by Joseph Martin in 1833. It was a main stop on the stage coach line, and its tavern was known far and wide by statesmen and brigands.*

Bleu Cheese Macaroni

Yield: 6 servings
1 7-ounce package elbow macaroni,
  cooked and drained
4 tablespoons butter
3 tablespoons flour
1 teaspoon salt
⅛ teaspoon pepper
2½ cups light cream
¾ cup Bleu cheese
1 cup shredded American cheese
¼ cup chopped pimiento
1 cup mushrooms, sliced
⅓ cup buttered, dry breadcrumbs

Preheat oven to 350 degrees F. Place cooked macaroni into 1½-quart buttered casserole and set aside. Melt butter over low heat. Blend in flour and seasonings. Add cream. Cook, stirring until smooth and thick. Add cheeses and stir. Add pimiento and mushrooms. Pour sauce over macaroni and mix. Top with buttered crumbs. Bake 40 minutes.

> *Virden, incorporated as a city in 1865, was a booming coal mining town. In October, 1898, a riot occurred which killed ten miners, six company guards, and wounded thirty others over the importation of non-union labor. Today Virden is a farming community.*

Cheesy Green Noodles

Yield: 8 servings

1 1-pound package green noodles, cooked and drained
1 small onion, chopped
1 cup sour cream

¼ pound (1 stick) butter, melted
1 cup grated Romano cheese
Salt and pepper to taste

Preheat oven to 350 degrees F. Place noodles into a buttered 9-by-13-inch casserole. Add onion and sour cream and mix. Add melted butter and Romano cheese. Season with salt and pepper. Bake for 20 minutes.

174

> *Monticello was born at a barbecue in 1837 when the lots were auctioned off. It was named after Thomas Jefferson, "The Sage of Monticello," and to carry it further, the high school teams are called "The Sages." It is the seat of Piatt County.*

Business District—St. Anne

Chili Powder Beef Roast

Mrs. Weygandt's grandmother, Corrine Adamson of East St. Louis in the Bottom, gave her this recipe which has been in the family for many years. "The roast is moist and richly flavored."

Yield: 6 to 8 servings

1½ ounces chili powder	5 bay leaves
5 pounds rump roast	1 onion, quartered
⅛ teaspoon garlic powder	1 cup water
Salt to taste	

Preheat oven to 325 degrees F. Rub chili powder into roast thoroughly. Place in roasting pan, sprinkle with garlic powder, and salt lightly. Place bay leaves on top of roast and onion along the sides. Pour water around roast and bake 4½ hours covered, turning roast every hour. Uncover during the last ½ hour for browning.

—*Vickie Weygandt*

Petersburg, the seat of Menard County, was platted in 1836 by Abraham Lincoln who lived nearby in New Salem.

175

Cornish Meat Pastry

Yield: 6 servings

1 pound round steak, cut in ½-inch pieces	Salt to taste
	Pepper to taste
1 pound potatoes, peeled and chopped	2 pie crusts for 7-by-11-inch pan
	2 heaping tablespoons suet, minced
1 large onion, chopped	2 tablespoons heavy cream

Preheat oven to 350 degrees F. Mix round steak, potatoes, onion, salt, and pepper together. Roll out two pie crusts and put one into a 7-by-11-inch pan. Fill with steak mixture and add suet, cream, salt, and pepper. Cover with remaining pie crust. Cut holes in top to let steam escape. Bake 2 hours.

Nokomis was incorporated in 1867 and was named for the narrator of Longfellow's Hiawatha. *The town was once a Kickapoo Indian settlement.*

Olive Beef Roll

Yield: 6 servings

2 pounds round steak
1 teaspoon salt
1 teaspoon paprika
¼ teaspoon pepper
½ pound mushrooms, thinly sliced
1¼ cup thinly sliced onions, divided
⅔ cup fine, dry breadcrumbs
½ cup (1 stick) butter, melted

1 tablespoon boiling water
1 egg
1 cup large almond stuffed olives, drained
6 tablespoons butter, divided
1 cup dry red wine
4 ounces mushrooms, thinly sliced

Preheat oven to 350 degrees F. Trim excess fat from meat. Pound meat with mallet until meat is about ¼ inch thick. Rub mixture of salt, paprika, and pepper into both sides of meat. Combine ½ pound mushrooms, 1 cup onions, and the breadcrumbs and spread over meat. Blend ½ cup melted butter, boiling water, and egg in a small bowl. Spoon mixture over meat. Place olives end to end on inside edge of long side of meat. Roll up meat from long side around olives and tie with string. Sauté beef roll in 4 tablespoons butter in a roasting pan until brown on all sides. Pour wine over beef roll. Bake, basting with pan juices twice, until meat is tender, about 1 hour. Remove beef roll to platter; keep warm. Reserve pan juices. Saute mushrooms and onions in 2 tablespoons butter in a medium-size saucepan until onion is transparent. Stir in reserved pan juices. Heat to boiling, stirring constantly. Serve with the sauce.

176

> *Pontiac was first settled in 1837 and is the seat of Livingston County. It was named for the Ottawa chief who fought the British in the French and Indian War.*

Round Steak Casserole

Yield: 4 servings

6 medium potatoes, peeled and sliced
2 large onions, peeled and sliced
1 green pepper, cut in 1-inch squares
4 tomatoes, cut in eighths
1 pound round steak, cut in 1-inch squares

1 10¾-ounce can beef gravy
2 tablespoons water
1 tablespoon tomato paste
2 teaspoons aromatic bitters
1½ teaspoons salt
¼ teaspoon pepper

Preheat oven to 375 degrees F. In a 2½-quart casserole arrange layers of half the potatoes, onions, green pepper, and tomatoes. Add all of the round steak; repeat the vegetable layers. Combine gravy, water, tomato paste, bitters, salt, and pepper. Pour over vegetables and steak. Bake for 2 hours or until meat is tender.

> *Hillsboro, the seat of Montgomery County, sits atop one of the largest known coal deposits in the United States. John Nussman settled here in 1817 after having arrived in a covered wagon from Hillsboro, North Carolina.*

Salisbury Steak

Yield: 4 servings
1 pound ground beef
½ cup soft breadcrumbs
¼ cup light cream
1 tablespoon minced onion

1 teaspoon salt
¼ teaspoon pepper
Melted butter for brushing

Combine all ingredients except butter; mix well. Shape into 4 patties, 1 inch thick. Broil 8 minutes on one side; brush with melted butter. Turn; broil 8 minutes longer, brushing again with butter.

177

> *Havana is the seat of Mason County and bears the legendary slogan "Catfish Riviera of the Corn Belt." It was first settled in 1831 by Major Ossian M. Ross who ran a ferry here.*

Stuffed Meatloaf

Yield: 6 servings
2 pound ground beef
1 egg
Dash dry vermouth
1 small onion, chopped
½ green pepper, chopped

Dash Worcestershire sauce
Dash steak sauce
Salt and pepper to taste
1 Gouda cheese, peeled
¼ cup wine vinegar

Preheat oven to 350 degrees F. Mix the beef with the egg, vermouth, onion, pepper, Worcestershire sauce, and steak sauce. Add salt and pepper to taste. Form the loaf around a peeled Gouda cheese. Top with a light coating of vinegar. Bake for 1 hour.

> *Gibson City was platted in 1870 on land owned by Jonathan B. Lott. The town was named after his wife, Margaret Gibson Lott.*

Snowy Beef Mounds

Yield: 6 servings

2 pounds ground beef
½ cup fine cracker crumbs
2 teaspoons salt
½ teaspoon pepper
⅓ cup minced onion
1 16-ounce can tomatoes

2 eggs, beaten
2 cups hot, seasoned mashed
  potatoes
⅓ cup mayonnaise
1 tablespoon chopped chives
¼ cup ketchup

Preheat oven to 350 degrees F. Combine ground beef, cracker crumbs, salt, pepper, onion, tomatoes, eggs and blend well. Shape mixture into 12 mounds. Place beef mounds in a shallow baking dish. Bake uncovered for 35 minutes. Combine mashed potatoes, mayonnaise, and chives. Place beef mounds on platter and top each mound with 1 teaspoon of ketchup and 3 tablespoons of potato mixture.

> *Bunker Hill was named after the famous battle and has battled major disaster ever since: fires in 1880, 1882, and 1893; a tornado in 1893; and another tornado which killed 30 people in 1948. Bunker Hill was first settled in 1833 when it was called Wolf Ridge.*

178

Meat Loaf with Almonds

Yield: 8 servings

1½ cups chopped onions
1 tablespoon butter
2 cups breadcrumbs
½ cup light cream
3 pounds ground round
2 eggs

1 tablespoon curry
1 tablespoon salt
2 tablespoons apricot jam
2 tablespoons lemon juice
¼ cup ground almonds
3 bay leaves

Preheat oven to 350 degrees F. Sauté onion in butter until translucent. Soak crumbs in cream. Combine meat, egg, onion, curry, salt, jam, lemon juice, almonds, and soaked crumbs and mix well. Place bay leaves on bottom of buttered 10-inch shallow casserole. Place meat mixture on top. Bake 1 hour. Drain moisture. Serve with lemon slices as garnish.

> *Auburn was incorporated in 1865 as a railroad town. It is now known as "Redbud City" by residents.*

Meat Loaf with Fruit

Yield: 8 servings

16 halves dried apricots
8 dried prunes, pitted, and halved
Water
1 pound ground beef
1 pound ground pork
1 egg beaten
½ cup beef stock
¼ cup maple syrup

2 tablespoons minced onion
½ cup chopped celery
½ cup chopped carrots
1 tablespoon chopped green pepper
½ cup dry breadcrumbs
1 teaspoon salt
¼ teaspoon thyme

Soak apricots and prunes 6 hours in water to cover. Preheat oven to 350 degrees F. Drain well. Arrange fruit in a checkerboard pattern on bottom of 9-by-5-by-2¾-inch loaf pan. Mix together remaining ingredients. Pack firmly on top of fruit. Bake for 1½ hours. Drain juice from pan into bowl. Turn meat loaf out so fruit will be on top. Skim fat from juice; pour over meat loaf.

> *Springfield is the capital of Illinois and the seat of Sangamon County. It was settled in 1818 by the Elisha Kelly family who named it after a spring in one of their fields. The city was chartered in 1840 after incorporation in 1832.*

179

Cheddar Beef Roll-Ups

Yield: 6 servings

1½ pounds ground beef
¼ cup dry breadcrumbs
2 tablespoons barbecue sauce
1 egg
½ teaspoon salt

1 cup shredded Cheddar cheese
¼ cup dry breadcrumbs
¼ cup chopped green pepper
2 tablespoons milk

Combine meat, breadcrumbs, barbecue sauce, egg, and salt; mix well. Pat meat mixture into a 14-by-8-inch rectangle on aluminum foil. Combine cheese, breadcrumbs, green pepper, and milk. Pat over meat mixture. Roll up jelly roll fashion. Chill overnight. Preheat oven to 350 degrees F. Slice into 6 servings. Bake in shallow pan for 30 minutes.

> *Carrollton, the seat of Greene County, was incorporated in 1861 and named for Charles Carroll who was the last surviving signer of the Declaration of Independence.*

Beef Stuffed French Bread

Yield: 4 servings

1 pound ground beef
1 medium onion, chopped
1 loaf French bread
1 egg
2 tablespoons prepared mustard
2 tablespoons chopped parsley

½ teaspoon salt
¼ teaspoon each pepper, garlic powder, and oregano
¼ cup light cream
2 tablespoons butter
1 garlic clove, crushed

Preheat oven to 400 degrees F. Sauté beef and onion until lightly browned; drain off fat. Cut off both ends of bread; cut loaf in half crosswise. Hollow loaf carefully, slowly pulling out dough with a long fork. Tear bread chunks into small pieces; mix with meat and remaining ingredients, except butter and garlic. Fill bread shell with mixture; replace ends of bread, using toothpicks. Melt butter with garlic; brush on loaf. Place on a cookie sheet, bake for 20 minutes.

> *Jacksonville was named for President Andrew Jackson. It was first settled in 1819 by Seymour and Elisha Kellogg.*

180

Mapled Beef in Acorn Squash

Yield: 8 servings

¼ cup brown sugar
1½ pounds ground beef or pork
1½ teaspoon nutmeg
¼ teaspoon ground cloves
Salt and pepper to taste

¼ pound (1 stick) butter, melted
⅓ cup maple syrup
4 acorn squash, halved
2½ cups boiling water

Preheat oven to 350 degrees F. In a small bowl combine sugar, meat, spices, butter, and syrup. Mix thoroughly and form into 8 balls. Place into squash halves. Pour boiling water into 9-by-13 pan. Place squash halves in water. Bake for 45 minutes or until squash is tender.

> *Chatham is now part of the Springfield complex and has become a "bedroom" community. It was platted in 1836 and its first post office opened in 1838.*

Baked Tortillas

Yield: 6 servings
1½ pounds ground beef
1 onion, chopped
1 garlic clove, crushed
1 16-ounce can tomato sauce
½ cup beef stock
1½ tablespoons chili powder
½ teaspoon cumin
¼ teaspoon salt
9 tortillas
½ cup sour cream
2 cups shredded Cheddar cheese

Preheat oven to 350 degrees F. Sauté meat with onion and garlic in skillet. Pour off fat. Add tomato sauce, stock, chili powder, cumin, and salt. Simmer for 10 minutes. Spoon ¼ of mixture into a 2-quart casserole. Arrange 3 tortillas over meat. Top tortillas with sour cream. Sprinkle with cheese. Repeat, ending with meat. Bake 25 minutes.

Arthur straddles the boundary of Douglas and Moultrie Counties. It is the shopping center for a large group of Amish people who are strict in their religious conviction. Since they do not drive automobiles, Arthur still has buggy shops and blacksmiths.

181

Main Dish Pie

Yield: 4 to 6 servings
½ cup chopped onion
1 clove garlic, minced
3 tablespoons butter
1 pound ground beef
½ cup canned tomato sauce
½ teaspoon salt
¼ teaspoon pepper
½ teaspoon sweet basil
1 pound elbow macaroni
1½ cups grated Cheddar cheese
1 10-ounce package frozen
 asparagus
1½ cups milk
2 eggs

Preheat oven to 350 degrees F. Sauté the onions and garlic in butter until transparent. Add the beef and stir until browned. Stir in tomato sauce, salt, pepper, and sweet basil. Simmer 3 to 4 minutes. Pack into the bottom of a buttered 2-quart casserole. Cook macaroni until just tender in boiling water. Drain. Add cheese and toss. Spread evenly over meat mixture. Cook asparagus until just tender. Arrange over macaroni. Beat milk and eggs together and pour over asparagus. Bake for 40 minutes or until custard is set. Unmold on a serving platter. Garnish with parsley and serve.

Waverly was settled in 1831 and platted in 1836 and was named for the Walter Scott Waverley novels, but the spelling of the name got changed through an oversight. The town is an underground storage station for the Panhandle Eastern Pipe Line Company.

Cabbage and Beef

Yield: 4 servings
1 large cabbage, coarsely chopped
1 pound ground beef
1 tablespoon butter
1 large onion, chopped
1 teaspoon salt
½ teaspoon pepper
1 teaspoon tarragon
1 12-ounce can vegetable juice
   cocktail
¼ cup vinegar

Preheat oven to 425 degrees F. Brown meat in butter with onion, salt, pepper, and tarragon. Place half of cabbage in a 2-quart casserole. Spoon meat mixture over cabbage. Cover with remaining cabbage. Pour juice and vinegar over all. Cover casserole tightly and bake for 30 minutes. Lower heat to 375 degrees F. and continue baking for 1 hour more. Serve hot.

Georgetown was platted in 1827 by James Haworth who, it is said, named the town after his son, George; however, more likely it was named after George Beckwith whose brother Dan gave Danville its name.

Beef and Corn Custard

Yield: 4 servings
1 pound ground beef
1 tablespoon butter
1 large onion, chopped
Salt and pepper to taste
½ teaspoon chili powder
1 9½-ounce can black olives, pitted
   and halved
1 34-ounce can of corn, drained
1½ cups heavy cream
2 eggs

Preheat oven to 375 degrees F. Sauté the ground beef in butter. When meat begins to brown, add the onion. Continue cooking until onion is transparent. Add salt, pepper, and chili powder. Add the olives and stir. Pack into a 2-quart casserole. Spread the drained corn over the meat. Beat the cream and eggs together. Pour over the corn. Bake 40 minutes or until custard is set.

Zucchini and Beef Casserole

Yield: 9 servings

1 pound lean ground beef
1 15-ounce can tomato sauce
1½ teaspoons minced garlic
1 teaspoon crumbled basil leaves
1 teaspoon crumbled oregano leaves
12 ounces Ricotta cheese
½ cup grated Romano cheese,

divided
1 egg
1½ pounds zucchini, cut lengthwise
 into ¼-inch slices
2 tablespoons flour
¾ cup shredded Mozzarella cheese

Preheat oven to 350 degrees F. Cook and stir meat in large skillet until brown. Drain off fat. Stir in tomato sauce, garlic, basil leaves, and oregano leaves; heat to boiling. Reduce heat and simmer about 10 minutes. In a separate bowl mix Ricotta cheese, ¼ cup Romano cheese, and egg. In a 9-by-9-by-2-inch pan, layer half each of zucchini, flour, cheese mixture, meat sauce, and Mozzarella cheese; repeat. Sprinkle remaining Romano cheese on top. Bake, uncovered, 45 minutes. Let stand 10 minutes before serving. Cut into squares.

183

Mexicali Casserole

Yield: 4 servings

1 pound ground round steak
2 onions, chopped
1 garlic clove, crushed
1 15-ounce can tomato sauce
½ teaspoon sweet basil

2 tablespoons chili powder
1 16-ounce can kidney or chili beans
1 bag corn chips
Bits of lettuce for topping

Preheat oven to 350 degrees F. Brown together in a little vegetable oil, meat, one onion, and garlic. Stir in tomato sauce, basil, and chili powder. Butter a 1-quart casserole and alternate layers of this mixture with layers of beans and corn chips, ending with corn chips. Bake covered for 45 minutes; uncover for the last 10 minutes.

Before serving, place some shredded lettuce and chopped raw onion on top.

Eggplant Casserole

Yield: 6 to 8 servings

½ cup chopped onion
1 garlic clove, crushed
1 pound ground meat
2 tablespoons butter
1 16-ounce can Italian style tomatoes, undrained
1 6-ounce can tomato paste
2 teaspoons oregano
1 teaspoon sweet basil
1½ teaspoons salt
¼ teaspoon pepper
1 tablespoon brown sugar
1 large eggplant, unpeeled
2 eggs, slightly beaten
½ cup breadcrumbs
1¼ cups Parmesan cheese, divided
¼ cup Lucca olive oil
8 ounces Mozzarella cheese

184

Sauté onion, garlic, and meat in butter until browned. Add tomatoes, paste, and seasonings and sugar. Simmer uncovered for 10 minutes. Preheat oven to 350 degrees F. Butter a 13-by-9-1¾-inch dish. Cut eggplant into ½-inch slices. Combine eggs with 1 tablespoon water. Combine crumbs with 1 cup Parmesan cheese. Dip slices into egg and then crumbs. Sauté in 1 tablespoon oil (add more as necessary) until golden brown and crisp. Arrange in a dish. Sprinkle with half of remaining cheese. Top with half of Mozzarella and half of tomato sauce. Layer remaining egg over sauce, then rest of Parmesan, tomato sauce, and Mozzarella. Bake 30 minutes.

Quick Spanish Rice

Yield: 4 servings

4 tablespoons butter
1 onion, thinly sliced
½ green pepper, chopped
½ pound ground beef
1 cup long grain raw rice
1 16-ounce can tomato sauce

1¾ cups hot water
½ teaspoon cumin
½ teaspoon sweet basil
1 teaspoon salt
Dash pepper

Heat butter in saucepan. Add onion, green pepper, beef, and rice. Stir over high heat until lightly browned. Add tomato sauce and remaining ingredients. Mix. Bring to a boil. Cover tightly and simmer 25 minutes.

> *White Hall was first settled in 1820, and is one of the world's largest producers of clay redware. It was named for the white washed home of Beverly Holliday who was the postmaster.*

Curried Beef

Yield: 4 to 6 servings

1½ tablespoons Lucca olive oil
1 Spanish onion, sliced in rings
3 teaspoons curry powder
1½ pounds lean flank steak, cut in 1-inch cubes
½ pound fresh mushrooms, sliced
1 tomato, chopped

2 garlic cloves, crushed
2 teaspoons salt
2 teaspoons sugar
2 cups beef stock
2 tablespoons cornstarch
2 tablespoons water

Heat oil in a heavy skillet. Sauté onion over medium heat until tender. Stir in curry powder; cook 1 minute. Add beef cubes and next five ingredients. Continue cooking until beef cubes are lightly browned. Add enough boiling stock to barely cover beef. Cover skillet and simmer gently about 1½ hours, or until beef is extremely tender. Thicken with cornstarch-water mixture. Serve with rice.

> *The town of Alvin was platted in 1876 and provided elevators to store the grain to be ground at the nearby mill which was still in operation until forty years ago.*

Round Steak Rosé

Mrs. Carpenter of Decatur in Breadbasket Flatlands makes this rich meal for special occasions. "There's never enough of it," she reports.

Yield: 8 servings

3 pounds round steak, ½ to ¾ inch thick
½ cup flour
1½ teaspoons salt
¼ teaspoon pepper
¼ cup vegetable oil
2 cups rosé wine
1 cup water
3 tablespoons (½ package) onion soup mix
1 can 6-ounce tomato paste
2 tablespoons brown sugar
½ cup water
1 cup shredded sharp Cheddar cheese
8 ounces fresh mushrooms, halved
2 tablespoons snipped parsley

Cut steak in strips ⅛ to ¼ inch thick and 3 to 4 inches long. Combine flour, salt, and pepper. Sprinkle over meat to lightly coat. Brown in hot oil in large skillet ⅓ at a time. Combine wine, 1 cup water and onion soup mix. Add to meat. Cover tightly. Cook slowly 45 minutes. Blend tomato paste, brown sugar, and ½ cup water. Add to meat; simmer covered 30 minutes or until meat is tender, stirring occasionally. Add cheese and mushrooms and simmer uncovered for 10 minutes. Sprinkle with parsley. Serve with rice or noodles.

—*Thelma Carpenter*

186

Meredosia, the legend says, is named after the French marais d'osier *which means swamp of reeds. It was settled in the 1830s on the banks of the Illinois River at the mouth of a backwater lake.*

Beef and Mushroom Skewers

Yield: 18 to 20 skewers

½ pound beef top round, cut ⅜-inch thick
½ pound mushrooms, sliced
2 tablespoons vegetable oil
2 tablespoons soy sauce
1 teaspoon crushed, toasted sesame seeds
1 garlic clove, crushed
½ teaspoon brown sugar
Dash pepper
2 bunches scallions, trimmed
1 cup flour
3 eggs, beaten
Vegetable oil for frying

Cut meat across grain in strips ½-inch thick, then cut in 2-inch lengths. Toss meat in bowl with mushrooms, oil, soy sauce, sesame seed, garlic, brown sugar, and a dash of pepper. Let stand 30 minutes. Cut scallions in 2-inch lengths. On toothpicks, skewer 2 pieces of meat (fold strips in half if too long), 2 pieces of scallion crosswise, and 2 mushroom slices. Repeat. Roll skewers in flour, then in beaten eggs. Cover bottom of frying pan with oil and heat until medium hot. Place skewers in pan and cook until golden, about 7 minutes on each side.

> *Clinton is the seat of DeWitt County, and, here on the courthouse square, the legend goes, Lincoln said, "You can fool all of the people some of the time; and some of the people all of the time; but you cannot fool all of the people all of the time."*

Beef Birds

Yield: 12 servings
3 pounds round steak, ½ inch thick
3 teaspoons salt
½ teaspoon pepper
3 slices bacon, minced
1 medium onion, minced

1 carrot, cut into 12 strips
2 large dill pickles, cut into 12 strips
1½ cups beef bouillon
Flour for gravy

187

Trim any fat from steak; render and use for browning. Pound steak to ¼ inch thickness, using a meat mallet or edge of a heavy plate. Cut into 12 rectangular pieces. Sprinkle with salt and pepper. Put a spoonful of bacon and onion on each piece; add a strip of carrot and pickle to each. Roll up and secure with wood picks or string. Brown beef birds on all sides in melted steak fat, adding drippings if necessary. Add beef bouillon, cover, and simmer for 1 hour or until meat is tender. Thicken pan liquid with flour for gravy.

> *Edinburg, which was incorporated in 1872, is a charming farming community complete with a town square, covered sidewalks, and a hotel building which was built as a bank in 1880.*

Pepper Steak

Yield: 4 to 6 servings

1½ pounds sirloin steak, 1 inch thick, all fat removed
¼ cup vegetable oil
2 garlic cloves, crushed
1 teaspoon salt
1 teaspoon ground ginger
½ teaspoon pepper
3 large green peppers, cut in strips
2 large onions, cut in strips

¼ cup soy sauce
½ teaspoon brown sugar
½ cup beef stock
4 scallions, cut in 1-inch slices
1 6-ounce can water chestnuts, sliced and drained
1 tablespoon cornstarch
¼ cup cold water

Cut meat into ⅛-inch slices. Heat oil in skillet; add garlic, salt, ginger, and pepper. Sauté until garlic is golden. Add steak slices. Brown lightly 2 minutes; remove meat. Add green peppers and onions. Cook 3 minutes. Return beef to pan; add soy sauce, brown sugar, beef stock, cornstarch dissolved in water, green onions, and chestnuts. Simmer 2 minutes or until sauce thickens. Serve with rice.

188

> *Neoga, known for its fruit growing, became a town in 1855 when it was given a station on the Illinois Central Railroad.*

Beef Stroganoff

Yield: 4 servings

1½ pounds fresh mushrooms, sliced
3 onions, chopped
¼ pound (1 stick) butter
2 pounds sirloin, cut in strips

Salt and pepper to taste
4 tablespoons flour
1 cup beef stock
1 cup sour cream

Sauté mushrooms and onions in butter. Remove from skillet. Toss beef in seasoned flour. Add beef to skillet and brown. Add stock and simmer about 30 minutes. Add sautéed vegetables and stir. Before serving, stir in sour cream. Serve over noodles.

> *Athens was settled in 1819 and in 1851 was nearly destroyed by a cholera epidemic. A two-story frame building here was the site of a banquet honoring Abraham Lincoln and the other legislators who had moved the state capital from Vandalia to Springfield.*

Conestoga Wagon

Steak in Wine Sauce

Yield: 5 servings
2 tablespoons butter
5 slices beef tenderloin (8–ounce)
2 teaspoons salt
1 teaspoon freshly ground black
   pepper
½ cup white wine

¼ cup cognac
½ cup beef stock
4 tablespoons butter
3 tablespoons heavy cream
2 tablespoons cognac

Heat 2 tablespoons butter in skillet. Season steaks with salt and pepper. Cook meat 4 minutes. Turn; cook 4 minutes longer. Pour off drippings. Add wine, ¼ cup cognac and stock; cook 3 minutes. Remove from heat; add remaining butter, stirring until melted. Add cream and remaining cognac. Stir until smooth. Serve immediately.

Marshall was founded by William B. Archer and was named after Chief Justice John Marshall of the Supreme Court. It was platted in 1835.

Goulash

Yield: 6 servings

2 pounds boneless beef, cut in 1-inch cubes
2 teaspoons soy sauce
2 teaspoons salt
1 cup sliced onions
2 tablespoons butter

½ cup chopped celery
1 8-ounce can tomato sauce
1 tablespoon paprika
1½ cups water
2 tablespoons cornstarch
¼ cup dry red wine or cold water

Sprinkle beef with soy sauce and salt. Toss to coat beef evenly. Sauté onions in butter until golden brown. Add meat and brown, turning often. Add celery. Blend tomato sauce, paprika, and water; add to meat mixture. Cook, covered, until meat is tender, about 1 hour. Blend cornstarch and wine; add to meat mixture. Stir until thickened.

Randolph bears the name of its first settler. Gardner Randolph brought his family from North Carolina to settle the land in 1822.

190

No Peek Stew

Mrs. Havlik of Oakbrook in Megalopolis says that this recipe has been in her family many years. "Don't peek! Or the steam escapes and the stew becomes less moist than it should."

Yield: 4 servings

6 tablespoons tapioca
1 10-ounce can consommé
1 15-ounce can tomatoes
2 whole onions, peeled

2 carrots, cut in large chunks
Potatoes, 4 to 6 medium
2 celery stalks, cut in large chunks
2 pounds beef stew meat

Preheat oven to 250 degrees F. Combine tapioca with consomme and tomatoes. Mix all ingredients in a heavy metal pan or dutch oven and bake covered for 6 hours.

—Mary Jane Havlik

Sullivan is the seat of Moultrie County. It was originally called Asa's Point. Legend has it that westward moving Asa Spencer Rice reached this point in his migration and said, "Of all the country I've seen, this is my choice."

Pot Roast with Cranberry Gravy

Yield: 8 servings

1 beef pot roast, about 4 pounds
¼ cup flour
1½ teaspoons salt
½ teaspoon pepper
3 tablespoons butter

2½ cups cranberry sauce
⅓ cup water
5 whole cloves
1 stick cinnamon

Dredge the roast in the flour, salt, and pepper and brown on all sides in the butter. Place in a dutch oven or crock pot. Stir together the cranberry sauce and water. Pour over meat. Add the cloves and cinnamon. Simmer 3 hours in the dutch oven or 8 to 10 hours in the crock pot, turning roast once. Serve with the gravy on the side.

> *Taylorville is the seat of Christian County. The town was platted in 1839 by John Taylor on land which had been purchased from the government for $1.25 an acre by Daniel C. Goode.*

Spicy Short Ribs

Yield: 4 to 6 servings

4 pounds beef short ribs
1 cup water
½ cup soy sauce
½ teaspoon salt
1 teaspoon basil

1 teaspoon brown sugar
½ teaspoon ground ginger
½ teaspoon pepper
1 garlic clove, crushed
3 teaspoons cornstarch

Brown ribs in deep heavy kettle. Pour off fat. Add water, soy sauce, salt, basil, brown sugar, ginger, pepper, and garlic. Cover and simmer 2 hours or until fork tender. Remove meat to center of large hot platter. Drain excess fat from juices. Blend cornstarch into meat juices. Continue stirring and cook over high heat until thick and clear. Serve with rice.

> *Mount Olive was first settled in 1826 but not incorporated until 1874. Its largest growth occurred because of the coal vein which was discovered during the year of incorporation.*

Liver Goulash

Yield: 6 servings
2 cups thinly sliced onion
5 tablespoons butter, divided
Salt and pepper to taste
1 8-ounce can tomato sauce
1 cup water
1½ pounds sliced beef liver, cut into

2-inch strips
3 tablespoons flour
½ teaspoon salt
2 tablespoons sour cream

Cook onion in 2 tablespoons butter in skillet; stir in salt, pepper, tomato sauce, and 1 cup water. Bring to a boil and simmer covered about 10 minutes. Roll liver in flour seasoned with ½ teaspoon salt. Brown in remaining butter, turning to brown on all sides and sautéing only to cook through. Add to sauce. Add sour cream. Heat through. Serve over noodles. Garnish with parsley.

> *Jerseyville was settled by James Faulkner in 1827 and is the seat of Jersey County. It was first named Hickory Grove but was later changed to New Jersey. The town was platted in 1834, and lots sold for $20.*

192

Liver Casserole

Yield: 6 servings
1 teaspoon poultry seasoning
2 tablespoons flour
⅛ teaspoon pepper
1 teaspoon seasoned salt, divided
1 pound beef liver, cut in 1-inch pieces

2 unpeeled apples, chopped
½ cup chopped onion
4 medium potatoes, peeled and thinly sliced
1 cup chicken stock

Preheat oven to 350 degrees F. In a paper bag, mix first 3 ingredients and ½ teaspoon seasoned salt. Add liver pieces and shake to coat each piece well. Butter a 1½-quart casserole and place in layers of meat, apples, onions, and potatoes, sprinkling final layer of potatoes with remaining salt. Boil stock and pour over top. Cover and bake ½ hour. Uncover and bake 15 minutes or until lightly browned.

> *Tolono was founded in 1856 and is famous for being the last place in Illinois that Abraham Lincoln spoke to the public before being inaugurated.*

Liver and Bacon

Yield: 6 servings

12 strips bacon
6 slices (2 pounds) calf or beef liver
¼ cup flour
1 teaspoon salt
⅓ cup bacon drippings
½ cup white wine

1 tablespoon basil
2 tablespoons butter
1 Spanish onion
4 tablespoons butter
½ teaspoon salt
¼ teaspoon pepper

Fry bacon until crisp. Drain, reserving drippings. Dredge liver in flour mixed with 1 teaspoon salt. Fry in drippings, about 3 minutes on each side. Arrange on platter with bacon. Add wine to drippings; stir well. Add basil and 2 tablespoons butter; heat. Pour wine mixture over liver. Slice onion thin and separate into rings. Saute in remaining butter until transparent. Season with remaining salt and pepper; arrange with meat.

> *Rossville is the home of an asparagus and corn packing company. It was first settled in 1829 and platted in 1859.*

Tongue

Yield: 4 to 6 servings

1 large calf tongue, about 2½ pounds
1 quart dry white wine
Water
1 large onion, chopped
4 garlic cloves, minced

1 tablespoon salt
8 grinds fresh pepper
6 whole cloves
2 tablespoons sugar
2 bay leaves

Wash the tongue and trim the root end. Place the tongue in a large stewing pan. Pour the wine over and add enough water to cover by 2 inches. Add the rest of the ingredients. Simmer for 2½ hours or until fork tender. Remove the tongue, peel it, and remove any bones or gristle at the root end. Slice length-wise and serve with horseradish.

> *Eureka is the seat of Woodford County and was established in 1830. It is the home of Eureka College which was founded in 1848.*

Spiced Tongue

Yield: 8 servings

4¼ pounds smoked beef tongue
Water to cover
1 large bay leaf
½ teaspoon whole black pepper
½ teaspoon whole allspice
½ teaspoon whole cloves
2 tablespoons chopped onion

1 garlic clove, minced
½ teaspoon salt
1 medium carrot, peeled and
  chopped
3 tablespoons flour
3 tablespoons butter, at room
  temperature

Wash tongue and simmer in boiling water to cover 2 hours. Remove tongue and reserve cooking water. Slip off skin and trim off root. Place tongue in saucepan with 1 quart tongue stock, bay leaf, pepper, allspice, cloves, onion, garlic, and salt. Cover and cook 1 hour or until tongue is tender, adding carrot 20 minutes before cooking time is up. Remove tongue. Blend flour with butter and add to the stock. Stir and cook until sauce is thickened. Slice tongue and serve with sauce.

194

> *Pana, "The City of Roses," was incorporated in 1856 and is the birthplace of Vincent Sheean, journalist; Florian Zabach, musician; and Leonard Crunelli, sculptor.*

Braised Beef Heart

Yield: 4 servings

1 5-pound beef heart
3 tablespoons butter
1 cup sliced onions
6 cups boiling water

2 teaspoons salt
½ teaspoon pepper
1 teaspoon celery seeds
2 teaspoons lemon juice

Remove fat veins and arteries from cleaned heart. Melt butter in Dutch oven. Add onions; sauté until browned. Add heart and brown on all sides. Add water, salt, pepper, and celery seeds. Cover, simmer 2½ to 3 hours or until tender. Lift out meat and strain liquid. Return 3 cups of liquid to pan; add lemon juice. Thicken for gravy.

> *Urbana, Champaign's twin city, is the home of the other half of the University of Illinois and was named by the same settlers for the town in Urbana, Ohio, from which they migrated.*

Braised Oxtails

Yield: 6 servings
2 teaspoons salt
¼ teaspoon pepper
½ cup flour
3 oxtails, cut into 2-inch lengths
½ cup drippings
2 medium onions, chopped

1 cup celery, cut into 1-inch pieces
½ cup water
2½ cups tomatoes
1 bay leaf
6 whole cloves

Add salt and pepper to flour. Dredge pieces of oxtails in flour and brown to a golden color in hot drippings. Add onions, celery, water, tomatoes, bay leaf, and cloves. Cover frying pan and simmer over low heat for 4 hours.

> *Mason City was platted in 1857 just as the Tonica, Petersburg, and Jacksonville Railroad laid down its tracks. The town is a trade center for farmers of the surrounding corn growing land.*

Chili Skillet Meal

Yield: 4 servings
2 slices bacon, halved
1 onion, sliced
1 green pepper, chopped
1 16-or 17-ounce can kidney beans
⅓ cup chili sauce
2 teaspoons chili powder
½ teaspoon cumin

¼ teaspoon salt
Pepper to taste
¼ pound sharp Cheddar cheese,
    shredded
1 pound frankfurters, sliced
4 large English muffins, halved and
    lightly toasted

Cook bacon until golden brown and crisp. Drain. Add onion and green pepper to fat in skillet. Cook until lightly browned, about 4 minutes. Add kidney beans. Reduce to low heat. Crumble bacon and add with remaining ingredients except muffins, stirring until cheese is melted. Cover; heat thoroughly. Serve on muffins.

> *Teutopolis was founded in 1838 by the German Company of Cincinnati. In 1860 a seminary was founded here, and priests still graduate from this theological institution.*

Iroquois County Court House—Watseka

Ham and Cheese Brunch

Yield: 8 servings

16 slices sandwich bread, trimmed
  and buttered
16 slices cooked ham
8 slices cheese
6 eggs

3 cups light cream
Salt and pepper
1 cup crushed potato chips
½ (1 stick) cup butter, melted

Preheat oven to 350 degrees F. Place 8 slices of bread on bottom of a
3-quart casserole. Layer slices of ham, cheese, and ham again over

bread; cover with remaining 8 slices of bread. Combine eggs with cream, salt, and pepper to taste. Beat well and pour over sandwich. Cover and refrigerate overnight. Mix potato chips and butter; spread over top of casserole. Bake for 1¼ hours.

> *Stonington was named after the town in Connecticut when it was settled in 1837. Little has changed here since 1878 when the village was incorporated.*

Monte Carlos

Yield: 4 servings

8 thin slices white bread	1 egg
8 slices Swiss cheese	1 egg yolk
4 slices ham	1 cup light cream
½ pound mushrooms, sliced and sautéed	3 tablespoons butter
	Hollandaise sauce
6 slices bacon, fried and crumbled	

Remove crusts from bread and make sandwiches: a slice of cheese, a slice of ham, sautéed mushrooms, bacon, and another slice of cheese. Blend the egg, egg yolk, and cream. Dip both sides of each sandwich in this mixture. Fry the sandwich in butter until golden brown on each side. Place in an oven-proof serving dish. Spoon Hollandaise sauce over each and brown under broiler.

197

> *Paris is the seat of Edgar County and was platted in 1853. The city is named after Paris, Kentucky, and not the French metropolis.*

Pork Chops and Pears

Yield: 6 servings

6 pork chops, 1 inch thick	1 cup sweet sherry wine
1 tablespoon butter	3 tablespoons brown sugar
1½ teaspoons salt	¼ teaspoon thyme
¼ teaspoon pepper	¼ teaspoon nutmeg
2 onions, cut in wedges	4 fresh pears, peeled and quartered
¼ cup seedless raisins	

Preheat oven to 375 degrees F. Fry chops for 5 minutes on each side in butter. Arrange in a baking dish. Sprinkle with salt and pepper. Top with onions and raisins. Add sherry, brown sugar, thyme, and nutmeg. Cover and bake 1¼ hours. Place pears over chops. Return to oven long enough to heat through.

Pork Chops and Cranberries

Yield: 8 servings

8 pork chops, 1 inch thick
1 tablespoon butter
1 teaspoon salt
¼ teaspoon freshly ground pepper
2 cups fresh cranberries, washed

2 tablespoons cornstarch
½ cup sugar
½ cup honey
1 cup dry red wine
3 teaspoons lemon juice

Preheat oven to 350 degrees F. Brown chops in butter and season with salt and pepper. Coat a 13-by-9-by-2-inch baking dish with pan drippings. Put in cranberries. Combine cornstarch and sugar. Sprinkle over cranberries. Drizzle honey over berries. Place browned chops on top of cranberries. Combine wine and lemon juice and pour over pork chops. Cover securely with foil and bake for 50 minutes. Serve chops with cranberries.

198

Baked Pork Chops with Apples and Raisins

Yield: 4 servings

8 pork chops
3 tablespoons vegetable oil
½ teaspoon salt
1½ teaspoons sage
4 tart apples, cored and sliced in rings

¼ cup brown sugar
2 tablespoons flour
1½ cups hot water
1 tablespoon vinegar
½ cup seedless raisins

Preheat oven to 350 degrees F. Brown chops in hot oil; sprinkle with salt and sage. Place in baking dish; top with apple rings; sprinkle with sugar and set aside. Add flour to oil in skillet; stir until brown. Add water and vinegar; cook until thickened. Add raisins. Pour over chops. Bake for 1 hour.

Pork Chops Stuffed with Bleu Cheese

Yield: 6 servings

1½ teaspoons minced onion
¼ cup mushrooms, thinly sliced
3 tablespoons butter, melted
½ cup crumbled Bleu cheese

1½ cups dry breadcubes
Dash salt
6 pork loin chops, 2 inches thick

Preheat oven to 350 degrees F. Sauté onion and mushrooms in butter. Stir in cheese, bread, and salt. Cut pocket in side of each chop. Stuff. Secure with wooden toothpicks. Place on bone end in a 13-by-9-by-2-inch baking pan. Bake 1¼ hours.

New Salem State Park is located near the Sangamon River. It is a faithful restoration of the pioneer settlement to which the young Abraham Lincoln came in 1831.

199

Baked Pork Tenderloin

Yield: 2 servings

2 onions, sliced
6 tablespoons bacon fat
2 medium pork tenderloins
flour for coating

6 whole cloves
2 cups water
½ cup sour cream
½ cup chili sauce

Preheat oven to 350 degrees F. Sauté sliced onions in bacon fat until brown. Coat tenderloins with flour; sauté in fat until well browned. Stick cloves in meat, add two cups water, cover pan, and simmer 30 minutes. Mix sour cream and chili sauce; pour over meat. Place uncovered in oven, and bake 30 minutes, basting occasionally.

Rantoul was named after Robert Rantoul, an official of the Illinois Central Railroad. It became a stop on that railroad in 1854 and soon developed into a thriving farm community.

Stuffed Roast Pork Shoulder

Yield: 6 servings
1 pork shoulder butt, about 5 pounds
2 cups soft breadcrumbs
2 tablespoons butter, melted
½ cup minced onion
½ teaspoon salt
¼ teaspoon pepper
½ teaspoon basil

Preheat oven to 350 degrees F. Remove bone from meat. Mix remaining ingredients together and place into cavity. Skewer cavity closed. Place on rack in shallow pan. Roast uncovered allowing 35 minutes per pound or until meat thermometer registers 185 degrees F.

> *Lake Shelbyville is fed by the Kaskaskia River as well as a number of smaller creeks and streams. The project was begun by the Army Corps of Engineers in the early 1960s. By 1971 fishing, boating, and other recreational facilities were open to thousands of campers and sportsmen.*

200

Cabbage Casserole

Mrs. Nordhielm of Galesburg in Land Between the Rivers brought this recipe with her from Sweden when she came to Illinois in the early 1900s.

Yield: 6 to 8 servings
1 large cabbage, chopped coarsely
2 large onions, chopped
3 tablespoons unsalted butter
3½ tablespoons flour
1½ cups milk, generous
Salt to taste
Pepper to taste
1 teaspoon dry mustard
1½ cups chopped broiled ham

Preheat oven to 325 degrees F. Drop the cabbage into boiling water and cook 5 to 8 minutes. Drain completely. Sauté the onions in butter until transparent. Stir in the flour and cook two minutes. Add the milk, more if necessary, to make a medium white sauce. Add the salt, pepper, mustard, and ham. Alternately layer the cabbage and white sauce in a 2-quart casserole dish. Bake for 20 minutes. Serve hot garnished with parsley.

—*Vendla Nordhielm*

Pork Cabbage Custard Casserole

Yield: 6 servings

1 small head cabbage
1 large onion, sliced
1 pound ground fresh pork, browned
  and drained

1 cup cracker crumbs
3 eggs
¾ cup light cream
Salt and pepper to taste

Preheat oven to 325 degrees F. Cook cabbage and drain. Layer cabbage, onion, pork, and then cracker crumbs. Beat eggs and cream with salt and pepper. Pour over mixture. Bake 30 minutes.

201

Sausage Patties in Fruit Sauce

Yield: 4 servings

1 pound bulk pork sausage
1 16-ounce can fruit cocktail
1 tablespoon brown sugar
1 tablespoon lemon juice
½ teaspoon cinnamon

½ teaspoon ground ginger
1½ teaspoons cornstarch
1 tablespoon cold water
4 buttered toast slices

Shape pork sausage into 8 cigar shapes, ½ inch thick. Brown in skillet and pour off drippings. Add fruit cocktail, brown sugar, lemon juice, cinnamon, and ginger. Cover and simmer for 10 minutes. Remove sausage from skillet. Pour in paste made of cornstarch and water; simmer until thick. Place 2 patties on each slice of butter toast and top with fruit sauce.

Apple Scrapple

Yield: 6 servings

1 pound pork sausage
1 cup yellow corn meal
1 cup cold water
1 cup boiling water
1 teaspoon salt

1 tablespoon grated onion
½ teaspoon sweet basil
1 cup applesauce
½ cup flour
Bacon drippings for frying

In a heavy skillet crumble sausage and cook until lightly browned. Drain off fat. Mix corn meal with cold water. Pour into a saucepan; add boiling water and seasonings. Cook, stirring until thickened. Cover and simmer 10 minutes. Fold in applesauce and sausage. Pour into buttered 9-by-5-by-3-inch loaf pan; chill until firm. Unmold and cut in ½-inch slices. Dip in flour and brown on both sides in hot bacon drippings.

> *Chebanse, as the legend goes, means "little duck" in Indian. It is divided by the county line of Iroquois and Kankakee Counties, causing its inhabitants to reside in two separate counties.*

202

Pawnhaas

Mrs. Rittenhouse of Chester in the Bottom says, "This was my father's recipe that was brought from Germany. It was so good on a cold winter morning, fried golden and covered with homemade molasses."

Yield: 3 loaves

1 hog head, cleaned
½ cup diced pork liver
½ cup diced pork heart
4 quarts water

2 teaspoons salt
1½ teaspoons pepper
4 cups yellow cornmeal

Simmer hog head, heart, and liver in 4 quarts water for 2½ hours or until meat falls from bone. Strain the meat and reserve the broth, adding more water if necessary to make 3 quarts. Chop the meat fine and discard bones. Bring the broth back to a boil in a heavy kettle and slowly add the cornmeal, stirring constantly until the consistency of mush has been reached. Add meat and seasonings and cook slowly for 45 minutes, stirring so that it does not burn. Pour into 3 bread loaf pans and refrigerate. When ready to serve, slice and fry slices in bacon grease until brown on both sides. Serve with molasses.

—Anna Rittenhouse

> *Tremont was first settled by Thomas Briggs and Hezekiah Davis who set up trade with the Indians. The town, legend has it, is named for the three hills upon which it is built.*

The Madonna of the Trail Monument—Vandalia

Mustard Rack of Lamb

Yield: 8 servings

2 racks of lamb, 8 chops each
1 5-ounce jar mustard
3 tablespoons soy sauce
2 garlic cloves, crushed

1 teaspoon tarragon
½ teaspoon ground ginger
2 tablespoons Lucca olive oil

Trim fat from meat. Make a cut between each chop, being careful not to cut through. Combine remaining ingredients. Mix until thick. Paint the racks with the mustard mixture. Cover and refrigerate for 2 days. Bring to room temperature. Place lamb, fat side down, on a rack in a shallow pan. Reserve marinade. Place lamb 6 inches from a preheated broiler and cook until brown. Remove, turn over, and paint the reserved marinade on the fat side and broil until brown, about 30 minutes.

> *Paxton was settled by Swedish immigrants in the mid-nineteenth century. Augustana College was located here at one time.*

204

Lamb with Eggplant

Yield: 6 servings

3 pounds lean shoulder of lamb, cut into cubes
3 onions, chopped
3 tablespoons butter
1 tablespoon Lucca olive oil

1 8-ounce can tomato sauce
1 cup beef stock
Salt and pepper to taste
2 large eggplants, peeled
2 garlic cloves, crushed

Sauté meat and onions in butter and oil until brown. Add tomato sauce, stock, salt, and pepper and bring to a boil. Cover; simmer 1 hour. Cut eggplant into cubes; add to meat with garlic. Cook 30 minutes or until meat and vegetables are tender.

> *Forrest was first settled in 1836. The coming of the railroads and later of the German-Amish immigrants gave the town stability and a future. It now is a center for cattle feed production and poultry.*

Lamb Teriyaki Kabobs

Yield: 8 servings
2 tablespoons pineapple juice
¾ cup lemon juice
2 tablespoons soy sauce
1 garlic clove, minced
3 pounds lamb, cut in 2-inch cubes

2 1-pound 13-ounce cans peach
  halves, drained
20 large mushrooms, washed and
  stemmed

Mix juices, soy sauce, and garlic. Pour over lamb. Cover. Marinate in refrigerator overnight. Thread lamb on skewers with peach halves and mushrooms. Brush with marinade. Place on a cookie sheet under broiler for 20 to 25 minutes, turning often.

Charleston is the seat of Coles County, and is the home of Eastern Illinois University. The town is filled with plaques commemorating the Lincoln family and their various activities.

Veal on a Stick

Yield: 6 servings
1½ pounds veal
1 teaspoon dry mustard
1 teaspoon chili powder
½ teaspoon ground ginger
1 cup soy sauce
½ cup chopped onion

¼ teaspoon turmeric
1½ teaspoons salt
½ teaspoon coriander
¾ tablespoon lemon juice
1 tablespoon sugar

Cut meat into 1½-inch cubes. Combine the other ingredients and marinate the cubes for several hours. Skewer the meat on butcher sticks. Boil until browned.

Greenup was incorporated in 1836 and named after William C. Greenup, the first clerk of the Illinois Territorial Legislature, who donated the land for the site of the town.

Veal Paprika

Yield: 8 servings

½ cup (1 stick) butter
2¼ cups thinly sliced onions
¾ pound mushrooms, chopped, or
   3 4-ounce cans
4 pounds boned veal leg or shoulder,
   cut in 1-inch cubes
3 cups chopped celery
¾ cup flour

2 tablespoons paprika
4 to 5 teaspoons salt
4½ cups chicken bouillon
¼ cup chopped parsley
3 bay leaves
¼ teaspoon pepper
⅓ cup lemon juice
3 cups sour cream

Heat butter in a large skillet. Add onions and mushrooms. Cook until tender but not browned; pour onion mixture into a large heavy saucepan. Place veal in skillet. Cook slowly until browned on all sides. Add veal to onion mixture. Add celery. Then stir in flour, paprika, and salt, mixing well. Gradually stir in chicken bouillon. Continue to cook and stir until mixture is thickened. Add parsley, bay leaves, pepper, and lemon juice. Bring to a boil, then reduce the heat. Cover and simmer gently, stirring occasionally, until veal is tender, about 1 hour. Remove bay leaves. Just before serving, stir in sour cream. Heat thoroughly. Serve over rice or Chinese noodles.

Vandalia was the second capital of the state from 1819 to 1839 and was the western terminus of the Cumberland Trail.

Veal with Crab and Asparagus

Yield: 4 servings

2 eggs
¾ teaspoon salt
½ teaspoon pepper
8 2-ounce pieces veal
1 cup flour
½ cup dry breadcrumbs

½ cup (1 stick) butter, divided
2 scallions, sliced
½ pound crab meat
Salt and pepper to taste
2 ounces sherry
16 asparagus spears, cooked

Bearnaise Sauce

Yield: 1 cup

4 egg yolks
2 tablespoons lemon juice
1 cup (2 sticks) butter, melted
¼ teaspoon salt

¼ teaspoon pepper
¼ teaspoon chives
½ teaspoon parsley flakes
¼ teaspoon dry tarragon leaves

Beat eggs. Salt and pepper veal. Dip veal into flour, then egg, and then into breadcrumbs. Melt ¼ cup butter in skillet; fry veal to golden brown. Melt remaining butter in another skillet; sauté scallions until tender. Add crab meat, salt, and pepper. Blend together until warm. Add sherry and simmer. Place 2 pieces of veal on plate. Place 2 tablespoons of crab meat in center of veal. Place 4 asparagus spears on crab meat; cover with Bearnaise Sauce.

To make Bearnaise Sauce, in top half of double boiler, beat egg yolks and stir in lemon juice. Cook over low heat. Add butter, a little at a time. Stir constantly with a wooden spoon. Add salt, pepper, chives, parsley flakes, and dry tarragon. Continue cooking slowly until thickened.

> *Altamont was named for a small hill not far from the town site and was incorporated in 1871. Once known as Mountville, its post office opened for business in 1870.*

Stuffed Veal Rolls

207

Yield: 6 servings

6 veal cutlets, pounded ¼-inch thin
Salt and pepper to taste
6 thin slices boiled ham
6 thin slices Swiss cheese
4 tablespoons butter
2 tablespoons flour
2 tablespoons minced onion
1 10¾-ounces can condensed beef consommé
¼ teaspoon basil

Preheat oven to 350 degrees F. Season cutlets with salt and pepper; top each with a slice of ham and a slice of cheese. Roll up; fasten with toothpicks. Brown rolls lightly in butter. Place in baking dish. Add flour and onion to remaining butter in skillet. Stir in consommé and basil; simmer 5 minutes. Pour over veal. Bake covered for 30 minutes.

> *Kickapoo State Park is one of the many recreation areas in the state which was developed from land previously used for strip mining. At a short distance from the park lie the salt springs used by early settlers who evaporated the water to get this precious commodity for seasoning and preserving.*

Veal Heart with Dumplings

Yield: 4 servings

1 veal heart, cut up
1 large onion, chopped
2 cups water

1 bay leaf
3 tablespoons vinegar
Salt and pepper to taste

Dumplings

1 cup flour
⅓ cup milk
1 egg

Place heart, onion, water, bay leaf, vinegar, salt, and pepper in dutch oven. Bring to a boil and cook over medium heat until heart is tender. Add dumplings and serve.

Combine flour, milk, and egg. Drop from tablespoon into hot stew. Boil about 10 minutes covered and 5 minutes uncovered.

> *Porter Martin came from Vermont to Iroquois County to plat the town of Martinton in 1871.*

Veal in Lemon-Wine Gravy

Yield: 4 servings

1½ pounds veal, very thinly sliced
1 cup flour
Salt and pepper to taste
1 tablespoon sweet basil
2 small garlic cloves, crushed

¼ (1 stick) pound butter
¼ cup chopped parsley
Juice of 1 lemon
⅓ cup dry vermouth

Dredge veal slices in flour seasoned with salt, pepper, and basil. Sauté garlic in butter. Add parsley and lemon juice. Saute veal 3 minutes on each side. Remove veal. Pour vermouth into skillet. Loosen pan drippings and boil 1 minute to deglaze pan. Pour over veal. Garnish with lemon slices.

> *Matthias Chrisman platted the town bearing his name in 1872. Chrisman's development was ensured by the railroads which came to crisscross his property.*

209

St. John The Baptist Church—L'Erable

Fruited Chicken Salad Sandwiches

Miss Ostrem of Brookfield in Megalopolis says that these party sandwiches are great with cocktails, but that they disappear rapidly.

Yield: 32 2-inch square sandwiches

1 cup cooked chicken, minced
½ cup celery, minced
½ cup apple, minced
⅓ cup crushed pineapple, well-drained
3 tablespoons mayonnaise
¼ teaspoon salt
⅛ teaspoon white pepper
1 teaspoon lemon juice
¼ teaspoon onion powder
8 slices bread, trimmed and buttered
1 Unpeeled apple, thinly sliced, for garnish
Crushed pineapple, for garnish

Combine chicken, celery, ½ cup apple, and ⅓ cup pineapple in a small bowl. Stir in mayonnaise, salt, pepper, lemon juice, and onion powder. To serve, spread chicken mixture on buttered bread. Cut as desired. Garnish with apple slices and pineapple.

—*Elaine L. Ostrem*

Cerro Gordo is a farming community which was settled in the mid 1850s. It was named for a battle which was fought in the Mexican War.

Chicken Sauté

Yield: 6 to 8 servings

6 pounds chicken, cut into pieces
½ cup flour
Salt and pepper to taste
½ cup (1 stick) butter
4 small scallions, chopped
1 garlic clove, crushed
2 tablespoons chopped parsley
½ teaspoon rosemary
1 cup Chablis
1 cup sliced mushrooms, sautéed in butter

Dust chicken with flour and seasonings and sauté in butter until brown on all sides. Add chopped onions, crushed garlic, parsley, and rosemary. When mixture starts to bubble, add wine. Cover tightly and simmer for ½ hour. Uncover and add sliced mushrooms. Cook about 10 minutes or until chicken is tender.

Manteno derives its name from the half Indian daughter of Francois Bourbonnais. It was founded in 1853, organized in 1855, and incorporated in 1878.

Chicken Oriental

Yield: 4 servings

2 tablespoons cornstarch, divided
½ teaspoon salt
2 whole chicken breasts, boned, skinned, and split
3 tablespoons vegetable oil
2 scallions, diagonally sliced
¼ pound fresh mushrooms, sliced
1 garlic clove, crushed

¼ teaspoon ground ginger
1 tablespoon soy sauce
1 tablespoon dry sherry
1 10¾-ounce can condensed chicken broth
1 7-ounce package frozen pea pods, thawed

In a medium-sized bowl combine 1 tablespoon of the cornstarch and salt. Cut chicken breasts into 1-inch cubes. Place chicken in bowl with cornstarch and toss lightly to coat pieces well. Heat oil in an electric skillet to 375 degrees F. Add chicken pieces and cook, stirring constantly, until chicken is lightly browned, about 2 to 3 minutes. Remove chicken; add scallions, mushrooms, garlic, and ginger. Cook, stirring occasionally, about 1 minute. In a small bowl combine soy sauce, sherry, and the remaining 1 tablespoon cornstarch and blend well. Stir chicken broth into skillet. Add cornstarch mixture gradually, stirring constantly, and cook until mixture thickens. Stir in pea pods and chicken. Cook a few minutes until thoroughly heated. Serve over rice.

211

> *Ashland was platted in 1857 by Richard Yates who became the Governor of Illinois during the Civil War. The town was named after Ashland, Kentucky.*

Baked Chicken Paprika

Yield: 4 servings

2½ or 3½ pounds chicken, cut up
¼ teaspoon salt
Dash pepper
4 tablespoons flour, divided
4 tablespoons butter
2 medium onions, chopped

1 teaspoon paprika
¼ cup water
1 4-ounce can mushrooms, with liquid
1 cup sour cream

Wash and dry chicken. Combine salt and pepper with 3 tablespoons flour in a bag; add chicken; shake until well coated with flour. Melt butter in a heavy skillet, add chicken, and brown on all sides. Add onion, paprika, water, and mushrooms, including liquids. Cover and simmer about ½ hour or until tender. Remove chicken to hot platter. Add remaining 1 tablespoon flour to mixture in skillet, blend well; add sour cream and stir over low heat 2 minutes. Pour over chicken. Sprinkle with paprika.

> *Streator was first known as Hardscrabble and later as Unionville. It was the home of George "Honey Boy" Evans, the composer of "In The Good Old Summertime."*

Chicken Burgundy

Yield: 3 to 4 servings

1 large frying chicken (about 3½ pounds) cut up
4 tablespoons butter
1 quart Burgundy wine
1 medium onion, chopped
2 celery stalks, chopped

1 tablespoon tarragon
1 teaspoon salt
6 grinds fresh pepper
1½ tablespoons dark molasses
½ pound mushrooms, sliced

In a heavy skillet, brown the chicken quickly in butter. In a large stew pan, combine all the other ingredients except the mushrooms. Bring to a boil. Then add the chicken and browning butter to the mixture. Boil together for ten minutes. Remove chicken and place in a large casserole dish. Preheat oven to 400 degrees F. Boil down wine mixture to one-half original amount. Add the mushrooms during the last 2 minutes of boiling. Pour over the chicken in casserole. Cover and bake for 35 minutes. Remove cover and bake for 10 minutes more. Serve over hot rice.

> *Chenoa was platted in 1856. Legend has it that its name is derived from the Indian word "chenowa" which means "white dove."*

Baked Chicken Breasts

Yield: 6 servings

6 chicken breasts, halved
2 cups sour cream
¼ cup lemon juice
4 teaspoons Worcestershire sauce
2 teaspoons paprika
1 teaspoon tarragon

4 garlic cloves, crushed
2 teaspoons salt
½ teaspoon pepper
1¾ cups breadcrumbs
1 cup (2 sticks) butter

Dry chicken breast halves with a towel. Combine sour cream, lemon juice, Worcestershire, paprika, tarragon, garlic, salt, and pepper.

Place chicken in sour cream mixture, coating each piece well. Cover with foil. Refrigerate overnight. Preheat oven to 350 degrees F. Remove chicken from sour cream mixture and roll in crumbs. Arrange in a single layer in a baking dish. Melt butter and drizzle over the chicken. Bake uncovered for 45 minutes.

> *Danville, the seat of Vermillion County, was first known as Salt Works because of saline wells here. It was named after Dan Beckwith who donated 100 acres of the original land for the town site.*

Honey Baked Chicken

Yield: 3 servings
1 fryer, cut in serving pieces
½ cup flour
1 teaspoon salt
¼ teaspoon pepper

½ cup (1 stick) butter
¼ cup honey
¼ cup lemon juice
1 tablespoon soy sauce

Preheat oven to 350 degrees F. Wash chicken, drain. Shake in mixture of flour, salt, and pepper in paper bag to coat well. Melt 4 tablespoons butter in baking dish, 13-by-9-by-2-inches; roll chicken pieces in dish to coat with butter. Place skin down in single layer. Bake 30 minutes. Melt remaining 4 tablespoons butter in small saucepan; stir in honey, lemon juice, and soy sauce. Turn chicken and pour honey mixture over all. Bake, basting several times with syrup and drippings, for 40 minutes longer or until tender and glazed.

213

> *Hoopeston is the "Sweet Corn Capital of the World." It was laid out in 1871 by three land companies on the farm of Thomas Hoopes who lent his name to the town.*

Native White Oak

Deviled Chicken

Yield: 4 servings

1 broiler-fryer chicken, cut up	¼ cup prepared mustard
4 tablespoons butter	1 teaspoon salt
½ cup honey	1 teaspoon curry powder

Preheat oven to 375 degrees F. Melt the butter in a large shallow baking pan. Stir in honey, mustard, salt, and curry powder. Roll chicken in sauce and place meaty side up in the same pan. Bake for 1 hour. Baste chicken with sauce while baking.

> *Morton was incorporated in 1877. It was the birthplace of David Lilienthal, the first chairman of the Atomic Energy Commission, and was named after Marcus Morton, a Governor of Massachusetts.*

Chicken with Artichokes and Mushrooms

Yield: 6 servings

Salt, pepper, and paprika to taste	pieces
9 chicken breasts	2 tablespoons flour
6 tablespoons butter, divided	1 cup chicken stock
12 artichoke hearts	4 tablespoons sherry
½ pound mushrooms, cut in large	

Preheat oven to 375 degrees F. Sprinkle salt, pepper, and paprika on chicken. Brown in 4 tablespoons butter and place in a shallow 9-by-11-inch pan. Arrange artichoke hearts around chicken pieces. Add 2 tablespoons butter to skillet and sauté mushrooms. Sprinkle flour over and stir in stock. When smooth and thickened, add sherry. Pour over chicken. Bake for 40 minutes.

> *Champaign was founded in 1822 by settlers from Champaign County, Ohio. The name in French means "flat, open country." It is the home of one-half of the University of Illinois. This is the hometown of Professor C. C. Wiley who was instrumental in the invention of the octagonal stop sign and the banked highway turn.*

Chicken in Wine

Yield: 4 servings
1 chicken, cut up
2 potatoes, chopped
½ cup (1 stick) butter
½ cup Sauterne wine

¼ cup chicken stock
½ teaspoon oregano
1 garlic clove, crushed

Preheat oven to 425 degrees F. Sauté chicken and potatoes in butter until brown. Remove. Mix wine, stock, oregano, and garlic. Pour over chicken and potatoes in casserole. Bake 25 minutes.

> *Girard was founded in 1831 by a Frenchman who built a sawmill here. The town did not prosper until coal was discovered, and then fell on hard times during the Great Depression.*

Chicken and Mushrooms with Cheese

Yield: 6 to 8 servings
4 whole chicken breasts, boned and
   skinned
3 eggs, beaten
½ cup flavored breadcrumbs
8 ounces fresh mushrooms

6 tablespoons butter
1 10¾-ounce can chicken broth
3 teaspoons lemon juice
6 ounces sliced Muenster cheese

Cut chicken breasts into bite-size pieces. Soak overnight in eggs. Preheat oven to 350 degrees F. Roll chicken pieces in breadcrumbs; sauté with sliced mushrooms in butter for 10 minutes. Place in casserole. Pour chicken broth over chicken and mushrooms. Sprinkle with lemon juice. Cover with sliced Muenster cheese. Bake uncovered for 40 minutes.

> *Morrisonville was incorporated in 1872 and named after Colonel J. L. D. Morrison, a veteran of the Civil War.*

Chicken Casserole

Yield: 6 to 8 servings

4 cups chopped cooked chicken or turkey
3 cups finely sliced celery
1 cup chopped toasted almonds
2 teaspoons salt
¾ teaspoon cracked black pepper
⅓ cup grated onion juice
⅓ cup lemon juice
1 teaspoon tarragon

1¾ cups mayonnaise
½ teaspoon hot pepper sauce
1 cup finely crushed potato chips
½ cup grated aged American Cheddar cheese
½ cup grated Parmesan or Romano cheese
Paprika for dusting

Preheat oven to 350 degrees F. Combine first 10 items and mix thoroughly. Turn into a 2-quart casserole or individual baking dishes; sprinkle top generously with grated Cheddar cheese, then potato chips about ¼ inch deep, then more Cheddar and some grated Parmesan or Romano. Dust top with paprika. Bake about 35 minutes.

216

> *Saint Elmo was settled in 1830 by Kentuckians of the Catholic faith and was named after the patron saint of mariners. It was first called Howards Point and was incorporated as a city in 1903.*

Baked Chicken Salad

Mrs. Giles of Oak Park in Megalopolis serves this chicken salad at buffets and says that it doubles well for larger groups.

Yield: 8 to 10 servings

2 cups cooked chicken, chopped
2 cups chopped celery
1 onion, chopped
1 tablespoon lemon juice
12 large mushrooms, sliced
1 cup seasoned croutons
½ cup water chestnuts, sliced

½ cup slivered almonds
1 tablespoon butter
1 cup mayonnaise
1 cup sour cream
Salt and pepper to taste
1 teaspoon sweet basil

Preheat oven to 350 degrees F. Combine chicken, celery, onion, lemon juice, mushrooms, croutons, and water chestnuts. Sauté the almonds in the butter and add to the chicken mixture. Blend the mayonnaise, sour cream, salt, pepper, and sweet basil. Fold into the chicken mixture. Place in a 2-quart casserole and bake for 40 minutes.

—*Marilyn Giles*

Chicken Livers and Celery

Yield: 6 servings

½ cup (1 stick) butter
2 cups sliced celery
1 tablespoon flour
½ teaspoon salt
Pepper to taste

1 pound chicken livers
1½ cups fresh mushrooms, sliced
½ cup dry sherry
½ cup sour cream

Melt butter. Sauté celery 5 minutes; remove from pan. Sprinkle flour, salt, and pepper over livers. Fry livers and mushrooms in remaining butter. Add celery and sherry; heat. Stir in cream; serve immediately over rice.

The Kankakee River

Chickory—Native Wildflower

Turkey Tetrazzini

Yield: 6 servings

4 tablespoons butter
¼ cup minced green pepper
½ pound fresh mushrooms, sliced
1 tablespoon finely minced onion
¼ cup flour
2 teaspoons salt
2 cups turkey broth

1 cup light cream
2 tablespoons sherry
2 cups turkey, cooked and cubed
½ pound spaghetti, cooked
⅓ cup grated Parmesan cheese
Parsley for garnish
Pimiento strips for garnish

Melt 2 tablespoons butter in skillet. Add green pepper, mushrooms, and onion. Cook until onions are transparent. Remove vegetables. Add flour and salt; mix well. Stir in broth, cream and sherry. Cook stirring constantly, until thickened. Reduce heat; cook 10 minutes. Add vegetables and turkey; heat thoroughly. Serve over hot spaghetti; sprinkle with Parmesan cheese. Garnish with parsley and pimiento strips.

> *Kankakee is the Indian word for "Beautiful Land." It is the seat of Kankakee County and the former home of Fred MacMurray, Casey Stengel, and Frank Waterman of fountain pen fame.*

Game Hens

Yield: 4 servings

4 Rock Cornish hens
Lemon peel
Juice of 1 orange

4 tablespoons butter
½ cup dry white wine
Salt and pepper to taste

Preheat oven to 375 degrees F. Place birds in roasting pan. Place a small piece of lemon peel in each bird's cavity. Combine and heat juice, butter, wine, salt, and pepper. Brush each bird with mixture. Roast birds for about 45 minutes or until brown and tender. Baste every 10 to 15 minutes while roasting. When birds are done, remove and keep warm. Strain pan juice into saucepan. Stir over moderately high heat until reduced to half. Spoon over birds to glaze.

> *Wenona is Sioux for "first born girl" and is spelled Winona or Wenonah, also. The early settlers of the town named it for the daughter of Nokomis, the mother of Hiawatha.*

Roasted Quail

Yield: 2 quail per serving

Quail

Butter

Small onions, cooked

Bacon slices

Salt and pepper

Preheat oven to 450 degrees F. Put a tablespoon of butter and an onion in cavity of each quail. Tie one bacon slice around the bird. Place bird on a rack in roasting pan and roast in oven for 20 minutes. Baste bird with juice in pan. Salt and pepper bird. Roast another 5 minutes. Baste again.

Arcola was platted in 1855 and named after the Italian town. Broom corn is grown abundantly to supply the broom manufacturing plant here.

Pheasant in Bourbon Cream

Yield: 2 to 3 servings

1 pheasant

Salt to taste

4 tablespoons butter

Freshly ground pepper

3 ounces bourbon whiskey

½ pint heavy cream

½ cup chopped parsley

Preheat oven to 350 degrees F. Rub pheasant with salt. Melt butter in a heavy metal roaster and roast pheasant for 1 hour, basting often and turning several times so all sides are browned. Carve. Season pieces with salt and pepper and arrange on a platter. Place in a warm oven. Heat juices in the pan and add bourbon. Add cream and stir over heat until sauce thickens. Pour sauce over the pheasant slices and sprinkle with parsley.

Saint Anne was first settled in 1850. Here, at the Church of St. Anne, rests the finger bone relic of le Bonne Sainte Anne. Legends surround the relic, and miracle cures have been attributed to it. Devoted pilgrims come every July 26 in veneration.

Roasted Wild Duck

Yield: 2 servings

1 1¼-pound wild duck
2 apples, peeled and quartered
1 slice onion

Salt to taste
Pepper to taste
½ cup orange juice

Preheat oven to 350 degrees F. Remove feathers from duck. Clean, singe and wash. Stuff with apple; skewer cavity closed. Rub with onion, salt, and pepper. Bake 1½ hours for rare. Baste every 10 minutes with orange juice.

> *Windsor's fortunes are tied to the Shelbyville Reservoir and the tourist trade. The town was founded in 1856 with the construction of the Penn Central Railroad.*

Duck in Wine

Yield: 4 servings

Salt and pepper to taste
2 wild ducks

¼ pound (1 stick) butter
2 cups red wine, divided

Salt and pepper the ducks inside and out. Brown in the butter. Place them breast down in skillet and add ½ of the wine. Simmering for 1 hour, turn ducks breast side up; add remainder of wine. Replace lid and simmer for 1½ hours.

> *Decatur is the "Soybean Capital of the World" in addition to being the seat of Macon County. The city was named after Stephen Decatur who said, "Our country . . . may she always be in the right; but our country, right or wrong."*

Stewed Squirrel

Yield: 6 to 8 servings

2 squirrels, cut in 8 pieces
½ cup vegetable oil
½ teaspoon salt

½ teaspoon white pepper
1 cup chopped onion
1 cube beef bouillon

Brown squirrel in oil. Add salt, pepper, and onion. Cover with water and add beef bouillon cube. Cook over low heat about 40 minutes until tender.

Fried Rabbit in Cream

Yield: 2 to 3 servings

1 rabbit, cut up	½ teaspoon pepper
½ cup flour	½ cup butter
1½ teaspoons salt	2 cups heavy cream

Skin, clean, and wash rabbit; drain well. Mix together flour, salt, and pepper; dredge rabbit. Reserve flour mixture. Melt butter in skillet. Brown rabbit about 20 minutes. Cover; simmer for 30 minutes. Remove rabbit. Stir remaining flour into fat in pan; add cream. Cook, stirring constantly, until gravy thickens. Return rabbit to pan; cook 10 minutes.

222

Hasenpfeffer I

Yield: 3 to 4 servings

1 rabbit, cut up	1½ teaspoon whole cloves
1 pint vinegar	½ small onion, sliced
½ teaspoon salt	⅓ cup flour
⅛ teaspoon pepper	½ cup butter or shortening

Skin, clean, and wash rabbit. Place in casserole. Add vinegar, salt, pepper, cloves, and onion. Cover; chill overnight. Drain; reserve ½ cup marinade. Dry rabbit; dredge in flour. Melt shortening in skillet. Brown rabbit about 20 minutes. Add reserved marinade; cover and simmer. Cook until tender. Gravy may be made from juices in pan.

Hasenpfeffer II

Yield: 2 servings
1 rabbit
3 tablespoons butter
½ cup chopped bacon
1 carrot, chopped
1 onion, chopped
1 bay leaf

½ garlic clove
¼ teaspoon ground cloves
Salt to taste
Pepper to taste
1 cup dry white wine
1 cup sour cream

Wash rabbit and cut into 6 pieces. Let stand in salted water for 1 hour. Then drain. Place butter in a skillet with bacon. When the bacon is fried, place the rabbit in skillet and brown on both sides quickly. Add carrot, onion, bay leaf, garlic, ground cloves, salt, and pepper to taste. Add dry wine. Simmer covered until meat is tender; if necessary, add a little hot water while simmering. Before serving add 1 cup sour cream.

> *Blue Mound was settled in 1870. A large glacial deposit is the mound it is named after. In the spring it is covered in blue flowers, and in the fall enveloped in a blue mist.*

223

Welsh "Rabbit"

Yield: 4 servings
1 tablespoon butter
1 pound Cheddar cheese, grated
¾ cup beer, divided
Dash pepper

1 teaspoon dry mustard
½ teaspoon salt
½ teaspoon Worcestershire sauce
1 egg, slightly beaten

Melt butter in top of double boiler. Add cheese and all but 1 tablespoon of beer. Cook over hot water, stirring until cheese melts. Combine seasonings with 1 tablespoon of beer and stir into cheese. Stir in egg. Serve over toast.

> *Mattoon was founded in 1855 and was named for the construction engineer, William Mattoon, of the Big Four Railroad. Mattoon marks the spot of the most southerly advance of the last glacier.*

Broiled Shrimp

Yield: 3 to 4 servings
¼ cup Lucca olive oil
1 teaspoon ground turmeric
1 garlic clove, crushed
¼ teaspoon pepper
1 teaspoon chili powder

1 tablespoon red wine vinegar
1½ teaspoons sweet basil
2 teaspoons crumbled spearmint
1 pound raw shrimp, shelled and
  deveined

Combine oil, turmeric, garlic, pepper, chili powder, vinegar, sweet basil, and spearmint. Pour over shrimp and marinate for at least 2 hours at room temperature. Broil for 10 minutes, basting with marinade sauce.

> *Watseka is the seat of Iroquois County and was platted in 1860. The name is Potowatomi for "pretty woman." Watseka was the wife of Gurdon S. Hubbard.*

Shrimp Kabobs

Yield: 6 servings
½ cup chili sauce
¼ cup vegetable oil
2 tablespoons dark corn syrup
2½ tablespoons vinegar
½ garlic clove, crushed

½ teaspoon salt
½ teaspoon pepper
2 pounds shrimp, peeled and cleaned
2 lemons, wedged

Blend chili sauce, oil, syrup, vinegar, garlic, salt, and pepper until smooth. Thread lemon wedges and shrimp on skewers. Broil 6 minutes on each side, brushing with sauce. To serve, squeeze juice from hot lemons over shrimp.

> *Dwight was founded in 1854 and named after the engineer who platted it. The town has been the site of the Keeley Institute for alcoholic treatment and Oakdale, a penal institute for women.*

A Breadbasket Flatlands Scrapbook

Shrimp De Jonghe

Yield: 4 servings

1 pound shrimp, cooked and cleaned
⅓ cup breadcrumbs
½ teaspoon salt
⅛ teaspoon pepper
1 tablespoon minced parsley
1½ teaspoons minced chives

1 teaspoon onion, chopped
2 tablespoons sherry wine
2 small garlic cloves, crushed
⅓ cup butter, melted
4 lemon wedges

Cut shrimp in half, crosswise. Combine breadcrumbs, salt, pepper, parsley, and chives. Mix together onion, wine, and garlic; let stand 5 minutes. Drizzle over crumb mixture; toss together. Toss 3 tablespoons butter with crumbs. Pour crumbs over shrimp; toss well. Brush a skillet with some of remaining butter. Brown shrimp 5 minutes on one side. Add remaining butter; toss well. Turn shrimp; brown 5 minutes on other side. To serve, arrange in 4 warmed shells or shallow individual casseroles. Garnish with lemon wedges.

> *Brighton was settled in 1826 and incorporated in 1869. Still standing is the James Gilson house which was erected in 1848.*

Shrimp and Egg Casserole

Yield: 4 to 6 servings

⅓ cup butter
⅓ cup sifted flour
2 cups warm milk
½ cup grated Parmesan cheese
2 tablespoons salt
3 tablespoons light dry wine
¼ teaspoon pepper
¼ teaspoon dried parsley

8 hard-cooked eggs, halved
½ pound fresh mushrooms, sliced
½ cup fresh scallions and greens, cut in ½-inch pieces
2 tablespoons butter
Salt and pepper to taste
1½ pounds fresh shrimp, cooked

Preheat oven to 350 degrees F. Melt butter, add flour, and blend until smooth. Add milk slowly. Cook until thick, stirring constantly. Let simmer about 3 minutes. Add cheese and all other seasonings and continue to simmer about 2 or 3 minutes. Sauté mushrooms and onions in 2 tablespoons butter about 5 minutes, turning often. Season with salt and pepper. Arrange egg halves with cut sides up on bottom of baking dish, 10-by-6-by-2-inches. Sprinkle eggs very lightly with salt and pepper. Combine cooked shrimp with sautéed mushrooms and onion and place over eggs. Pour sauce over top. Bake for 20 minutes if ingredients are warm or about 30 minutes if prepared in advance and cold. Place under broiler to brown top if necessary.

Broiled Crab Open-Facers

Mr. Nichols, once from St. Elmo in Little Egypt tells this story: The Durbin side of his family was traveling on the National Road in 1847 in a covered wagon on their way to St. Louis. The horses escaped at St. Elmo. The family liked the area so much they never left.

Yield: 6 servings
3 English muffins
2 tablespoons butter, at room
  temperature
1 8-ounce can crab meat
¼ cup mayonnaise
1 3-ounce package cream cheese, at
  room temperature
1 egg yolk
1 teaspoon minced onion
¼ teaspoon prepared mustard
Dash pepper
Dash salt

Split, toast, and butter English muffins. Stir together crab meat and mayonnaise. Set aside. Beat together cream cheese, egg yolk, onion, mustard, and seasonings. Spread toasted muffin halves with crab mixture. Top with cream cheese mixture. Place on a baking sheet and broil 5 inches from heat for 2 to 3 minutes or until bubbly and golden.

—*Chet Nichols*

227

Deviled Crab with Almonds

Yield: 6 servings

3 hard-cooked eggs
1 7½ ounces can crab meat
3 tablespoons butter
3 tablespoons flour
2 cups light cream
1½ cup thinly sliced celery

¼ cup minced green pepper
2 tablespoons minced onion
2 tablespoons lemon juice
¼ cup soft breadcrumbs
¼ cup grated Swiss cheese
½ cup blanched slivered almonds

Preheat oven to 350 degrees F. Chop eggs coarsely. Drain and flake crab. Make a roux of the butter and flour. Gradually stir in cream; add salt. Cook, stirring constantly, until thickened. Stir in eggs, crab meat, celery, green pepper, onion, and lemon juice. Spoon into 6 individual ramekins. Combine breadcrumbs, cheese and almonds; sprinkle over top. Bake for 15 minutes, or until crumbs and almonds are lightly browned.

> *Roodhouse was named for John Roodhouse who founded it in 1866 as a division point on the Alton Railroad. It prides itself on the large number of Army officers it has produced.*

Mushrooms Stuffed with Crab Meat

Yield: 6 servings

3 tablespoons butter
5 tablespoons minced scallions
1½ cups crab meat
1 cup bechamel sauce

½ teaspoon lemon juice
Salt and white pepper to taste
1 pound 2-inch mushroom caps

Preheat oven to 350 degrees F. In a heavy 8 to 10-inch skillet, melt butter over moderate heat and sauté scallions, stirring constantly until soft. Stir in crab meat and toss with scallions for 10 seconds. Transfer mixture to a large bowl. Stir in Bechamel sauce, then season to taste with lemon juice, salt, and pepper. Lightly butter a shallow pan large enough to hold mushroom caps in one layer. Sprinkle inside of caps with salt and arrange in pan. Spoon in crab filling. Bake for 10 to 15 minutes or until mushrooms are tender and filling is bubbly.

> *Lake Vermillion with its cottage and resorts belies the fact that it is a man-made lake formed by a dam stretching across the Vermillion River.*

Oyster and Crab Casserole

Yield: 6 servings

1 pint oysters and liquor
3½ tablespoons butter
¼ cup flour
½ teaspoon salt
Pinch pepper
1 cup heavy cream (approximately)

¼ cup coarsely shredded Cheddar
  cheese
2 6½-ounce cans crab meat
1 cup fine, soft breadcrumbs
2 tablespoons butter, melted

Preheat oven to 350 degrees F. Drain and pick over oysters; save oyster liquor. Melt 3½ tablespoons butter in saucepan. Stir in flour, salt and pepper and cook until bubbly. Add enough cream to oyster liquor to make 1½ cups liquid. Stir into flour-butter mixture. Cook, stirring constantly, until thickened. Add cheese; stir until melted. Flake crab meat; remove membrane. Spread crab meat in a 1½-quart casserole. Add oysters. Pour sauce over. Combine breadcrumbs and 2 tablespoons melted butter. Sprinkle over mixture. Bake 40 minutes or until crumbs are browned.

> *Carlinville is the home of the legendary "White Elephant," the imposing courthouse which was budgeted at $50,000 and, by the time of its completion in 1870, had cost $1,380,500. The town was incorporated as a city in 1837.*

229

Scalloped Oysters

Yield: 6 servings

1½ cups cracker crumbs
⅓ cup butter, melted
1 pint oysters, drained
Salt and pepper to taste

⅓ cup Chablis
½ cup heavy cream
1 cup grated mild Cheddar cheese

Preheat oven to 350 degrees F. Mix crumbs and butter. Spread half of crumb mixture over the bottom of an 8-by-8-by-2-inch baking dish. Cover with half the oysters and seasonings. Repeat layers of crumbs, oysters, and seasonings. End with crumbs. Pour wine over, then cream. Sprinkle with cheese. Bake for 25 minutes.

> *Washburn has been known as Half Moon Prairie, Stringtown, and Uniontown. The first settler was William Maxwell in 1834, but the town was not incorporated until 1866.*

Oven-Fried Catfish

Yield: 6 servings
2 pounds catfish fillets
1 cup Sauterne wine
1 tablespoon salt
1 cup toasted breadcrumbs

⅓ cup vegetable oil
1 tablespoon chopped parsley
4 lemons, quartered

Preheat oven to 450 degrees F. Cut fillets into serving size pieces. Dip in wine; roll in salted breadcrumbs. Place on well-oiled baking sheet. Sprinkle with oil and remaining wine. Bake 15 minutes. Serve sprinkled with parsley and garnished with lemon quarters.

> *Atlanta was originally called New Castle, but was named after the Georgia city when it moved to the railroad tracks nearby in 1855. The local library is filled with books inscribed in memory of past residents.*

Fillet of Sole

Yield: 4 servings
2 tablespoons Lucca olive oil
2 onions, minced
½ pound mushrooms, sliced
Salt and pepper to taste
¼ teaspoon soy sauce
4 fillets sole or flounder

Pinch paprika
½ cup sherry
½ cup orange juice
½ cup orange liqueur
2 tablespoons chopped parsley

Preheat oven to 375 degrees F. Put olive oil in bottom of a baking dish and cover with half of onions, mushrooms, salt, and pepper. Sprinkle with soy sauce. Add the fillets in a layer and then the rest of the onion, mushrooms, seasonings, sherry, orange juice, and ¼ cup liqueur. Bake uncovered for about 40 minutes or until fish is golden brown. Sprinkle with parsley. Bring fish to the table in the same dish and flame with the remaining ¼ cup liqueur.

> *Bourbonnais was named after coureur de bois François Bourbonnais who founded it in 1832. French influence is strongly felt here, and French still spoken in many homes.*

Fish Fillets in Banana Sauce

Yield: 4 servings

4 large pieces fillet of sole
Flour, salt, pepper, paprika
4 tablespoons butter
½ cup sherry
½ teaspoon ground ginger

2 tablespoons lemon juice
2 tablespoons brown sugar
½ teaspoon sweet basil
2 bananas
Almonds

Roll fillets well in combined flour, salt, pepper, and paprika. Melt butter in a skillet. Sauté fillets 2 or 3 minutes or until brown on each side and flaky. Remove to platter. In skillet combine sherry, ginger, lemon juice, brown sugar, sweet basil, and bananas which have been cut in quarters lengthwise. Simmer 2 minutes. Pour over fish. Sprinkle with almonds.

Toluca was platted in 1889. The first residents were mostly Italians who came to work the booming coal mines. The town was named by railroad laborers, after the city in Mexico.

The Rolling Northwest

The stamp of the geological past is etched intriguingly on the pitching landscape of northwestern Illinois, throwing into bold relief an unglaciated finger of land pointing downward from the driftless stretches of southern Wisconsin. Rolling hills, steep bluffs, and undulating roadways crisscross the area in sharp contrast to the flat and unbroken plains to the east and to the south. Bordered by the Great Mississippi River and its pallisades to the west, the troubled surface of the land gradually becomes pacific and tranquil as it stretches into the Apple River Valley to the south and gentles into a more peaceable kingdom as it approaches and traverses the Rock River country to the east.

Jo Daviess County, the bastion of this irregular-for-Illinois terrain, boasts the containment of both an unique historic site and an equally unique geographic phenomenon. The nineteenth century boom town of Galena clings precariously to the multi-level landscape carved out by the once commercially important Galena (Fever) River. Further north and close to the Wisconsin border a 1200 foot elevation, Charles Mound, rises out of the land mass to form the highest point in Illinois.

Galena is an attraction for history and architecture buffs alike. It grew to be a teeming shipping and mining center in the first half of the nineteenth century, and retained its economic importance well into the second half of the century until Chicago's rise to prominence diminished its strategic trade position. The structures in Galena encompass almost every genre of American architecture, but the homes and public buildings in the Greek Revival style are the greatest attractions for visitors. Although some of the structures still bear reminders of the devastating Black Hawk War, they are for the most part beautifully preserved and represent possibly the largest collection north of the Mason-Dixon Line of that most favorite pre-Civil War architectural style. The Old Customs House and the DeSoto House Hotel are among the antebellum structures which draw many visitors to inspect their design and construction. Even the home of its most illustrious citizen, Ulysses S. Grant, though unmistakably Victorian in design, attracts its share of admirers to savor its furbelows and gingerbread.

The rushing waters of the Mighty Mississippi are a constant and kinetic presence as one travels south. The bluffs become less stark as the pleasant valleys of the Apple and the Plum Rivers signal a more modified land formation spreading into a grassy plain on the banks of the great river where the town of Savanna idles. Like Galena, it grew up in the early nineteenth century and enjoyed its place in the sun until the emergence of Chicago as a trade center. But, unlike Galena, Savanna was regenerated by the expansion of the railroad and it still retains commercial importance as a shipping terminus for farm produce throughout the Midwest.

Moline and Rock Island, together with East Moline and Davenport, Iowa, form what are affectionately known as the Quad Cities. The Mississippi River runs almost due west where these four cities merge into a continuous and extensive metropolitan area. Although each has its own government and city boundaries, it is almost impossible to tell where one begins and the other ends. The arsenal and the twin farm implement industries of John Deere and International Harvester have traditionally been the sources of employment and economic prosperity for the Quad Cities. The long, grim limestone island for which the city and Rock Island County were named houses the arsenal. The island was fortified by the U. S. Government at the beginning of the Black Hawk War and served as a prison camp for Confederate soldiers during the Civil War.

The Rock River Valley provides a backdrop for the Quad Cities and gradually slopes out into the flat prairie farm land of Henry County. Nestled comfortably in the cornfields, and not far from the peaceful old railroad town of Kewannee, is the historic little Swedish settlement of Bishop Hill. Originally, the little village was established in 1846 by Eric Jansson. A religious fundamentalist,

Jansson persuaded a group of followers to leave their native Sweden to seek religious freedom in a new country. The settlement provided its constituents with food, clothing, and shelter on a communal basis. Leadership disputes finally caused the dissolution of its tightly-knit membership, and the colony disintegrated. Many of the original inhabitants remained to purchase their own land and to conduct their own businesses. Several of the common buildings of the original settlement were destroyed by fire but the buildings which remain are being restored and are a palpable testimony to their European cultural heritage. One of the most haunting of the remaining structures is the Steeple Building. The elaborate molded stucco of its tower, bearing a clock with no minute hand, thrusts skyward and hovers as a specter of the past over a span of silent but waving fields of corn.

Princeton, the seat of Bureau County, was settled by New England expatriots in the early nineteenth century. The tranquility of its tree-lined streets belies the fiercely abolitionist conflicts which characterized it before the Civil War. Owen and Elijah Lovejoy, noted for their political activism in the abolitionist cause, were prominent citizens. The Lovejoy home has been preserved and serves as a monument to the patriotism of its early inhabitants.

Starved Rock looms like some prehistoric tell 140 feet above the Illinois River. It was here that Fort St. Louis was established in 1683 making it the first major center of French influence in Illinois. The aura of the legendary band of Indians who were trapped and starved still seems to hang over its summit. Not far from The Rock lies the town of Ottawa at the joining of the Illinois and the Fox Rivers. Noted as the site of the first Lincoln-Douglas Debate, it stretches comfortably on the banks of the two rivers in some of the most valued farm land in LaSalle County.

Oregon, seat of Ogle County, provided the setting for one of Illinois's earliest art colonies, The Eagle's Nest. In 1898 Laredo Taft, together with other sculptors, painters, and writers chose a rustic tract close to the Rock River near Oregon to serve as Thoreau-esque retreat for their creative endeavors. The Oregon area is still a haven for artists and art students and has become synonomous with Illinois art development. Taft's forty-foot brooding sculpture of an Indian gazes down from a lofty bluff overlooking the river. Although Taft intended the statue to represent the idealization of the Indians of the Illinois Territory, the popular belief holds that the statue immortalized the great Indian chief, Black Hawk, and it is commonly referred to as the Black Hawk Monument by natives and visitors alike.

Long before the city of Rockford was begun, its location was marked by a shallow, rocky crossing in the Rock River used by the stage coach line that traveled between Galena and Chicago. Situated not far from the Wisconsin border, in the northernmost part of the state, it is the seat of Winnebago County and one of the largest cities in the state. Early settlement of Rockford was made by New Englanders seeking opportunities in the West. Later, the town welcomed large numbers of Swedish immigrants who soon formed a sizable percentage of Rockford's population.

In spite of its being one of the largest industrial and manufacturing centers of northern Illinois, Rockford retains its old nickname of "The Forest City" for the trees which shade the residential areas. Many of the older residences are built from rocks quarried from the river and arranged in the old cobblestone style. One glorious exception is the house built by Robert Tinker, an early mayor of Rockford. Tinker returned to Illinois after a Grand Tour of Europe and decided to build a chalet in the Swiss style which he had so admired in Europe. The Swiss Cottage, which has been preserved and restored with many of the original furnishings, is both an architectural and historical attraction to visitors to Rockford.

235

The Rolling Northwest is atypical of the rest of Illinois geographically and emotionally. Here the phantasmic beauty and unglaciated remnants of a past misted forever with vaguely remembered saber-tooths and wooly mammoths is constantly in evidence. There is a feeling of the "forever land" here, not scoured and purged by relentless ice, but invigorated and renewed by the healing and encouraging sun. The Rolling Northwest is an Illinois dreamscape.

Vegetables

Picnic Potato Salad

Mrs. Flynn of Freeport in Rolling Northwest writes, "While engaged to my husband I tasted this salad numerous times at his family's picnics. After we were married I finally convinced my mother-in-law to divulge the family secret recipe. We think it's the best made."

Yield: 8 servings

6 to 8 medium-size cold, boiled
   potatoes in their jackets
1 medium onion, minced
3 ribs celery, minced

Salt and pepper to taste
4 hard-cooked eggs
2 tablespoons chopped parsley

Dressing

2 eggs
1 cup sugar
1 tablespoon flour
½ teaspoon mustard

¼ cup vinegar
Salt and pepper to taste
2 tablespoons butter
⅔ cup milk

Peel and chop the potatoes and combine with the onion and celery. Season to taste. Chop two of the eggs and add to the potato mixture along with the parsley. Toss with dressing and garnish with the remaining eggs.

Combine all dressing ingredients into a saucepan. Cook until thickened and chill.

—*Barbara Flynn*

Woosung in Ogle County has been operating a post office since 1855. It used to be called Juniata City.

The Old Customs House—Galena

Sour Cream Potato Salad

Yield: 12 servings
6 cups sliced, cooked potatoes
1 sliced, unpeeled cucumber
1 cup shredded carrots
Dash pepper
2 teaspoons salt

1 tablespoon chopped chives
½ teaspoon dill seed
⅓ cup basic mayonnaise
1 cup sour cream

Combine ingredients and chill several hours before serving.

> *Rockford, named after a shallow spot in the Rock River which allowed stagecoaches to ford, is the second largest city in Illinois. A leader in manufactured goods, the city is one of the principal producers of machine tools and machine parts. It was incorporated in 1852.*

German Potato Salad

Yield: 8 servings

9 strips bacon, chopped
2 tablespoons flour
3 tablespoons sugar
1½ teaspoons salt
½ cup vinegar
½ cup water

8 medium-sized potatoes, cooked
  and sliced
¼ cup minced onion
½ cup chopped celery
Parsley

Fry bacon until crisp and brown; drain. To bacon drippings, add flour, sugar, and salt; cook until bubbly. Stir in vinegar and water. Cook, stirring constantly, until thickened. Layer in order ⅓ of potatoes, onion, celery, and sauce in a 1½-quart serving dish. Repeat until all ingredients are used. Garnish with parsley. Serve warm.

Starved Rock State Park is the oldest park in the Illinois State Park System. The story of the Illini Indians forced to starve on the summit of the Rock by their Ottawa and Potowatomi adversaries is a classic in Illinois folklore and legend.

238

Creamed Potatoes

Yield: 6 servings

2 cups chopped onions
⅔ cup chopped green pepper
½ cup chopped celery
½ cup (1 stick) butter
6 tablespoons flour

4 cups heavy cream
2 teaspoons salt
¼ teaspoon pepper
6 cups cubed, cooked potatoes
1 cup shredded Cheddar cheese

Preheat oven to 350 degrees F. Sauté onions, green pepper, and celery in butter until soft. Stir in flour. Add cream and cook, stirring constantly, until mixture is thickened. Stir in salt and pepper. Place potatoes in a buttered 3-quart casserole. Pour sauce over. Top with cheese. Bake until hot and bubbly.

Milledgeville, located on Elkhorn Creek, is a center for both dairy and fertilizer products. It was incorporated as a village in 1887.

Mushroom Bake

Yield: 6 servings

2 pounds raw mushrooms
5 slices bread, toasted, buttered and
   cut into cubes

Salt and pepper to taste
1 pint heavy cream
½ cup sherry

Preheat oven to 350 degrees F. Wash mushrooms, and slice thickly. Cover bottom of buttered 1½-quart casserole with ⅓ of bread. Sprinkle with salt and pepper. Add ⅓ of mushrooms. Repeat until all the bread and mushrooms are used. Pour the cream over all. Bake 35 minutes. Add sherry and bake 5 minutes more.

Galena means lead sulphide in Latin. Large deposits of this mineral and Galena's strategic location made it a booming metropolis at the beginning of the nineteenth century. One of its more prominent favorite sons was Ulysses S. Grant. It incorporated as a city in 1835.

Mushrooms and Artichokes

Yield: 6 servings

3 cups mushrooms, sliced
¾ cup sliced scallions with tops
5 tablespoons butter
2 tablespoons flour
Salt and pepper to taste
¾ cup chicken stock
¼ cup heavy cream

1 teaspoon lemon juice
⅛ teaspoon nutmeg
1 10-ounce package frozen artichoke
   hearts, cooked and drained
¾ cup breadcrumbs
1 tablespoon butter, melted

Preheat oven to 350 degrees F. Cook mushrooms and scallions in 5 tablespoons butter. Remove vegetables and set aside. Blend flour, salt, and pepper into pan drippings. Add stock, cream, lemon juice, and nutmeg. Cook and stir until bubbly. Add vegetables. Place into 1-quart casserole. Combine breadcrumbs and melted butter; sprinkle on top. Bake for 20 minutes.

LaSalle was named for the French explorer, Robert Cavelier, Sieur de la Salle. It became a city in 1852, even though the settlement had been founded in the 1830s.

Baked Mushrooms I

Yield: 6 servings

½ cup chopped celery
¼ cup chopped onion
3 tablespoons butter
¾ pound fresh sliced mushrooms

4 cups stale bread, cubed
2 cups grated sharp Cheddar cheese
2 eggs
2 cups heavy cream

Preheat oven to 350 degrees F. Sauté onions and celery in butter. Add mushrooms and cook until tender. Butter a 2-quart casserole, and layer half of bread, mushroom mixture, and cheese. Repeat. Beat eggs and cream; pour over top. Bake for 45 minutes.

> *Dakota derives its name from the Dakota Territory. It was incorporated as a town in 1869.*

Baked Mushrooms II

Yield: 4 servings

1½ pounds fresh mushrooms, sliced
1 onion, chopped
5 tablespoons butter
½ cup beef stock, boiling
½ cup heavy cream

2 eggs, beaten
Salt and pepper to taste
1 cup breadcrumbs
½ cup chopped pecans

Preheat oven to 350 degrees F. Sauté mushrooms and onions in butter. Combine stock with all remaining ingredients except nuts. Pour mixture into a buttered 1-quart casserole and bake covered for 20 minutes. Uncover and top with pecans. Bake 15 minutes longer.

> *Bureau County's name came from the French trader Pierre Buero.*

Cauliflower with Mustard Sauce

Yield: 4 servings

1 whole cauliflower, washed and
   trimmed
¾ cup mayonnaise
Salt and pepper to taste

2 tablespoons mustard
Juice of 1 lemon
¾ cup whipped cream
Paprika to taste

Steam the cauliflower until tender. Drain and keep warm. Combine mayonnaise, salt, pepper, mustard, and lemon juice. Fold in whipped cream. Pour sauce over cauliflower. Sprinkle with paprika.

Sesamed Cauliflower

Yield: 6 servings

1 medium cauliflower, cooked and
   drained
Salt and pepper to taste

1 cup sour cream
1 cup shredded Cheddar cheese
2 teaspoons sesame seeds, toasted

Preheat oven to 400 degrees F. Break cauliflower into flowerettes. Place half of the floweretts in a buttered 1-quart casserole. Season with salt and pepper. Spread half of sour cream over top. Add half the cheese and half of the sesame seeds. Repeat. Bake uncovered about 5 minutes, or until cheese melts.

Cauliflower Stuffed Tomatoes

Yield: 8 servings

1 small head cauliflower
8 medium tomatoes
1 tablespoon chopped scallion
1 tablespoon butter
2 tablespoons flour

¼ teaspoon salt
1 cup heavy cream
1½ cups shredded Cheddar cheese
2 tablespoons browned breadcrumbs

Preheat oven to 400 degrees F. Cook cauliflower in boiling salted water. Drain. Separate flowerettes; set aside. Cut out centers of tomatoes. Turn upside down to drain. Sauté scallion in butter. Blend in flour and salt. Add cream slowly. Cook until thick. Remove from heat, add cheese, and let melt. Cool slightly. When ready to serve, place tomatoes in a 7-by-11-by-2-inch pan and heat in oven 3 to 4 minutes. Fill each tomato with 2 tablespoons sauce and 2 or 3 pieces of cauliflower. Top with more sauce, sprinkle with crumbs, and return to oven until browned on top.

Sautéed Tomatoes

Yield: 6 servings

2 large tomatoes
1 large egg, beaten with 1 tablespoon
water
¼ cup grated Parmesan cheese
½ cup breadcrumbs
1 teaspoon basil

½ teaspoon salt
½ teaspoon pepper
½ teaspoon marjoram
¼ teaspoon thyme
3 tablespoons butter

Slice each tomato into 3 slices, removing stem ends. Beat egg with water. Combine Parmesan cheese, crumbs, and spices. Pat crumb mixture onto tomato slices; dip in egg, then again in crumbs. Sauté in butter until bottom is brown. Turn carefully; brown other side. Serve hot.

> *Somonauk means "paw paw" in Potowatomi. In the 1850s Alvirus Gage platted the town and began a real estate development. In 1865 it was incorporated as a village.*

Creamed Whole Onions

Yield: 6 servings

16 small onions, peeled
½ cup water
1 teaspoon salt
4 tablespoons butter
3 tablespoons flour
1 teaspoon salt

Dash white pepper
2 cups heavy cream
½ cup coarsely grated Cheddar
cheese
Paprika to taste

Preheat oven to 325 degrees F. Place onions in saucepan with water and salt. Cover. Cook gently until onions are tender, 25 to 30 minutes. Drain; pour into a 6½-by-9¾-inch casserole. Make a roux of the butter and flour. Add salt and pepper. Cook until bubbly. Add cream. Cook, stirring constantly, until thickened. Reduce heat; cook 5 minutes. Add sauce to onions. Sprinkle top with cheese. Bake 5 minutes or until cheese is melted. Sprinkle with paprika.

> *Marseilles was one of the towns on the Illinois River visited by the floating theaters in the nineteenth century. Showboats traveling down Illinois waterways brought variety theater and melodrama to those who could not travel to the metropolitan centers.*

Sherried Onions

Yield: 2 servings

5 medium onions, peeled and sliced
½ teaspoon sugar
½ teaspoon salt
½ teaspoon freshly ground pepper

⅓ cup butter
½ cup sherry
2 tablespoons Parmesan cheese

Season onions with sugar, salt, and pepper. Melt butter in a 2-quart saucepan. Sauté onions in butter until barely tender, 8 minutes. Separate rings. Add sherry and cook quickly 2 to 3 minutes. Sprinkle with cheese and serve.

> *Tampico in Whiteside County claims a famous son, President Ronald Reagan. It was incorporated as a village in 1875.*

Onion Tart

Yield: 6 servings

30 soda crackers
¾ cup butter, melted
3½ cups thinly sliced onion
½ pound grated Cheddar cheese

3 eggs, beaten
1½ cups heavy cream, scalded
Salt and pepper to taste

243

Preheat oven to 350 degrees F. Crush the crackers and mix with ½ cup butter. Press on the bottom and side of an 8-inch pie plate. Sauté the onions in remaining butter until transparent. Place the onions on the cracker crust. Sprinkle the cheese over the onions. Combine eggs, cream, salt, and pepper. Pour over cheese and onions. Bake for 35 to 40 minutes or until custard is set.

> *In 1856 the DeSoto House in Galena was the scene of Abraham Lincoln's speech in support of the newly organized Republican Party and its anti-slavery candidate. More luxurious in its appointments than any hotel outside of Chicago when it was built in 1855, the hotel, in somewhat altered state, still operates as a hostelry to intrepid visitors to Galena.*

Pioneer House in Winter

Potato Casserole

Yield: 8 servings

6 medium-sized potatoes, peeled and boiled
1 pint sour cream
1 bunch scallions, chopped
10 ounces sharp Cheddar cheese, grated

3 tablespoons heavy cream
1 teaspoon salt
⅛ teaspoon pepper
3 tablespoons butter, melted
⅓ cup breadcrumbs

Preheat oven to 300 degrees F. Grate potatoes. Add sour cream, onions, cheese, cream, salt and pepper. Mix thoroughly. Pour into a buttered 9-by-13-inch pan. Combine melted butter and crumbs; spread over top. Bake 50 minutes.

> *Port Byron was originally called Canaan. It was important as a refueling stop on the river for wood burning boats. It became a village in 1876.*

Cheesy Potatoes

Yield: 6 servings

9 tablespoons butter, divided
4 tablespoons flour
2 cups heavy cream
⅔ cup chicken broth
5 tablespoons Parmesan cheese

Salt and pepper to taste
2 pounds potatoes, cooked, peeled, and diced
6 tablespoons Bleu cheese
Paprika for dusting

Preheat oven to 425 degrees F. Make a roux of 5 tablespoons butter and flour. Add the cream and broth and stir until thick. Add

Parmesan cheese, salt, and pepper. Fold in potatoes. Pour into a 2-quart casserole. Sprinkle with Roquefort and dot with remaining butter. Dust with paprika. Bake for 20 to 30 minutes or until hot and bubbly.

> *Andalusia provided the river crossing where a ferry carried countless settlers into the Iowa Territory in the 1830s. It was incorporated as a village in 1884.*

Potato Bacon Loaf

Yield: 8 servings
8 large potatoes
2 eggs, beaten
1 tablespoon salt
¼ teaspoon pepper
¼ pound bacon, chopped

Preheat oven to 350 degrees F. Grate potatoes. Add eggs and seasonings. Fry bacon. Add bacon and grease to potatoes. Mix well. Pour into an 8-inch square pan and bake 1 hour.

> *A sawmill using the water power of the Rock River drew settlers to Morrison in 1839. It was incorporated as a city in 1867.*

Potato Croquettes

Yield: 6 to 8 servings
1½ pounds potatoes
2 cups farina
4 eggs
1 cup warm milk
2 teaspoons salt
Melted butter, for brushing
1 cup grated Romano cheese

Preheat oven to 375 degrees F. Boil potatoes in skins. Peel and mash well. Add farina, eggs, salt, cheese and milk. Mix well. Shape into round patties and place on buttered baking sheet. Before baking brush with melted butter and sprinkle with grated cheese. Bake 15 minutes.

> *In 1835 Byron was settled by New Englanders. It was named for Lord Byron, the romantic English lyric poet, who was currently in vogue. It was incorporated as a city in 1904.*

The Clock Tower Building—Bishop Hill

Sidecar Carrots

Yield: 6 servings
24 baby carrots
1 ounce Cointreau
3 ounces lemon juice

2 ounces brandy
2 ounces honey
Chopped parsley for topping

Preheat oven to 350 degrees F. In a saucepan place carrots in cold, salted water to cover; bring to a boil and cook until just tender. Drain carrots and arrange in a single layer in a buttered 7-by-12-by-2-inch baking dish. Mix the Cointreau, lemon juice, brandy, and honey. Pour over the carrots and bake for 15 minutes, basting occasionally with the syrup. Sprinkle with parsley and serve.

Caramel Carrots

Yield: 6 servings
16 medium carrots, sliced
½ cup boiling water
10 slices bacon
1 medium onion, minced

1 teaspoon salt
Dash pepper
⅓ cup brown sugar
⅔ cup butter, melted

Simmer carrots in water 15 minutes. Fry bacon crisp and onion transparent. Remove; drain. Crumble bacon; mix with carrots and onion. Stir in salt, pepper, sugar, and butter. Cover. Cook 10 minutes or until sugar is melted and carrots are glazed.

Minty Carrots

Yield: 6 servings
2 tablespoons butter
2 tablespoons flour
1 cup chicken stock
½ cup grated Cheddar cheese
Dash hot sauce

7 large carrots, washed, scraped, and
  cut into matchsticks
8 fresh mint leaves, minced
2 ounces white creme de menthe

In double boiler melt butter, stir in flour, and slowly add stock until thick. Add cheese and hot sauce. Keep hot while preparing carrots. Cover carrots with water and simmer for 10 minutes. Drain and arrange in serving dish. Sprinkle with minced mint. Lace the hot sauce with the crème de menthe. Pour sauce over carrots and serve.

Buffalo Cooking Pouch

248

Spinach and Cream Cheese

Yield: 6 servings

2 10-ounce packages frozen chopped spinach, cooked and drained
2 3-ounce packages cream cheese, at room temperature
5 tablespoons minced onions
¼ teaspoon nutmeg
¼ cup breadcrumbs

Preheat oven to 350 degrees F. Mix spinach, cream cheese, onions, and nutmeg together. Place in a 1-quart casserole and sprinkle with breadcrumbs. Bake for 20 minutes.

Spinach and Cheese

Yield: 8 servings

1 10-ounce package frozen spinach, cooked, drained, and chopped
¼ cup flour
1 teaspoon salt
¼ teaspoon pepper

3 eggs
1 16-ounce container small curd cottage cheese, drained
2 cups grated sharp Cheddar cheese

Preheat oven to 350 degrees F. Blend first four ingredients. Stir in remaining ingredients. Turn into an 11-by-7-inch buttered dish. Bake for 45 minutes or until set.

> *Malta is the site of Kishwaukee Community College. It became a village in 1869.*

Spinach-Broccoli Casserole

Yield: 6 servings

1 10-ounce package frozen chopped spinach
1 10-ounce package frozen chopped broccoli
1 cup shredded Cheddar cheese
1 pint large curd cottage cheese

3 eggs, beaten
3 tablespoons flour
Salt to taste
½ cup dry breadcrumbs
3 tablespoons butter

249

Preheat oven to 350 degrees F. Thaw spinach and broccoli and drain. Combine cheeses, eggs, and flour. Add to spinach and broccoli. Salt lightly, mixing well. Place mixture in a buttered 1-quart soufflé dish. Spinkle breadcrumbs on top and dot with butter. Bake uncovered 1 hour.

> *Depue was an important riverboat port in the nineteenth century. The erratic movement of long ago glaciers formed the abrupt bend in the Illinois River where Depue is located.*

Baked Spudonions

Yield: 4 servings

4 large baking potatoes, peeled
½ cup butter, at room temperature
3 large onions, sliced into fourths

Salt to taste
Freshly ground black pepper to taste

Preheat oven to 375 degrees F. Cut each potato crosswise into 4 slices. Butter between slices and on top. Reassemble with onion rounds between. Season with salt and pepper. Secure with toothpicks. Wrap each potato in a double thickness of foil. Bake 1½ hours until done. Remove toothpicks and serve.

> *In Amboy two immigrants from the British Isles, Samuel Carson and John Pirie opened a store in 1854. A few years later they were joined by a fellow countryman, J. E. Scott and the firm of Carson, Pirie, Scott and Company was born. The* Amboy News *began publication in 1854 with Noel Dickens, brother of Charles, as its editor.*

Potato Pancakes

This recipe is from Mrs. Rowe's grandmother's "homemade" cookbook which is almost 100 years old. Mrs. Rowe is from Kewanee in Rolling Northwest.

Yield: 8 to 10 pancakes

4 large potatoes, peeled and grated
2 eggs, beaten until light
Pinch salt

3 tablespoons flour
½ teaspoon baking powder
Hot shortening for frying

Mix all ingredients together. Pour into hot shortening on griddle. Bake, turning until done on both sides.

—*Mrs. J. Raymond Rowe*

> *Mount Carroll is the home of Shimer College where an unusual liberal arts experiment carried out in the 1950s and 1960s was developed. Settlement was platted in 1843 and it became a city in 1867.*

Potato Dumplings

Yield: 50 pieces

2 pounds potatoes, peeled and grated
1 cup flour
2 eggs, slightly beaten

Salt and pepper to taste
½ cup (1 stick) unsalted butter
1 large onion, chopped

Press grated potatoes to squeeze out excess moisture. Combine with flour, eggs, and seasonings. Mix thoroughly. Drop by spoonfuls into boiling salted water in a 2-quart saucepan. Cover and steam until dumplings rise to the top, about 10 minutes. Remove dumplings with a perforated spoon and drain. Melt butter in a saucepan. Add onions and cook until limp. Pour over the dumplings and serve.

Savanna was founded by settlers from Kentucky in 1838. It was incorporated as a city in 1874.

Sweet Potato Casserole

Yield: 6 to 8 servings

6 sweet potatoes, cooked and peeled
¾ cup butter, at room temperature
½ cup light brown sugar
1 teaspoon salt
1 teaspoon cinnamon

½ teaspoon nutmeg
½ cup half and half
¾ cup chopped pecans
½ cup dark seedless raisins

Preheat oven to 350 degrees F. Whip together sweet potatoes, butter, brown sugar, and seasonings until light and fluffy. Stir in half and half, pecans, and raisins. Pour into a 1-quart baking dish. Bake for 35 minutes.

Jane Addams, the feminist social reformer who began Hull House in Chicago, grew up in Cedarville. Her gravesite and family home have been restored and maintained, attracting numbers of visitors to the village that was founded in 1848 and incorporated in 1849.

Walnut Sweet Potatoes

Yield: 6 servings

9 medium sweet potatoes
¾ teaspoon salt
¼ teaspoon paprika
6 tablespoons butter

½ cup heavy cream
¾ cup chopped walnuts
8 thin slices bacon

Preheat oven to 400 degrees F. Scrub potatoes well and bake for 1 hour, or until tender. Peel and mash potatoes. Add salt, paprika, butter, and cream; beat until fluffy. Fold in nuts. Place in a buttered 1½-quart casserole. Arrange bacon over potato mixture. Bake 20 minutes or until bacon is crisp.,

> *At an elevation of 1241 feet, Charles Mound in Jo Daviess County is the highest point in the state.*

Sweet Potato Stuffed Oranges

Yield: 10 servings

6 medium sweet potatoes, pared
Water to cover
2 tablespoons grated orange rind
½ cup orange juice
½ cup (1 stick) butter

½ teaspoon salt
Pinch pepper
5 naval oranges
½ cup slivered almonds, toasted

Place potatoes in saucepan with water. Cover. Simmer 35 minutes. Preheat oven to 350 degrees F. Drain and mash potatoes. Add orange rind, juice, butter, salt, and pepper. Beat. Cut oranges in halves in zigzags. Remove pulp. Fill with potato mixture. Bake 15 minutes. Serve topped with almonds.

> *Hanover, named for the town in New Hampshire from which its first settlers came, was platted in 1837. It was located on the portage between the Apple and Mississippi Rivers. It became a village in 1849.*

Lemon Yam Casserole

Yield: 6 servings

4 pounds yams, cooked, drained, and
   peeled
1 cup brown sugar
¾ cup butter, at room temperature

½ teaspoon salt
3 teaspoons grated orange rind
3 teaspoons grated lemon rind

Preheat oven to 350 degrees F. Mash yams until smooth. Add other ingredients and beat until light. Pour mixture into a buttered 2-quart casserole. Bake 30 minutes.

> *The Mississippi Palisades is named after the Hudson River Palisades which it resembles with its rugged terrain and thickets which rise and fall with dramatic irregularity as the land slopes finally to the great Mississippi River.*

Sweet Yams in Cream

Yield: 8 servings

8 medium yams
2 cups sugar
1 cup water

½ cup heavy cream
4 tablespoons sherry
1 teaspoon salt

Drop unpeeled yams in boiling water. Cook 10 minutes. While cooking, put sugar and water in large skillet and bring to a boil. Then lower heat and let boil gently 8 minutes. Peel yams and cut in half. Place in sugar and water syrup. Cook 10 minutes slowly. Pour off ½ of syrup and pour in cream, salt, and sherry mixture. Cook until yams are done. Serve hot with the sauce.

> *Pearl City was formerly known as Yellow Creek. It was incorporated as a village in 1891.*

Deviled Carrots with Water Chestnuts

Yield: 6 servings

1 pound carrots
½ cup (1 stick) butter
2 tablespoons light brown sugar
2 tablespoons chopped onions

1 teaspoon dry mustard
½ teaspoon salt
⅛ teaspoon pepper
1 4-ounce can water chestnuts

Wash, peel, and cut carrots in lengthwise halves. Sauté in butter 8 minutes. Add remaining ingredients except water chestnuts. Reduce heat, cover, and cook over low heat 12 minutes or until carrots are tender. Toss with water chestnuts. Serve.

> *Princeton was started in 1833 by Massachusetts settlers. It was the home of a well-known abolitionist preacher, Owen Lovejoy whose brother Elijah was killed by an anti-abolitionist mob in Alton in 1837. Princeton was incorporated as a city in 1849.*

Carrots and Grapes

Yield: 6 servings

6 cups coarsely shredded carrots
⅓ cup butter
¼ teaspoon anise seed
1 teaspoon salt

1 teaspoon honey
4 tablespoons water
3 cups seedless green grapes

Combine carrots, butter, anise, salt, honey, and water in a 2-quart saucepan. Cover and cook 6 minutes until carrots are tender. Stir in grapes. Serve.

> *Winnebago, named for the Indian tribe, was settled by travelers from New England, Canada, and the British Isles at the end of the Black Hawk War in 1832. It became a village in 1855.*

Carrot and Apricot Casserole

Yield: 8 servings

1 8-ounce package dried apricots
1 12-ounce can apricot nectar
2 16-ounce cans carrots, drained
¾ cup light brown sugar, firmly

packed
3 tablespoons butter
¾ cup slivered almonds

Preheat oven to 350 degrees F. Soak apricots in the nectar overnight. Put half of the carrots in a buttered 2-quart casserole. Top with half of the apricot nectar mixture and half of the sugar and butter. Repeat and then top with almonds. Bake 30 to 40 minutes.

> *Instead of the conventional town square, Erie has a town triangle. Three Indian trails which intersected the region have left their legacy in the arrangement of its streets. Erie became a village in 1872.*

Corn Pudding

Yield: 6 servings

3 egg yolks
3 tablespoons butter, at room
   temperature
1 teaspoon flour
½ teaspoon baking powder

6 ears corn, grated
½ teaspoon salt
1 cup milk
¾ cup chopped green pepper
3 egg whites, stiffly beaten

Preheat oven to 325 degrees F. Add egg yolks to butter and mix well. Add flour, baking powder, grated corn, and salt, blending thoroughly. Add milk gradually. Mix well until smooth. Add green pepper and lastly fold in egg whites. Pour into a buttered 3-quart casserole and bake for 30 minutes.

255

> *In the Pecatonica Valley, one of the oldest developed sections of the state, lies the Seward Forest Preserve. A winding brook, stone bridges, and dense woodlands give the area a primitive, natural look.*

Corn Pudding Puff

Yield: 12 servings

3 cups fresh corn
6 eggs, beaten
⅓ cup sugar
1 teaspoon salt
Pepper to taste

3 cups heavy cream
3 teaspoons baking powder
½ cup (1 stick) butter, at room
   temperature, divided

Preheat oven to 350 degrees F. Cut corn off cob. Scrape ears. Combine eggs, sugar, salt, pepper, cream, and baking powder and add to corn. Butter 2-quart baking dish with ½ stick butter. Add remaining butter to mixture and pour into baking dish. Bake for ½ hour. Reduce heat to 300 degrees F. and bake for 30 minutes more.

Broccoli Casserole

Yield: 4 servings

¾ cup white sauce
¾ cup cubed medium Cheddar
cheese, cubed
1 cup sour cream
2 tablespoons butter
1 teaspoon sugar

1 teaspoon lime juice
¼ teaspoon salt
1 cup cashew nuts
1 bunch broccoli, cleaned and
chopped

Preheat oven to 325 degrees F. Prepare white sauce. Add all other ingredients except nuts and broccoli. Heat to melting. Place raw broccoli in a 2-quart dish; pour sauce over broccoli. Bake 45 minutes, stirring in nuts during the last 15 minutes of baking.

Sandwich, as the legend goes, was named for the town in New Hampshire where "Long John" Wentworth was born. It was incorporated in 1859.

Baked Broccoli and Mushrooms

Yield: 6 servings

2 10-ounce packages frozen
chopped broccoli, cooked and
drained
3 tablespoons butter, melted
½ teaspoon salt
Dash pepper
2 eggs, beaten

½ teaspoon tarragon
¼ cup seasoned breadcrumbs
2 4-ounce cans mushroom pieces,
drained
1 2-ounce jar pimiento, chopped
⅓ cup breadcrumbs

Preheat oven to 350 degrees F. To broccoli, add all ingredients except breadcrumbs. Mix thoroughly. Place into a buttered 1½-quart casserole. Top with breadcrumbs. Bake for 30 minutes.

During the Civil War more than twelve thousand Confederate prisoners were held in the prison on the limestone island in the Mississippi River which gives Rock Island its name.

Broccoli and Cheese Custard

Yield: 4 servings

1 bunch broccoli, washed, trimmed, and split into half stalks
3 eggs, beaten

⅔ cup heavy cream
1¼ cup grated sharp Cheddar cheese
Salt and pepper to taste

Preheat oven to 350 degrees F. Cook broccoli uncovered in ¾ cup boiling salted water in a 2-quart saucepan until just tender. Drain and put into a 3-quart buttered casserole. Combine eggs, cream, cheese, salt, and pepper. Mix well and pour over broccoli. Set casserole in pan of hot water. Bake for 30 minutes or until firm.

> *Freeport got its name, as legend has it, when the wife of William Baker became so distressed with her husband's generosity in giving food and aid to travelers along the Chicago to Galena Trail that she said, "This place is getting to be a regular free port for everybody coming along the trail. You'd best call your new town 'Freeport' because that is exactly what it will be."*

Creamy Broccoli and Zucchini

Yield: 4 to 6 servings

2 cups chopped fresh broccoli
2 cups chopped zucchini
½ cup chopped onion
1 garlic clove, minced
2½ tablespoons butter
3 tablespoons flour
2 tablespoons chopped parsley

½ teaspoon salt
¾ cup heavy cream
1½ cups Ricotta cheese
8 ounces green noodles, cooked and drained
Grated Parmesan cheese for topping

In a 3-quart saucepan, cook broccoli and zucchini together, covered, in 1½ cups of boiling salted water until tender. Drain well. In a 4-quart saucepan, cook onion and garlic in butter until onion is tender, but not brown. Blend in flour, parsley, and salt; add cream all at once. Cook and stir until thickened and bubbly. Add Ricotta cheese. Cook and stir until cheese is nearly melted. Stir in cooked vegetables. Heat through. Serve over hot, cooked green noodles. Top with Parmesan cheese.

Zucchini

Yield: 4 servings

1 pound zucchini, peeled
2 tablespoons butter
1 medium onion, chopped
1 green pepper, sliced
3 medium tomatoes, quartered

½ teaspoon ground ginger
1 pinch basil
1 pinch oregano
½ teaspoon salt
Grated Cheddar cheese for topping

Slice zucchini into 1-inch cubes and cook in one inch of water 10 minutes. Drain if necessary. In skillet add butter, onion, and green pepper. Sauté until tender. Add zucchini and cook 5 minutes. Add tomatoes; add spices and cook 3 minutes. Serve with grated cheese.

258

Zucchini Pancakes

Yield: 4 to 6 servings

½ cup flour
¾ teaspoon salt
⅛ teaspoon pepper

2 eggs, separated
2 cups shredded zucchini
Oil for frying

Mix flour, salt, pepper, and egg yolks. Combine with zucchini. Beat egg whites until stiff but not dry. Fold in zucchini mixture. Drop by spoonfuls into ¼-inch hot oil and brown both sides. Serve with butter and ketchup.

Zucchini and Onions

Yield: 2 servings
1 large zucchini, sliced
1 medium onion, sliced
2 tablespoons butter
1 8-ounce can tomato juice
1 teaspoon fennel seed

1 teaspoon dried basil leaves
Salt and pepper to taste
3 tablespoons grated Romano
 cheese

In a large skillet, sauté zucchini and onion in butter, cooking until zucchini and onion are tender. Add tomato juice and seasonings; top with cheese. Cover and cook until heated thoroughly.

Rockton was settled on both sides of the Rock River in 1835. It wasn't until the mid-nineteenth century that the two areas were joined by a connecting bridge. It was incorporated as a village in 1847.

Italian Zucchini

259

Yield: 4 servings
2 tablespoons Lucca olive oil
1 onion, sliced
1 pound zucchini, washed
1 teaspoon salt

¼ teaspoon pepper
2½ teaspoons sweet basil
1¼ cups canned tomatoes

Heat oil in a skillet. Add onion. Cook until transparent. Cut zucchini in ¼ to ½-inch slices. Add with remaining ingredients to onion. Cover. Simmer 8 minutes. Uncover. Simmer 5 minutes or until tender.

Coleta in Whiteside County was incorporated as a village in 1914. Its post office, in existence since 1855, serves White Pigeon.

A Farm in the Rolling Northwest

Zucchini in Sour Cream

Yield: 6 to 8 servings

6 tablespoons butter, divided
8 medium zucchini, sliced ¼ inch
  thick
3 tablespoons grated onion
½ teaspoon salt
¼ teaspoon white pepper

¼ teaspoon celery seed
1 cup sour cream
1 cup small bread cubes
¾ cup blanched almonds
Garlic salt to taste

Heat 2 tablespoons butter in skillet. Sauté zucchini and onion. Add salt, pepper, and celery seed. Gradually stir in sour cream, blending well. Heat thoroughly without boiling. Place in a serving dish. Heat remaining butter in skillet. Add bread cubes and nuts. Sprinkle with garlic salt. Stir frequently until brown. Sprinkle on top of zucchini.

Apple River Canyon State Park was established in 1932. The land it encompasses includes the river itself, sloping bluffs, craggy limestone formations, and a multitude of wild flowers and wildlife.

260

Asparagus Casserole

Yield: 4 to 6 servings

2½ pounds asparagus
1 pint boiling water
¼ teaspoon salt
Pepper to taste
8 chicken livers, sautéed and

  chopped
¾ cup mayonnaise
½ cup chopped onion
¾ cup grated Cheddar cheese
3 tablespoons butter

Cook asparagus in boiling water until just tender. Drain; season with salt and pepper. Place asparagus in 8-cup casserole. Blend chicken livers, mayonnaise, and onion; spread over asparagus. Sprinkle with grated cheese and dot with butter. Brown under the broiler.

Ottawa, on the joining of the Fox River with the Illinois River, was platted in 1830. It is widely known for its glass production. Because of its location it became a center of water transportation after the end of the Black Hawk War. It became a city in 1837.

Asparagus with Cheese

Yield: 6 servings

40 asparagus spears, cooked until
  tender
Butter for dotting
Lemon juice to taste

1 pound Swiss cheese, sliced
Grated Romano cheese
Melted butter to taste

Preheat oven to 400 degrees F. In a buttered baking dish, arrange a layer of asparagus, dot with butter, and sprinkle with lemon juice. Cover asparagus with slices of cheese and sprinkle with a small amount of Romano. Alternate layers of asparagus and cheeses, ending with a cheese layer. Sprinkle with melted butter. Bake 10 minutes until cheese is melted and bubbling.

> *In 1853 Pecatonica was settled on the banks of the river bearing the same name. Residents disagree as to the meaning of the word. Some claim that it means "river of many bends" while others maintain that it means "muddy." Pecatonica was incorporated as a village in 1869.*

Creamed Asparagus

Yield: 10 servings

5 tablespoons butter
4 tablespoons flour
2½ cups heavy cream
1 6-ounce can mushrooms, drained
¾ cup cubed Cheddar cheese
1 tablespoon chopped pimiento
Salt and pepper to taste

Dash nutmeg
2 tablespoons chopped celery
2 tablespoons chopped onion
3 10-ounce packages frozen
  asparagus, cooked
2 hard-cooked eggs, sliced
⅔ cup buttered breadcrumbs

Preheat oven to 350 degrees F. Melt butter in a saucepan. Stir in flour. Slowly stir in cream until thickened. Stir in mushrooms, cheese, pimiento, seasonings, celery, and onion. Butter a 2-quart casserole. Put asparagus in casserole and cover with sliced eggs. Cover with the sauce and top with buttered crumbs. Bake for 30 minutes.

> *Whiteside County was named after Samuel Whiteside, Brigadier General of the Militia during the Black Hawk War. Whiteside also was a representative in the First General Assembly.*

Muffined Asparagus and Cheese

Yield: 10 servings

10 slices Swiss cheese
5 English muffins, split and buttered
30 asparagus spears, cooked
4 eggs, separated

1 tablespoon prepared mustard
1 teaspoon Worcestershire sauce
Salt and pepper to taste
¼ cup sour cream

Preheat oven to 350 degrees F. Place one slice of cheese on each muffin half. Lay 3 stalks asparagus on cheese. Beat egg yolks. Add mustard, Worcestershire, salt, pepper, and sour cream. Beat egg whites until stiff. Fold yolk mixture into whites. Spoon a tablespoon of mixture on top of asparagus. Bake until brown and puffed.

> *Fulton was named for the inventor of the steamboat, Robert Fulton. It was developed by real estate speculators in 1839. It long enjoyed prosperity as a river port and railroad terminus. It was incorporated as a city in 1859.*

Green Bean Casserole

Yield: 10 servings

¾ cup chopped onion
2 tablespoons butter
2 tablespoons flour
1 teaspoon salt
¼ teaspoon pepper
1 teaspoon grated lemon rind

1 cup sour cream
2 10-ounce packages frozen green beans, cooked
½ cup coarsely grated Cheddar cheese
¾ cup breadcrumbs

Preheat oven to 325 degrees F. Sauté onion in butter until tender. Stir in flour, salt, pepper, and lemon rind. Add sour cream and mix well. Add drained beans. Heat and stir. Spoon mixture into a buttered 2½-quart casserole. Sprinkle cheese and crumbs across the top. Bake until cheese melts and crumbs brown.

> *Sycamore was named for the trees growing in the surrounding forests when it was settled in 1835. In earlier days the Indians had named the nearby river Kishwaukee, which in Indian means "sycamore." Sycamore became a city in 1859.*

Saucy Green Beans

Yield: 6 servings

2 10-ounce packages frozen French style green beans
½ cup mayonnaise
2½ tablespoons prepared mustard
2½ teaspoons prepared horseradish

Cook beans as directed on package. Drain. Combine mayonnaise, mustard, and horseradish. Fold into drained beans. Serve hot in a 2-quart serving dish.

> *Prophetstown was named for Wabokieshiek, the Winnebago chief whose name meant White Cloud. The Indians called him Prophet for he correctly predicted that the white settlers would overcome the Indians in the Black Hawk War.*

Green Beans and Bacon

Yield: 4 servings

1 pound green beans
4 slices bacon, cut into 1-inch squares
4 tablespoons butter
½ cup minced onion
⅓ cup chopped celery
1 garlic clove, crushed
½ teaspoon dried rosemary
½ teaspoon sweet basil

In a 1½-quart pot, cook beans and bacon in lightly salted water until tender. Melt butter in saucepan. Add onion and celery and sauté for 10 minutes. Add garlic, rosemary, and basil and cook slowly 10 minutes. Just before serving, drain beans and bacon; add herb mixture and toss.

> *Genoa was named by its early residents for the city in New York state from whence they came. In 1836 it prospered as a stop on the Chicago-to-Galena coach line. It became a city in 1911.*

Green Bean, Onion, and Tomato Casserole

Yield: 6 to 8 servings

2 tablespoons butter
2 tablespoons flour
½ teaspoon salt
½ teaspoon hot pepper sauce
1 16-ounce can seasoned stewed
  tomatoes

2 16-ounce cans cut green beans,
  drained
1 16-ounce can small whole onions,
  drained
½ cup Parmesan cheese
¼ cup Romano cheese

Preheat oven to 350 degrees F. Melt butter; stir in flour, salt, and hot pepper sauce to make a roux. Stir in tomatoes and cook over low heat, stirring, until thickened. In a 1½-quart casserole, alternate layers of green beans, onions, and tomato mixture. Top with cheeses. Cover and bake about 30 minutes.

> *Roscoe was settled in the Rock River Valley at the end of the Black Hawk War, and it began postal service in 1837. It did not officially become a village until 1965.*

264

Green Beans with Almonds and Mushrooms

Yield: 8 servings

1½ pounds green beans
¼ cup coarsely chopped toasted
  almonds
½ pound mushrooms, sliced

¼ cup (½ stick) butter
¼ teaspoon dried savory
1 teaspoon lemon juice
Salt and pepper to taste

Wash beans and remove ends. Cut in 1-inch pieces and place beans in 1 inch of salted water in a 2-quart saucepan. Heat to boiling. Cook, uncovered, 5 minutes. Cover and cook until tender, about 10 minutes. Sauté almonds and mushrooms in butter until golden. Drain beans well, add mushroom mixture, savory, and lemon juice. Salt and pepper to taste. Toss to blend.

> *Families from a New York settlement of the same name settled Geneseo in 1836. The name is an Indian word meaning "pleasant valley." It became a city in 1855.*

The Black Hawk Monument—Oregon

Lettuce and Peas

Yield: 6 servings
2 heads romaine lettuce
1 10-ounce package frozen peas
3 tablespoons butter
3 tablespoons flour

1 cup beef bouillon
Salt and pepper to taste

Wash lettuce leaves and place in a 4-quart kettle. Add water to cover leaves. Bring to a boil. Boil until tender, 10 minutes. Drain leaves, reserving 1 cup cooking liquid. Chop leaves. Cook frozen peas according to package directions. Drain. Make cream sauce of butter, flour, bouillon, and vegetable liquid. Add romaine, peas, salt, and pepper.

Cherry was the scene of a devastating mine disaster in 1909. Two hundred seventy men died in a fire which blocked the mine shaft. It had been incorporated as a village in 1905.

Rice and Peas

Yield: 6 servings
1 cup chopped onion
4 tablespoons butter
1 cup long grain rice
2 cups chicken stock

1 teaspoon salt
¼ teaspoon pepper
1 10-ounce package frozen peas
⅓ cup grated Romano cheese

Sauté onion in butter in a 3-quart saucepan for about 5 minutes until softened. Stir in rice. Cook 2 minutes. Stir in stock, salt, and pepper. Cook, covered tightly, over low heat for 10 minutes. Mix peas through rice. Cook, covered, for 15 minutes or until rice and peas are tender. Place in a serving dish and sprinkle with cheese.

Lena, a dairy producing center, was formerly known as Terre Haute. It was incorporated as a town in 1869.

Green Peppers and Raisins

Yield: 4 servings

4 green peppers, washed, seeded, trimmed, and cut into spears

1 cup white raisins

⅓ cup butter, melted

Salt and pepper to taste

In a 2-quart saucepan, steam pepper spears covered in ¾ cup of water until just tender. Add raisins; heat through. Drain. Season with butter, salt, and pepper.

> *Lanark was once known as Cherry Grove. It grew up at the junction of two lines of the Milwaukee Road in 1861. It was incorporated in 1867.*

Roast Peppers

Yield: 6 servings

8 whole, sweet peppers (green, red or yellow)

⅓ cup Lucca olive oil

1 garlic clove, crushed

½ teaspoon sweet basil

Salt and pepper to taste

Roast the peppers by placing them under broiler. Keep turning them until the outer skin has turned black. Peel. Remove the stems, seeds, and white membrane. Cut into strips and place in serving dish. Heat the olive oil with remaining ingredients until their flavors are absorbed into the oil (about 2 minutes). Pour over pepper strips. Serve with frilled toothpicks.

> *In 1836 Kewanee was settled by representatives from a New England association bent on "promoting the education and piety of the State of Illinois": It became a city in 1855.*

Stuffed Pickled Peppers

Yield: 6 quarts

24 medium-size green peppers
6 quarts water
½ cup salt
1 cup white vinegar
¼ cup brown sugar
¼ teaspoon whole cloves
1 tablespoon salt

2 tablespoons white mustard seed
2 cups chopped celery
1 cup chopped sweet red pepper
4 cups finely shredded cabbage
2 cups chopped green tomatoes
¼ cup chopped onion

Syrup

2 pounds sugar
1½ pints vinegar
3 to 4 sticks cinnamon

Wash and cut tops from peppers; remove seeds and veins. Let stand in brine made of 6 quarts of water and ½ cup salt. Bring vinegar, sugar, cloves, salt, and mustard seed to boiling point. Pour over vegetables. Remove peppers from brine and stuff with vegetable mixture. Replace tops on peppers and fasten with toothpicks or tie with string. Pack into hot sterilized jars.

To make syrup, combine ingredients. Bring to boil; simmer 20 minutes.

> *De Kalb was named for Baron Johann De Kalb who fought in the American Revolutionary War. It was incorporated as a village in 1856. Northern Illinois University, begun as a normal school in 1895, forms an important part of the community.*

Celery Loaf

Yield: 6 servings

1½ cups celery, chopped
⅓ cup parsley
¾ cup pecans
1 large white onion, chopped
½ green pepper

1 cup whole wheat breadcrumbs
2 eggs, slightly beaten
3 tablespoons butter, melted
1 teaspoon salt
1½ cups heavy cream

Preheat oven to 350 degrees F. Grind celery, parsley, pecans, onion, and green pepper together. Mix with dry breadcrumbs. Combine eggs, butter, salt, and cream and stir into first mixture. Turn into a well buttered 5-by-9-inch loaf pan. Bake 1 hour. Serve with a cheese or tomato sauce.

Father Marquette said mass for the Kaskaskia Indians during the Easter season of 1675 at the site of what is now Utica. He had promised the Indians to return even though he was suffering from an illness which took his life a few weeks later.

Celery with Sesame Seeds

Yield: 8 servings

3 tablespoons butter
3 tablespoons minced leeks
6 cups celery, cut into ½-inch diagonal
   slices
1 tablespoon cornstarch
¼ teaspoon ground ginger

2 tablespoons soy sauce
¾ cup chicken stock
⅓ teaspoon salt
1 6-ounce can water chestnuts,
   drained and sliced
2 tablespoons toasted sesame seeds

In a large skillet, melt butter. Add leeks and sauté 2 minutes. Add celery and stir-fry 8 minutes until celery is just tender. In a small bowl combine cornstarch and ginger. Blend in soy sauce, chicken stock, and salt. Add to celery along with water chestnuts. Cook and stir over low heat until sauce is thickened and coats celery. Stir in sesame seeds.

269

Belvidere dates back to the 1830s. It was a stop on the Chicago-to-Galena stagecoach line. It incorporated as a city in 1852.

Celery with Mushrooms and Almonds

Yield: 6 servings

8 cups sliced celery
½ cup boiling water
1 cup fresh mushrooms, sliced
⅓ cup butter

2 teaspoons salt
½ teaspoon pepper
¼ cup toasted almond halves

Cook celery in water 8 to 10 minutes. Drain. Sauté mushrooms in butter, about 5 minutes. Add celery, salt, pepper, and almonds. Toss together lightly.

Green Rock is a suburb of the Quad Cities named for the Green and the Rock Rivers. It became a city in 1950.

Cabbage with Almonds

Yield: 6 servings

3 tablespoons butter, divided
¼ cup chopped blanched almonds
1½ cups heavy cream

5 cups shredded cabbage
1 teaspoon salt
2 tablespoons flour

Melt 1 tablespoon butter in a skillet over low heat. Add almonds and cook until lightly browned. Set aside. Heat cream in a 2-quart saucepan over moderately low heat. Add cabbage and salt; cover and simmer 2 minutes. Add remaining butter; sprinkle flour over cabbage. Mix and simmer 3 minutes, stirring frequently. Stir in almonds.

> *Jo Daviess County was named for Joseph Hamilton Daviess who was killed at Tippecanoe in 1811. He had been a well known lawyer in Kentucky and a United States District Attorney.*

Fried Cabbage

270

Yield: 6 servings

¼ pound bacon, chopped
1 large onion, chopped
1 medium cabbage, sliced

Salt to taste
Pepper to taste
4 tablespoons brown sugar

Sauté bacon and onion until crisp but not brown. Add cabbage and continue to fry 5 minutes. Add salt, pepper, and brown sugar. Cover and simmer for 15 minutes.

> *Boone County's name honored the legendary hunter, Indian fighter, and pathfinder, Daniel Boone.*

Sweet Sour Sauerkraut

Yield: 4 servings

1 29-ounce can sauerkraut
Few pinches caraway seed
1 small onion, minced
3 to 4 slices bacon, cut small

2 tablespoons white flour
2 tablespoons brown sugar
Salt and pepper to taste

Rinse sauerkraut. Place in quart saucepan. Add enough water to cover. Add caraway seed. In a skillet, brown onion with bacon. When bacon becomes slightly crispy and onions are browned, remove and add to sauerkraut. To bacon drippings add flour and

cook until browned. Stir in brown sugar. Add juice from sauerkraut
slowly, stirring to form a smooth gravy. Add to sauerkraut and
simmer 30 minutes.

> *Mendota is an Indian word meaning "where trails meet." It was so named because the Burlington, the Illinois Central and the Milwaukee Railroads all converged here. It was incorporated as a city in 1859.*

Milkweed—Native Wildflower

Brussels Sprouts in Marjoram Butter

Yield: 4 servings

1 10-ounce package frozen brussels
   sprouts
½ teaspoon salt
3 tablespoons butter

½ teaspoon marjoram
1½ teaspoons lemon juice
1 tablespoon minced parsley

Cook brussels sprouts with salt added, according to directions on package. Drain well. Place in a serving dish. Melt butter and stir in marjoram and lemon juice. Pour over brussels sprouts. Sprinkle with parsley.

> *Henry County owes its name to Patrick Henry, a member of the Continental Congress and Governor of Virginia.*

Escalloped Eggplant

Yield: 4 servings

1 medium eggplant, peeled and
   chopped
3 slices bread, trimmed
1 egg

½ cup heavy cream
3 dashes Worcestershire sauce
Salt and pepper to taste
½ pound Cheddar cheese, grated

Preheat oven to 350 degrees F. Cook eggplant in salted water until tender. Soak bread in egg and cream. Blend the drained eggplant, bread, egg-cream mixture, Worcestershire sauce, salt, pepper, and cheese with an electric mixer. When mixture is fairly smooth, pour into a buttered 1½-quart casserole and bake uncovered for 1 hour.

> *Bishop Hill was an experiment in communal living by a group of Swedish immigrants who first settled the region in 1846. It was named after Biskopskulla, the birthplace of their founder, Eric Jansson. It was incorporated as a village in 1893.*

Turnip Casserole

Yield: 8 servings
3 pounds turnips, peeled and
  chopped
4 tablespoons butter
1½ teaspoons sugar
1 teaspoon salt

Dash pepper
3 eggs
1 cup breadcrumbs
1½ teaspoons lemon juice

Preheat oven to 375 degrees F. Boil turnips in salted water for 30 minutes or until soft. Drain. Place in a large bowl with butter, sugar, salt, and pepper. Beat until smooth. Add eggs, one at a time. By hand stir in crumbs and lemon juice. Pour into buttered oblong 2-quart casserole. Bake for 50 minutes uncovered.

> *The Quad Cities complex in reality encompasses five towns clustered together on both sides of the Mississippi River. Bettendorf and Davenport make up the Iowa part of the complex, while Rock Island, Moline, and East Moline sprawl on the Illinois side of the River.*

Kale

Yield: 6 servings
1 large bunch kale
1 large yellow onion, peeled and
  sliced

1 garlic clove, crushed
2 tablespoons butter
1 tablespoon prepared mustard

Wash kale; remove and discard stalks. Chop kale coarsely. Steam 25 minutes. Sauté onion and garlic in butter. Add kale to onion and stir in mustard.

> *Shabbona was incorporated as a village in 1875. It was named for the Ottawa Indian chief who aided white settlers during the Black Hawk War.*

Okra

Yield: 6 servings

6 slices bacon
1 quart okra, stems removed
2 onions, sliced
5 tomatoes, sliced

1 cup water
2 tablespoons sugar
Salt and pepper to taste

Fry bacon crisp. Remove from pan, crumble and set aside. Leave 4 tablespoons bacon drippings in the skillet. Add okra, sliced onions, sliced tomatoes, and water. Sprinkle on sugar, salt, and pepper. Cover and cook over medium heat 30 minutes. Reduce heat and simmer another 30 minutes. Serve with crumbled bacon.

> *York and Sandville were former names for the village of Thomson in Carroll County. It was incorporated in 1865.*

Artichoke Hearts in Bleu Cheese Sauce

Yield: 6 servings

2 10-ounce boxes frozen artichoke
    hearts, cooked and drained
½ pound (1 stick) butter

6 to 8 ounces Bleu cheese
Juice of 1 lemon
Salt and pepper to taste

In a double boiler, melt butter; add Bleu cheese, lemon juice, salt, and pepper. Add hearts to cheese sauce and serve hot.

> *Loves Park was named for Malcolm Love whose real estate development began the settlement in 1909. It was incorporated as a city in 1909.*

Vegetable Medley

Yield: 4 servings

½ cup (1 stick) butter
2 large onions, chopped
2 green peppers, chopped
1 eggplant, peeled and chopped
6 ripe tomatoes, peeled and chopped
4 zucchini, cut in ½-inch slices

Salt and pepper to taste
2 tablespoons chopped parsley
¼ teaspoon tarragon
¼ teaspoon basil
1 large garlic clove, crushed
1 cup shredded Cheddar cheese

In a 4-quart saucepan sauté onion in butter until transparent. Add green peppers and eggplant. Sauté for 5 minutes. Add tomatoes and zucchini. Simmer, covered, for 30 minutes. Add salt, pepper, herbs, and garlic. Cook uncovered for 10 minutes. Add cheese and stir until melted.

> *Rock Falls and Sterling are twin cities joined by bridges spanning the Rock River. They were both founded in 1837. Sterling became a city in 1841, while Rock Falls became a city in 1889.*

Vegetable Plate

Yield: 6 servings

2 8-ounce packages frozen Chinese pea pods
Butter and salt to taste
¾ pound fresh mushrooms, sliced

4 tablespoons butter
2 pints cherry tomatoes
1 8-ounce can chopped black olives, drained

Steam pea pods. Drain. Season to taste with butter and salt. In a 3-quart saucepan brown mushrooms in ¼ cup butter. After mushrooms are browned, add tomatoes and olives. Cover and steam for 3 minutes, using no water. Remove from heat just before tomato skins pop. Salt to taste. Place pea pods in center of round platter. Spoon mixture around edge.

> *The village of Millville is deserted. Once a prospering stop on the stagecoach line, the village was bypassed when the railroad came through the region. When a flood inundated the village in 1892, most of the remaining residents fled.*

Garden Pie

Mrs. Lavenau of Westchester in Megalopolis says that this quick vegetable pie makes any meal an elegant repast.

Yield: 6 to 8 servings

2 10-ounce packages frozen vegetables, thawed
½ cup chopped onion
⅓ cup grated cheese
1½ cups milk

¾ cup biscuit mix
3 eggs
¼ teaspoon salt
¼ teaspoon pepper

Preheat oven to 400 degrees F. Lightly butter a 10-inch pie plate. Sprinkle vegetables, onion, and cheese into pie plate. Beat remaining ingredients until smooth. Pour over vegetables. Bake 30 minutes or until golden. Let stand 5 minutes. Serve.

—*Louise Lavenau*

German settlers from Maryland and Pennsylvania founded Mount Morris in 1841. It was incorporated as a village in 1857.

A Rolling Northwest Scrapbook

Exotic Rice

Yield: 4 servings
¾ cup chopped onion
4 tablespoons butter
1¼ cups uncooked rice
½ teaspoon curry powder
½ cup white raisins

1¼ teaspoons salt
2½ cups water
½ cup shredded fresh coconut
½ cup salted peanuts

Preheat oven to 400 degrees F. Sauté onion in butter. Place rice, curry powder, raisins, salt, and water in 1½-quart casserole; add onion-butter mixture. Blend. Cover and bake 5 minutes. Reduce heat to 350 degrees F. and bake 40 minutes. Cool slightly and sprinkle coconut and peanuts over top.

> *Galva was settled by former residents of Bishop Hill after dissention caused the dissolution of that Swedish commune. The town's name is derived from Gefle, a seaport in Sweden. It incorporated as a city in 1867.*

Rice Casserole

Yield: 4 servings
1 onion, minced
1 6-ounce can mushrooms or ½ fresh mushroom caps and stems
4 tablespoons butter
¾ cup uncooked rice

1 12-ounce can consommé
¾ cup water
1 teaspoon salt
½ teaspoon pepper

Preheat oven to 350 degrees F. Brown onion and drained mushrooms in butter. Put rice, consommé and water into greased 1½-quart casserole. Add onion and mushrooms, salt, and pepper. Bake covered for 1 hour.

> *Stillman Valley gets its name from Major Isaiah Stillman who led his militia of 300 men in a rout of 50 Sauk warriors led by Chief Black Hawk himself. The Battle of Stillman's Run took place in 1832. It incorporated as a village in 1911.*

Wild Rice Casserole

Yield: 6 servings

½ pound wild rice
3 eggs, beaten
½ cup chopped onion
½ cup chopped celery

½ cup chopped green pepper
3 cups heavy cream
Salt to taste

Wash rice carefully and soak overnight. Preheat oven to 350 degrees F. Mix all ingredients. Place in a 2-quart casserole and set in a pan of hot water. Bake for 2 hours. Serve with a mushroom sauce.

> *As legend has it, Elizabeth on the site of the Apple River Fort was named for Mrs. Elizabeth Armstrong, a pioneer woman. In the absence of her husband and children, she defended the fort from an Indian attack during the Black Hawk War; Elizabeth was incorporated as a village in 1881.*

Polynesian Rice Casserole

278

Yield: 6 servings

2 tablespoons butter, melted
¾ cup wild rice, washed and drained
¾ cup long grain white rice, washed and drained
½ cup minced onion

3½ tablespoons soy sauce
3 chicken bouillon cubes
4 cups boiling water
½ cup macadamia nuts, chopped
Parsley for garnish

Preheat oven to 325 degrees F. Mix butter with rice in a 2-quart casserole. Add onion and soy sauce. Dissolve bouillon cubes in water; stir into rice mixture. Cover. Bake 1 hour. Serve garnished with nuts and parsley.

> *Orangeville had a post office in 1854 but did not incorporate as a village until 1867.*

Macaroni Mousse

Mrs. Van Dyke of Galesburg in Rolling Northwest says that her mother, Mrs. Garnet Butterwick, made this mousse as an extra special company dish during the 1920's.

Yield: 6 to 8 servings
2 cups elbow macaroni
1½ cups milk, scalded
1 cup breadcrumbs
¼ cup melted butter
1 red pepper, chopped
1 tablespoon chopped parsley

1 tablespoon chopped onion
1½ cups grated American cheese
Salt and pepper to taste
¼ teaspoon paprika
3 eggs, beaten

Preheat oven to 350 degrees F. Cook macaroni and rinse. Pour milk over breadcrumbs; add butter, pepper, parsley, onion, cheese, and seasonings. Stir in eggs. Place macaroni in a 6-cup buttered loaf pan. Pour milk and cheese mixture over. Bake for 50 minutes or until firm.

—*Frances Van Dyke*

279

Alanson Parker gave the name Stockton to the settlement he envisioned at a stock raising center. It incorporated as a village in 1890.

Hollandaise Sauce

Yield: 1 cup
2 egg yolks
1 tablespoon vinegar
Salt to taste

⅛ teaspoon cayenne pepper
1 tablespoon heavy cream
10 tablespoons butter

Put egg yolks into top of a double boiler and beat in vinegar, salt, and cayenne pepper. Beat in cream. Simmer and beat until mixture begins to thicken. Beat in butter a little at a time.

Dixon was named for its first white settler, John Dixon, who brought his family to the region in 1830. Both Abraham Lincoln and Jefferson Davis served at the fort located here during the Black Hawk War. It was incorporated as a village in 1843.

Megalopolis

A network of sophisticated transportation systems links Chicago at its front yard, Lake Michigan, to the farthest reaches of the several counties which form this most heavily populated region of northeastern Illinois. Many of these transportation systems closely parallel the old plank roads, Indian trails, and stage and trade routes which were so important to the early development of the state. Suburbs and towns grew up along these early trails and roads which led out of the city. Like the rest of Illinois, this area, though later in development than some of the central and southern sections of the state, has its part of the historic and cultural inheritance of the past.

Cook County has the largest concentration of population, commerce, cultural activities, and industry, but the "collar" counties have their share as well. With the dynamic growth and consequent population displacement in Chicago, vacant areas and farm lands are rapidly giving way to urban complexes which used to separate Chicago from her sister cities. Highways, railroads, and rapid transit lines make accessibility of distant places a reality, and it is not uncommon for a McHenry County resident to travel across several counties to seek out a new restaurant in southern Cook County, or for a shopper from Will County to visit a shopping center in Lake County to sample the bargains there.

Traveling around the periphery of Megalopolis, one finds a variety of communities each with its own justifiable pride in local history, yet linked by a common bond and contributing to the diversity which is Illinois.

The Chain of Lakes region represents another aspect of the beneficence of the glacier. These natural lakes are dimples in the glacial moraines spanning McHenry and Lake Counties. Cottages and summer homes are numerous in this resort area, and ownership is held not only by local people but by residents of other counties in the megalopolitan sprawl. The town of McHenry on the Fox River borders the lake region on the west. It was settled as early as 1836, and like many other towns it was located on a road called the Chicago Pike which led from the city on the lake to the northwest reaches beyond it.

Waukegan in Lake County was well-known as a French outpost during the eighteenth century. Established on the site of a Potowatomi Indian village, the little fort was given status as a U. S. port of entry in 1846 and prospered with traffic in furs, hides, and grains. Waukegan, located on a bluff overlooking Lake Michigan, has become a bustling industrial center sharing the lake front with a continuum of affluent, venerable old communities of the North Shore such as Glencoe, Kenilworth, Wilmette, and Winnetka extending southward to Evanston at the northern limits of Chicago.

Evanston is separated from Chicago only by a cemetery. It is an archetype of the typical college town. The sprawling campus of Northwestern University set amidst the tree-shaded streets flanked by gracious old houses could have been the setting for any of the Hollywood "Campus Movie Musicals" of the 1930s and 1940s. Evanston has experienced industrial and commercial growth too, owing to its proximity and transportational linkage to the teeming metropolis to the south.

Elgin lies at the western perimeter of Megalopolis on the subtly sloping bluffs of the Fox River in Kane County. Before it was incorporated as a village in 1854, its early settlers had seen to it that Elgin became a stop on the Chicago-to-Galena stage line, ensuring its independence from Chicago and a firm place in the economic and commercial growth of northern Illinois. Dairy production and other industries contributed to Elgin's economic prominence and, although the lovely old Gothic building that was the watch factory is no more, for many years Elgin and watches were synonomous.

Before turning west through Kendall County, the Fox River flows unhurriedly through Kane County to Aurora which spreads out on both sides of the river in the gently bottoming valley. Aurora is a perfect example of the numerous towns in Illinois whose fame and fortune were made by the railroads. In the mid-nineteenth century, the Chicago Burlington and Quincy Railroad extended its run to the town, contributing to Aurora's emergence as an industrial shipping center for the northern part of the state and the prairie farmlands which surround it.

Located on the DesPlaines River in Will County is the town of Joliet. The opening of the Illinois-Michigan Canal in the mid-nineteenth century brought unprecedented commercial opportunities to its doorstep. Later the arrival of several railroad extensions aided Joliet in the shipping of its valuable paper and steel products. Steel production in both Joliet and Morris in Grundy County to the south was facilitated by the large deposits of soft coal in the area.

Perhaps one of the most unique towns in Illinois is Summit, southwest of Chicago in Cook County. The town was named because of its location on the crest of the watershed which represents the continental divide of two great water systems.

Precipitation which falls on the east side of Summit is drained into streams which empty ultimately into the Atlantic Ocean, while that falling on the west side of the town is drained by the Mississippi River system into the Gulf of Mexico.

The towns and communities to the south of Chicago represent the heartbeat of its industrial growth from the 19th into the 20th century. Many of these population centers grew up along old well-traveled Indian routes such as Sauk or Hubbard Trails. Others sprang up along the newly laid railroad beds. The steel mills and other related industries brought newly arrived immigrants to the vicinity with the promise of employment and a share in the good life. The industrial conglomerate south of Chicago includes communities such as Calumet Park, Harvey, Calumet City, and Chicago Heights, finally spilling out of the boundaries of Illinois to continue around the southern tip of Lake Michigan into northern Indiana.

The story of the Chicago Portage and its importance to trade routes and the development of early Illinois is a well-known one. As early as the seventeenth century the Indians and French *voyageurs,* fur trappers, *coureurs du bois,* and missionaries forded the nine mile neck of land stretching from the Chicago River to the Des Plaines River on their travels between the great waterways in Canada to the north and east and the Gulf of Mexico to the south. The little trading post at the fork of the Chicago River on the banks of Lake Michigan gradually drew more settlers, only to be savaged by Indian attacks and other disasters time and time again. Finally, when it was incorporated as a town in 1833 the settlement became stable and the real growth of Chicago began. Immigrants began to stream in via the Erie Canal to the new harbor at the joining of the Chicago River with Lake Michigan. Many of these newcomers settled in Chicago while others pushed on farther to establish farms or homesteads in the country surrounding the city. The construction of the Illinois-Michigan Canal opened the area outside the city to further growth, settlement, and development.

After the Chicago Fire in 1871, large numbers of Chicagoans left the city to build new homes in the "country" surrounding Chicago, and suburban Chicago and the outlying areas began to develop. Some suburbs such as Hyde Park and Austin were annexed and became part of the city itself, while others such as Cicero, Oak Park, and Evanston opted for separation and became towns and villages on their own. Although, like Chicago, many of these outlying towns demonstrate a diversity of ethnic origins in their populations, others, like microcosms of the ethnic neighborhoods which are so uniquely Chicago, reflect a predominance of one ethnic flavor in their settlement. For example, the town of Geneva on the Fox River retains a distinctly Scandinavian flavor harkening back to its settlement by immigrants from northern Europe. The towns of Cicero and Berwyn reflect their predominance of Czechs. Italians make up most of the population of Melrose Park, while Oak Lawn has a heavy concentration of people whose ethnic origins are Irish.

The dynamic city on the western edge of its own inland sea has been described by visitors as "the most American of cities," and with its diversity of population it has retained a unique character of its own while contributing to the enrichment of state and country to an almost staggering degree. This is Louis Sullivan and Frank Lloyd Wright country. It is the City of Skyscrapers, but it is also a haven for architecture like the Kimball House on historic Prairie Avenue. American literature has been embellished by contributions of Chicago-area writers such as Ernest Hemingway, Archibald MacLeish, Saul Bellows, Gwendolyn Brooks, and Theodore Dreiser. The talents of Ivan Albright, George Bellows, and Laredo Taft have enriched the visual arts in Chicago, while its place in the development of music in America has been fortified by the birth of the

Chicago blues and the world fame of the Chicago Symphony. To the performing arts Chicago has given such gifted performers as Mercedes McCambridge, Charleton Heston, Jack Benny, and many others.

The vitality of the city has always been likened to the legendary phoenix rising from the ashes. This philosophy is perhaps most aptly stated in the words of that visionary Chicago planner and supporter Daniel Burnham.

> Make no little plans; they have no magic to stir men's blood and probably themselves will not be realized. Make big plans; aim high on hope and work, remembering that a noble and logical diagram once recorded will never die, but long after we are gone will be a living thing, asserting itself with growing intensity. Remember that our sons and grandsons are going to do things that would stagger us. Let your watchword be "order" and your beacon "beauty."

Megalopolis is diversity. It is quiet and serene, loud and nerve-wracking, awe-inspiring and heart-rending. It is everything that is American. The whole history of the nation is written large in Megalopolis. Other Megalopolitan areas get their "feel" from geography and climate; the Chicago Megalopolis gets its feel from people: people who are here now and people who have passed through, staying a while to leave their mark and going on better for having been here.

Desserts and Sweets

Coconut Pound Cake

Yield: 10 servings

1½ cups (3 sticks) butter, at room temperature
2½ cups sugar
5 eggs, at room temperature
3 cups sifted flour
1 teaspoon baking powder
1 teaspoon almond extract
1 teaspoon vanilla extract
1 cup light cream
1 cup shredded coconut

Cream butter and sugar for 15 minutes. Add eggs, one at a time, and beat just enough to blend. Sift the flour and baking powder together. Add alternately with the cream. Mix until blended. Add the almond and vanilla extract. Fold in the coconut. Pour into a buttered and floured tube pan. Place cake in cold oven and set it for 300 degrees F. Bake 1 hour and 45 minutes or until cake tests done.

> *The Chicago White Sox played baseball for the first time in 1900. White Sox Park is still a landmark in that area of the city known as Armour Square.*

Bourbon Pound Cake

Yield: 6 to 8 servings

1 pound (4 sticks) butter
3 cups sugar, divided
8 eggs, separated
3 cups flour
2 teaspoons vanilla extract
2 teaspoons almond extract
⅓ cup bourbon
¾ cup chopped pecans

Preheat oven to 350 degrees F. Cream butter and 2 cups sugar. Add egg yolks one at a time, beating after each. Add flour alternately with flavoring and bourbon, beating after each. Beat egg whites until stiff. Beat remaining sugar into egg whites gradually. Fold egg yolk mixture into the whites. Sprinkle pecans in the bottom of a well buttered 10-inch tube pan. Carefully turn batter into the pan. Bake 1½ hours. Do not frost.

> *Lockport, incorporated as a city in 1853, enjoyed a livelihood as an important port on the Illinois and Michigan Canal. It now provides the sophisticated lock system which controls the water diverted from Lake Michigan.*

Apple Poundcake

Mr. Messler of Downers Grove in Megalopolis says that this old-fashioned cake is "great," and despite some changes in it, it has been in the family for many years.

Yield: 8 to 10 servings

3 cups flour
1 teaspoon baking soda
1 teaspoon salt
½ teaspoon cinnamon
½ teaspoon nutmeg
1½ cups (3 sticks) butter, at room temperature
2 cups sugar
3 eggs
2 teaspoons vanilla extract
2 cups finely chopped and pared apples
1 cup chopped pecans
½ cup raisins
½ cup applejack
½ cup apple juice
¼ cup brown sugar
2 tablespoons butter

Preheat oven to 325 degrees F. Combine flour, soda, salt, cinnamon, and nutmeg; set aside. In a large bowl beat together butter, sugar, eggs, and vanilla. Add flour mixture and beat until smooth. Fold in apples, pecans, and raisins. Put in a buttered and floured bundt pan. Bake for 1 hour and 15 minutes. Cool in pan 10 minutes; remove and finish cooling. Combine applejack, apple juice, brown sugar, and butter. Boil. Prick cake and pour through.

—*Robert Messler*

286

> *Tinley Park was known as Bremen when it was settled by German immigrants prior to the Civil War. It became the village of Tinley Park in 1892. The replica of a golf ball which adorns its water tower underlines its fame as "The Golf Ball Capital of the World."*

Peach Custard Cake

Yield: 6 servings

1½ cups flour
½ teaspoon salt
½ cup (1 stick) butter
1 pound 4 ounce can sliced peaches
½ teaspoon cinnamon
½ cup sugar
½ cup peach syrup
1 egg
1 cup heavy cream

Preheat oven to 375 degrees F. Mix flour and salt in a small bowl. Cut in butter until mixture resembles coarse meal. Pat onto bottom and halfway up the sides of a buttered 8-inch square baking pan. Arrange peaches on crust. Sprinkle with cinnamon and sugar. Bake for 20 minutes. Mix peach syrup, egg, and cream and pour over peaches. Return to oven and bake 30 minutes or until firm. Cool before serving.

Mokena, as legend has it, is similar to the Algonquin word for turtle. Although postal service was provided as early as 1853, it was not incorporated as a village until 1880.

Banana Split Cake

Yield: 1 10-inch cake

1½ cups sugar
1 cup (2 sticks) unsalted butter, at
   room temperature
4 eggs
½ cup mashed banana
½ cup sour cream
½ cup heavy cream

1 teaspoon vanilla extract
3 cups flour
2 teaspoons baking powder
1 teaspoon salt
½ teaspoon baking soda
½ cup strawberry preserves
½ cup cocoa

Preheat oven to 350 degrees F. Cream together sugar and butter. Add eggs, one at a time, beating after each addition. Combine banana, sour cream, cream, and vanilla. Sift together flour, baking powder, salt, and soda. Add sifted ingredients alternately with banana mixture to creamed mixture. Beat until blended. Add preserves to 1 cup batter. Add cocoa to another cup of batter. Spoon half of the plain batter into a well buttered 10-inch tube pan. Spoon strawberry batter over plain batter. Top with remaining plain batter. Spoon chocolate batter over top. Bake for 1 hour and 15 minutes, or until done. Cool in pan for 15 minutes. Remove from pan and cool on rack. Sift confectioners' sugar over cake.

287

Oak Park was originally named Kettlestrings Grove after its first settler. It boasts two famous literary sons in Ernest Hemingway and Edgar Rice Burroughs. Its streets are graced with many fine examples of Frank Lloyd Wright's architectural design. The architect's house and studio are open to the public.

Rhubarb Cake

Yield: 8 to 10 servings
1½ cups sugar
½ cup (1 stick) butter
2 eggs
1 teaspoon baking soda
2 cups flour
½ teaspoon salt

1 cup sour milk
2 cups minced rhubarb
¾ cup sugar
1 teaspoon cinnamon
½ cup chopped pecans

Preheat oven to 350 degrees F. Cream sugar and butter; add eggs. Sift dry ingredients and add alternately with sour milk. Mix 2 tablespoons flour with rhubarb and add to remaining ingredients. Place in a buttered and floured 13-by-9-inch pan; cover with mixture of sugar, cinnamon, and nuts; bake for 45 minutes.

> *Barrington in northwest Cook County was established as a village in 1865. Quaker settlers from Great Barrington, Massachusetts, gave the town its name.*

Dump Cake

Yield: 12 servings
1 16-ounce can cherry pie filling
1 16-ounce can crushed pineapple
  with juice
1 18½-ounce box yellow cake mix

1 cup (2 sticks) butter, melted
1½ cups coconut
1 cup chopped pecans or walnuts

Preheat oven to 350 degrees F. Layer ingredients in a 13-by-9-inch pan in order given. Bake for 1 hour. Serve warm with ice cream.

> *By the turn of the century, fashionable Prairie Avenue, between 16th and 22nd streets, displayed many mansions of Chicago's elite. The elaborate homes of Marshall Field, W. W. Kimball, and John J. Glessner can still be seen in the historic district which echoes the past elegance of Chicago.*

Fruit Cake

This recipe from Modoc in the Bottom for Romona Melliere's fruit cake has been in her family for over one hundred years.

Yield: 1 loaf cake
5 egg yolks
1 cup sugar
1 cup molasses
1 cup (2 sticks) butter, at room temperature
⅔ cup wine
⅔ cup whiskey
1 teaspoon baking soda
2 tablespoons hot water

2 cups flour, sifted
½ teaspoon each of cloves, allspice, cinnamon, ginger, and nutmeg
5 egg whites, stiffly beaten
1 pound raisins
1 pound currants
½ pound chopped citron
1 pound walnuts
½ cup flour

Preheat oven to 325 degrees F. Beat egg yolks with sugar. Blend in molasses, butter, wine, and whiskey. Add baking soda and water mixture. Stir in sifted flour and spices. Add stiffly beaten egg whites. Roll fruits and nuts in ½ cup flour and stir into mixture. Bake in a large buttered loaf pan for 1½ hours or until done.
—*Romona Melliere*

289

Jackson Park was the site selected for the elaborate designs of Frederick Law Olmstead for the World Columbian Exposition in 1893.

Tomato Cake

Yield: 1 10-inch cake
2½ cups flour
½ cup cocoa
2½ teaspoons baking powder
2 teaspoons baking soda
1 teaspoon salt
1 teaspoon cinnamon
1 cup minced walnuts
¾ cup butter, at room temperature

2 cups sugar
3 eggs
2 cups coarsely grated or minced green tomatoes
2 teaspoons grated orange peel
2 teaspoons vanilla extract
½ cup light cream

Preheat oven to 350 degrees F. Sift dry ingredients together. Add nuts. Cream butter with sugar. Beat in eggs, one at a time. Beat in tomatoes, orange peel, and vanilla. Add cream alternately with dry ingredients. Pour into a 10-inch buttered tube pan. Bake 1 hour. Cool in pan 15 minutes.

Walnut Sour Cream Cake

Yield: 8 slices

1 cup (2 sticks) butter, at room
   temperature
1 cup sugar
2 eggs
1 teaspoon vanilla extract

2 cups sifted flour
1 teaspoon baking powder
1 teaspoon baking soda
½ teaspoon salt
1 cup sour cream

Filling and Topping

⅓ cup brown sugar
¼ cup sugar

1 teaspoon cinnamon
1 cup chopped walnuts

Cream butter and sugar until light and fluffy. Add eggs and vanilla; beat. Sift dry ingredients and add alternately with sour cream, beating until smooth after each addition. Spread half of batter in a buttered and floured pan, 9-by-12-by-2 inches. Preheat oven to 350 degrees F.

Mix sugars, cinnamon and nuts; sprinkle half over batter. Spread remaining batter on top gently. Sprinkle with remaining sugar and nut mixture. Bake for 35 minutes.

290

Nut Cake

Mrs. Hamm of Freeport in Rolling Northwest says that this is an old family favorite. "My mother used this recipe of her mother's. It dates back before 1927."

Yield: 8 servings

2 cups dates
2 cups English walnuts
1 scant cup flour
2 teaspoons baking powder

4 eggs, beaten
1 cup sugar
1 teaspoon vanilla extract

Preheat oven to 325 degrees F. Combine all ingredients. Spread in a buttered 9-by-13-inch baking dish. Bake 1 hour.

—Violet (Mrs. Harold) Hamm

> In the mid-1860s Potter Palmer arranged for the demolition of residential housing on State Street near Randolph. By 1870 the block stretching from Randolph to Washington Street and from State to Wabash Avenue was leased to Marshall Field, Leiter, and Company. The block now contains the original Marshall Field's Store.

Toffee Cake

Yield: 8 to 10 slices
2 cups brown sugar
2 cups sifted flour
½ cup (1 stick) butter
1 egg
1 cup heavy cream

1 teaspoon baking soda
½ teaspoon salt
1 teaspoon vanilla extract
6 ¾-ounce bars toffee candy bars, chopped

Preheat oven to 350 degrees F. Mix brown sugar and flour; thoroughly cut in batter. Reserve 1 cup of the mixture. To remaining mixture add egg, cream, soda, salt, and vanilla. Beat until blended. Pour into a buttered 9-by-13-inch pan. Sprinkle with reserved crumbs and toffee. Bake for 35 minutes.

291

> Antioch is located in the Chain-of-Lakes region. It was originally settled in the 1830s at the end of the Black Hawk War. Its name owes its inspiration to the town of Bible times. Hollywood's "Oscar" is manufactured here.

Graham Cracker Cake

Yield: 8 to 10 slices

20 squares graham crackers
1 cup milk
½ cup (1 stick) butter, at room
 temperature
1 cup sugar

2 eggs
1 teaspoon vanilla extract
1 cup flour
2½ teaspoons baking powder
1 teaspoon salt

Preheat oven to 375 degrees F. Break crackers into small pieces and pour milk over. Cream butter and sugar; add eggs and vanilla. Beat until fluffy. Sift together flour, baking powder, and salt. Add cracker mix and flour mixture. Stir. Pour into 2 8-inch buttered and floured pans and bake 25 minutes. Cool and frost.

> *The town of Mundelein was named after a former cardinal and archbishop of Chicago, George William Cardinal Mundelein. It was known as Area when it became a village in 1909.*

Chocolate Rum Cake

Yield: 8 servings

1 cup (2 sticks) butter, at room
 temperature
3 cups sifted confectioners' sugar
3 3-ounce squares unsweetened
 chocolate, melted and cooled
½ cup rum

3 eggs
2 tablespoons heavy cream
1 10-inch angel food cake
1 cup heavy cream, whipped
½ teaspoon vanilla extract
1 tablespoon sugar

Cream butter and sugar. Add chocolate and rum; beat well. Beat eggs until thick and lemon colored; blend with first mixture. Fold in 2 tablespoons cream. Cut cake into 3 layers. Spread filling between layers and on top. Chill overnight. To whipped cream add vanilla and sugar. Frost sides of cake with cream mixture.

> *Libertyville, which had a postal service as early as 1839, was known as Independence Grove in its earlier days. Both Daniel Webster and Samuel Insull were landowners in the area at one time or another.*

Cottage Cheese Fudge Cake

Yield: 8 to 10 slices

1¾ cups sugar
⅔ cup butter, at room temperature
2 eggs
1 teaspoon vanilla extract
½ cup buttermilk
½ cup creamed cottage cheese

½ cup cocoa
½ cup boiling coffee
2½ cups sifted flour
1½ teaspoons baking soda
½ teaspoon salt

Preheat oven to 350 degrees F. Cream sugar and butter; add eggs and beat well. Add vanilla, buttermilk, and cottage cheese and mix thoroughly. Make a heavy, smooth paste of cocoa and boiling coffee. Cool slightly. Add to mixture and blend well. Add flour, baking soda, and salt. Pour into a well buttered and floured 9-by-13-inch pan. Bake for 25 minutes or until done.

> *Naperville was named for Joseph Naper who came to build a sawmill and plat the town in 1832. During World War II troops were trained at nearby Camp McDowell for espionage activities behind the lines in Germany.*

293

Log Cake

Yield: 8 to 10 servings

4 eggs, separated
¾ cup sugar, divided
½ teaspoon vanilla extract
¾ cup sifted cake flour

1 teaspoon baking powder
¼ teaspoon salt
½ pint heavy cream, whipped
Confectioners' sugar for coating

Filling

1 cup sugar
3 tablespoons cornstarch
2 2-ounce squares unsweetened
    chocolate

Dash salt
1 cup boiling water
3 tablespoons butter
1 teaspoon vanilla extract

Preheat oven to 375 degrees F. Beat egg yolks until thick and lemon colored. Gradually beat in ¼ cup sugar. Add vanilla. Beat egg whites. Gradually add remaining cup sugar and beat until stiff. Fold yolks into whites. Sift together flour, baking powder, and salt. Fold into egg mixture. Spread batter in buttered, wax-papered jelly roll pan. Bake for 12 minutes or until done. Turn out on linen towel sprinkled with sifted confectioners' sugar. Peel off waxed paper. Starting at narrow end, roll cake and towel together. Cool on rack.

Mix sugar, cornstarch, chocolate, and salt. Add boiling water. Cook until thick. Remove from heat. Add butter and vanilla. Unroll cake and spread with filling. Roll up again without towel and spread whipped cream over log.

> *Des Plaines grew up along the river which French explorers had called the Rivière aux Plaines. In the 1840s it was given the name Rand by the New England settlers who came to cut timber there for the plank road which led to Chicago. When the Illinois and Wisconsin Railroad arrived in 1869, the town had been renamed Des Plaines.*

Sunshine Angel Cake

Sunshine cake has been the birthday cake in the Welch/Metzger family of Collinsville in the Bottom for 45 years. Mrs. Metzger warns, "Make two cakes; one is never enough."

Yield: 1 10-inch cake
1½ cups sugar, divided
6 eggs, separated
¾ teaspoon cream of tartar
1½ cups flour

1 teaspoon salt
½ cup water
¼ teaspoon almond extract

Preheat oven to 350 degrees F. Divide sugar in half. Beat egg whites until frothy; add the cream of tartar and beat until soft peaks form. Add half of the sugar and beat until stiff. In another bowl, beat egg yolks until lemon colored. Add remaining sugar and beat until thickened. Into the yolk mixture beat the flour and extract alternately with the water. Fold in the egg whites carefully by hand. Pour into an unbuttered 10-inch tube pan and bake for 1 hour or until done. Remove from pan and frost.

—*Lois Welch Metzger*

> *Coal City was so named for the coal deposits in the region and is a favorite spot for fossil hunters. It became a village in 1881.*

Indian Summer Cake

Yield: 1 8-inch round cake
½ (1 stick) cup butter, at room
    temperature
1 cup sugar
⅓ cup seedless raisins
1 egg
1 cup unsweetened applesauce
1¾ cups sifted flour

1½ teaspoons cinnamon
1 teaspoon allspice
1 teaspoon nutmeg
¼ teaspoon ground cloves
½ teaspoon salt
1 teaspoon baking soda
½ cup pecans

Cream Cheese Frosting

1 3-ounce package cream cheese, at
    room temperature
1 tablespoon lemon juice

1 egg white, slightly beaten
1½ to 2 cups confectioners' sugar

Preheat oven to 350 degrees F. Cream butter and sugar until fluffy. Stir in raisins. Beat egg until light; add and mix well. Add applesauce. Sift together the flour, spices, salt, and baking soda; add and mix well. Stir in nuts. Pour into two buttered and floured 8-inch layer cake pans. Bake for 35 to 45 minutes. Cool and frost.

    Make Cream Cheese Frosting: Blend cream cheese with lemon juice and egg white. Add sugar gradually, blending well.

295

> Cicero was incorporated as a town in 1867. At one time some of Chicago, Oak Park, and Berwyn were a part of this present-day working class community. Immigrants from Eastern Europe formed the early basis of its population.

Sour Cream Spice Cake

Yield: 1 8-inch round cake

½ (1 stick) cup butter, at room
   temperature
1 cup sugar
2 eggs
2¼ cups sifted cake flour
½ teaspoon baking soda

½ teaspoon salt
1 teaspoon baking powder
½ teaspoon nutmeg
1 teaspoon ground cloves
2 teaspoons cinnamon
1 cup sour cream

Foamy Icing

1 cup sieved firmly packed light
   brown sugar
2 egg whites

3 tablespoons cold water
¼ teaspoon vanilla extract

Preheat oven to 375 degrees F. Cream butter and sugar, until fluffy.
Add eggs, one at a time; beat well after each addition. Sift together dry
ingredients; add alternately with sour cream to creamed mixture.
Turn into 2 buttered and floured 8-inch layer cake pans. Bake 30
minutes. Cool.

    Make Foamy Icing: Combine sugar, egg whites, and water in
top of double boiler; stir well. Place over boiling water. Beat
constantly until mixture holds a point. Remove from heat. Add
vanilla and beat a minute longer.

296

> *In 1875 a contemporary writer described Kenwood as "the Lake
> Forest of the South Side."*

Mince Meat Cake

    Mrs. Bundy of Mounds in Egypt says, "My parents were
farmers near Iuka when I was a child back in the 1930s and made
their own mincemeat. Mother made this cake at Christmas, and it
was a treat."

Yield: 12 servings
1½ cups sugar
½ cup (1 stick) butter
2 eggs
½ cup milk
1 teaspoon vanilla extract
1½ cups mincemeat

2½ cups flour
2 teaspoons baking powder
1 teaspoon cinnamon
½ teaspoon baking soda
1 tablespoon cocoa

Preheat oven to 350 degrees F. Cream sugar and butter. Add eggs and beat well. Beat in milk and add vanilla and mincemeat. Sift together dry ingredients and thoroughly stir into liquid mixture. Pour into a buttered and floured 9-by-13-inch pan and bake 40 minutes or until it tests done.

—*Reta Bundy*

> *Fox Lake is the largest in the Chain-of-Lakes. Both the Fox and the Potowatomi Indians occupied the region. It became a village in 1906.*

Fruitcake

Yield: 2 loaf cakes

1 cup (2 sticks) butter, melted
1⅓ cups sugar
¼ cup molasses
4 eggs
3 cups sifted flour, divided
1 teaspoon baking powder
2 teaspoons salt
2 teaspoons cinnamon

1 teaspoon nutmeg
½ teaspoon mace
1 cup orange juice
2⅔ cups seedless raisins
2 cups dates, chopped
2 cups mixed candied fruit
1½ cups walnuts broken in half

297

Preheat oven to 275 degrees F. Line two buttered 8½-by-4½-by-2½-inch loaf pans with brown paper. Mix butter, sugar, molasses, and eggs with mixer for two minutes. Sift together 2 cups flour, baking powder, salt, spices and add alternately with orange juice. Mix 1 cup flour into fruit and nuts. Pour batter over fruit, mixing thoroughly. Pour into prepared pans. Place pans in a pan of water on lower oven rack. Bake cakes 2½ to 3 hours. Remove from oven. Let stand 15 minutes before removing from pans. Cool thoroughly before removing paper.

> *Palos Park was settled in the 1830s by German and Irish immigrants who had worked on the Illinois-Michigan Canal. It was not incorporated as a village until 1915.*

The Old Graue Mill—Hinsdale

Cream Cheese Frosting

Yield: 2 cups

1 8-ounce package cream cheese, at
   room temperature
1 8-ounce box confectioners' sugar

½ teaspoon almond or vanilla extract
Chopped pecans

Cream together cream cheese, sugar, and extract. Spread over top
and sides of cake. Sprinkle with nuts.

Butter Cream Icing

Yield: 1½ cups

6 tablespoons butter, at room
   temperature
3 cups confectioners' sugar

3 tablespoons heavy cream
1 teaspoon vanilla extract

Blend together butter and sugar. Stir in remaining ingredients. Beat until smooth and fluffy.

Egg White Frosting

Yield: 1 cup frosting

1 egg white
½ cup white corn syrup
½ teaspoon vanilla extract

Combine ingredients and beat until mixture is thick and forms peaks.

Pink Frosting

Yield: enough for 2 8- or 9-inch layers

1 4-ounce bottle of maraschino
   cherries

½ pound miniature marshmallows
½ pint heavy cream, whipped

Reserving juice, drain and chop cherries. Pour juice of cherries over marshmallows and let stand for 1 hour. Drain. Add the cream to the marshmallows. Frost cake. Sprinkle with chopped cherries. Place in refrigerator overnight.

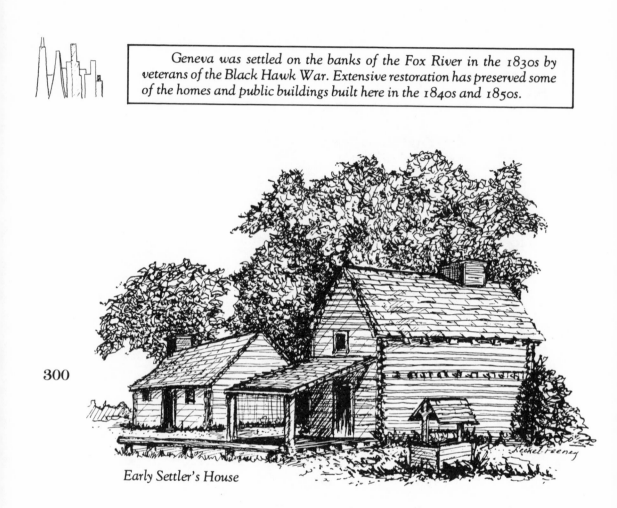

Geneva was settled on the banks of the Fox River in the 1830s by veterans of the Black Hawk War. Extensive restoration has preserved some of the homes and public buildings built here in the 1840s and 1850s.

300

Early Settler's House

Raspberry Dessert

Yield: 6 servings
20 macaroons
¾ cup blanched almonds
1 cup white grape juice

1¾ cups heavy cream
3 cups raspberries

Chop macaroons and almonds together in a food chopper or processor. Pour the grape juice over the macaroons and almonds. Whip one cup of cream until almost stiff and fold into macaroon mixture. Place in six serving glasses. Spoon crushed raspberries over the top and place a large dollop of stiffly beaten whipped cream over the raspberries.

Apricot Pecan Dessert

Yield: 10 servings

½ cup (1 stick) butter
1 cup confectioners' sugar
2 eggs, beaten
1½ pounds vanilla wafers, crushed

2 12-ounce cans apricots, drained
2 cups heavy cream
1 cup chopped pecans

Melt butter; stir in sugar and eggs. Cook until thickened, about 4 minutes. Reserving ½ cup crumbs, spread wafer crumbs in a 13-by-9-inch pan. Pour cooked mixture over crumbs in pan; arrange apricots, flat side down, on cooked mixture. Whip cream; fold in pecans. Spread on apricots; top with reserved crumbs. Chill.

301

Chocolate Tortoni

Yield: 6 servings

1 teaspoon cornstarch
2 tablespoons sugar
Pinch salt
½ cup heavy cream
1 egg yolk, slightly beaten
½ 1-ounce square unsweetened
  chocolate, melted

½ teaspoon vanilla extract
2 teaspoons rum
10 candied cherries, divided
5 macaroons, crushed
½ cup heavy cream, whipped
1 egg white, stiffly beaten

Sift together cornstarch, sugar, and salt. Stir in cream. Cook 8 minutes. Add some hot mixture to slightly beaten egg yolk; mix well. Stir into remaining hot mixture. Cook 2 minutes. Add chocolate, vanilla, and rum. Beat and cool. Finely chop 4 cherries. Stir cherries and macaroons into chocolate mixture. Fold in whipped cream and stiffly beaten egg white. Pour into 6 crinkled paper cups. Top with remaining cherries. Freeze.

Chocolate Soufflé

Yield: 6 servings
2 tablespoons butter
1 tablespoon flour
¾ cup heavy cream
⅓ cup sugar
2 tablespoons boiling water
2 1-ounce squares unsweetened
   chocolate, melted

1 1-ounce square sweet chocolate,
   melted
4 egg yolks, well beaten
½ teaspoon vanilla extract
4 egg whites
1½ teaspoons baking powder

Rum Whipped Cream Sauce

2 egg yolks
3 tablespoons rum
1 cup heavy cream

3 tablespoons sugar
1 teaspoon vanilla extract

302

Preheat oven to 300 degrees F. Make a roux of the butter and flour. Stir in cream. Cook, stirring constantly, until thickened. Reduce heat and cook 5 minutes. Blend sugar and water into chocolate; stir until smooth. Add some hot mixture to well-beaten egg yolks; mix well. Stir into remaining hot mixture. Add vanilla. Cool to room temperature. Beat egg whites until frothy. Add baking powder; beat until stiff. Fold into unbuttered 1½-quart soufflé or casserole dish. Bake 1 hour. Serve immediately with Rum Whipped Cream Sauce.

   To make sauce, beat egg yolks until thick. Add rum; mix well. Whip cream; beat in sugar and vanilla. Fold in egg mixture.

Coffee Gelatin Dessert

"This was a quick dessert made so that not even leftover coffee was wasted," says Mrs. Robbins of Elgin in Megolopolis.

Yield: 6 servings
1 tablespoon unflavored gelatin	3½ ounces whiskey
2 cups black coffee	Heavy cream
4 tablespoons sugar	

Soften gelatin in ½ cup coffee. Heat remaining coffee and dissolve sugar in it. Add whiskey; bring to a boil and remove from heat. Stir in the gelatin until completely dissolved. Pour into individual molds and chill until firm. Unmold and serve with a dollop of heavy cream.

—*Anna Robbins*

A settlement was begun at Crete in 1836 by Willard Wood who opened a tavern near the intersection of the Hubbard Trail and the Chicago-Vincennes Military Road. It was incorporated in 1880.

Apple Crisp Granny Magee

Mrs. Pyzik of Bolingbrook in Megalopolis says, "As a child, I helped pick apples for my grandparents. As a treat, my grandmother would make me her apple crisp and serve it warm with a scoop of vanilla ice cream."

Yield: 6 servings
5 to 6 cups apples, sliced and pared	¾ teaspoon salt
1 cup flour, sifted	1 egg
1 cup sugar	⅓ cup butter, melted
1 teaspoon baking powder	½ teaspoon cinnamon

Preheat oven to 350 degrees F. Place apples in a 6-by-10-inch baking dish. In a separate bowl, mix other ingredients until crumbly. Place on top of apples. Spoon melted butter over topping and sprinkle on cinnamon. Bake for 30 to 40 minutes or until golden.

—*Glenna Magee Pyzik*

Peach Cobbler

Yield: 6 servings

1 cup sugar	1 cup sifted flour
2 tablespoons cornstarch	1 tablespoon sugar
½ cup water	1½ teaspoons baking powder
4½ cups peeled and sliced peaches	½ teaspoon salt
2 tablespoons butter	3 tablespoons butter
¾ teaspoon cinnamon	½ cup heavy cream

Mix together sugar and cornstarch. Stir in water and peaches. Bring to boil; boil 1 minute stirring constantly. Place in 1½-quart shallow casserole. Dot with butter. Sprinkle with cinnamon. Preheat oven to 400 degrees F. Sift together flour, sugar, baking powder, and salt. Cut in butter. Stir in cream; mix to soft dough. Drop by spoonfuls onto hot mixture. Bake 30 minutes.

Spiced Fruit Compote

Yield: 8 servings

2 29-ounce cans cling peaches, halved	¼ teaspoon ground ginger
2 cinnamon sticks	2 29-ounce cans pear halves, drained
½ teaspoon allspice	1 17-ounce can figs, drained
¼ teaspoon nutmeg	½ cup brandy
	3 bananas, sliced

Drain syrup from peach halves. Combine syrup with cinnamon sticks, allspice, nutmeg, and ginger. Cook over medium heat to boiling. Reduce heat to low; cover and simmer for 10 minutes, stirring occasionally. Remove from heat and cool. In large bowl, combine pears, figs, peaches, and brandy. Pour peach syrup mixture over fruit. Mix well. Cover and refrigerate overnight. To serve, slice bananas into 1-inch chunks. Stir into fruit mixture.

Raspberry Sherbet

Yield: 6 servings

1 16-ounce package frozen
   raspberries, in syrup
1 cup boiling water
1 3-ounce package raspberry gelatin

½ cup sugar
¼ cup lemon juice
2¼ cups milk

Thaw raspberries; push through sieve to remove seeds. Pour water over gelatin; stir until gelatin is dissolved. Add sugar and lemon juice. Stir in puréed raspberries. Chill. Blend slowly into milk. Pour into an 8-by-8-by-2-inch pan. Freeze to a mush. Beat. Return to pan; freeze till firm.

Caramel Ice Cream

Yield: 1½ quarts

1 cup sugar
½ cup water
3 tablespoons flour
¼ teaspoon salt

3 cups heavy cream, scalded
1 egg, beaten
1½ teaspoons vanilla extract
1 cup heavy cream, whipped

Spread ½ cup sugar evenly in skillet. Heat until sugar melts and turns light brown; stir constantly. Gradually add water; cook until sugar is dissolved. Mix together flour, salt, and remaining sugar; stir gradually into hot cream. Cook, stirring constantly, until mixture thickens. Cook 8 minutes longer. Add some hot mixture to egg; mix well. Stir eggs into remaining hot mixture. Blend in caramel sauce and vanilla. Strain into an 8-by-8-by-2-inch pan. Freeze to a mush. Beat well. Fold in whipped cream. Return to pan; freeze firm.

Custard Ice Cream

Yield: 1 quart

½ cup sugar
Dash salt
4 egg yolks, beaten

2 cups heavy cream, scalded
1 teaspoon vanilla extract
1 cup heavy cream, whipped

Beat sugar and salt into egg until dissolved. Slowly add cream to egg mixture; stir well. Strain mixture into saucepan. Cook over low heat, stirring constantly, until custard coats the spoon. Chill. Add vanilla to whipped cream; fold into cold custard mixture. Pour into 8-by-8-by-2-inch pan; freeze.

The first major steel production center in the Chicago area was Chicago Heights. Although steel production has spread to other towns south of Chicago, the steel mills are still associated with Chicago Heights.

306

The Kimball House—Prairie Avenue Historic District—Chicago

White Cookies

Mrs. Pierce of Monmouth got this recipe from her mother who won first prize with it in the county fair of 1920.

Yield: 3 dozen

1½ cups sugar
½ cup (1 stick) butter, at room
   temperature
2 eggs
1 cup sour cream

1 teaspoon vanilla extract
4 cups flour
1 teaspoon baking soda
1 teaspoon baking powder
⅛ teaspoon salt

Preheat oven to 350 degrees F. Cream sugar and butter. Beat in eggs, sour cream, and vanilla. Sift dry ingredients and stir into liquid ingredients. Roll out and cut in circles with a glass or cookie cutter. Place on cookie sheet and bake 10 to 12 minutes or until done.

—N. D. Pierce

Winnetka was founded on the land evacuated by Indians in accordance with the treaty framed after the Black Hawk War. In 1837 an early settler, Johann Happ, succeeded in calling the settlement New Trier, after an historic German city. When the town was platted in 1857, the name Winnetka was adopted.

Old Fashioned Sour Cream Cookies

Mrs. Gareau of Berwyn in Megalopolis says that this recipe which her mother-in-law makes has been a family favorite for years. Mrs. Gareau's mother-in-law says, "I usually take a small glass, rub the bottom with any kind of shortening, dip in cinnamon mixture, and flatten each cookie."

Yield: 6 dozen

3 cups sifted flour
1 teaspoon baking powder
½ teaspoon baking soda
½ teaspoon salt
1 cup (2 sticks) butter, at room
   temperature
1½ cups sugar

2 eggs
1 cup sour cream
1 teaspoon vanilla extract or 2
   teaspoons grated lemon peel
½ cup sugar
2 tablespoons cinnamon

Sift flour with baking powder, baking soda, and salt. Set aside. In large bowl of electric mixer, at high speed, beat butter, sugar, and eggs until light and fluffy. At low speed beat in sour cream and vanilla or lemon peel until smooth. Gradually beat in flour mixture until well combined. Refrigerate 1 hour or more. Preheat oven to 375 degrees F. Lightly butter 2 cookie sheets. Drop batter by slightly rounded tablespoonfuls on cookie sheets, 2 inches apart. For topping sprinkle unbaked cookies with sugar-cinnamon mixture. Bake 10 to 12 minutes. Remove to wire rack to cool.

—*Berenice Gareau*

> *Hinsdale was begun as an organized community in the 1860s and became incorporated as a village in 1873. In 1923 the tiny settlement of Fullersburg with its Old Graue Mill was annexed to the village. This historic water-driven grist mill began operating in 1850. It has been restored and is open to the public during the summer.*

Toffee Grahams

Mrs. Korshak, of Springfield, says that these rich crackers were a delight served by her mother to all the kids in the neighborhood.

Yield: 4 dozen
24 honey graham crackers
½ pound (2 sticks) butter, melted
1 cup fully packed light brown sugar
1 teaspoon vanilla extract
1 cup chopped pecans

Preheat oven to 350 degrees F. Line an unbuttered jelly roll pan 15-by-10-inches with crackers. Be sure the lines are all going in one direction. Combine butter and brown sugar. Bring to a boil and boil for 2 minutes. Stir continuously until sugar is absorbed by the butter. Remove from heat and add vanilla and nuts. Mix well. Spread over crackers. Bake for 10 minutes. Cool. Cut along creases while warm and place on rack to cool further.

—*Stella Korshak*

> *In the 1830s Wheeling began as a stagecoach stop to change horses on the road between Chicago and Milwaukee. Although it became a village in 1894 it was not until the 1950s that the population began to increase. "La Française," one of the world's finest French restaurants, draws countless gourmets each year to Wheeling.*

Angel Wings

Yield: 1½ dozen
1 cup sifted flour
2 egg yolks, well beaten
4 tablespoons heavy cream

¼ teaspoon salt
2 to 3 cups vegetable oil
Confectioners' sugar for dusting

Sift flour into bowl. Add egg yolks, cream, and salt. Mix into smooth, stiff dough. Set aside and let stand ½ hour. Roll pieces of dough thin and cut into 4x3-inch pieces. Prick with fork and drop into hot oil and fry until puffy and golden. Drain on paper and sprinkle with confectioners' sugar.

> *Pullman, the first planned industrial town, was built in the 1880s. It was the brainchild of George Pullman, who invented and manufactured the first railroad sleeping car. Pullman was annexed to Chicago's south side in 1905.*

Margurites

Mr. Wiley of Champaign in Breadbasket Flatlands remembers this childhood treat from before World War I as an after school snack.

Yield: 1½ dozen
3 egg whites
¼ cup sugar
1 1-ounce square sweet chocolate,

grated
16 soda crackers

Preheat oven to 375 degrees F. Beat egg whites until stiffening; add sugar and beat until stiff peaks form. Place a mound of the meringue on each cracker and sprinkle some chocolate over each. Bake until golden, about 12 minutes.

—L. E. Wiley

> *Batavia on the Fox River was begun as a settlement shortly after the Black Hawk War. It provided the area for many years with stone quarried from its limestone deposits and paper and flour produced by its water-driven mills. It became a town in 1856.*

Fried Cookies

Yield: 3 dozen
2 cups flour
2 tablespoons confectioners' sugar
½ teaspoon salt
3 tablespoons butter, melted
Grated rind of 1 lemon

2 eggs
6 egg yolks
3 cups vegetable oil for deep frying
Confectioners' sugar for dusting

Combine flour, sugar, salt, and melted butter. Add lemon rind and mix well. Whisk whole eggs and egg yolks together. Make a depression in center of flour mixture and add eggs. Mix into a paste. Place on a lightly floured board and knead until satiny. Roll out very thin. Cut diagonally in strips 1 inch wide and 4 inches long. Slit each piece 1 inch down and pull one end through the slit. Fry in 2 to 3 inches deep hot fat until delicately brown. Dust with confectioners' sugar.

> *Chicago Heights, incorporated in 1892, once bore the names Thorn Grove and Bloom. The original settlement was at the crossing of the Sauk Trail and Hubbard Trail, a busy intersection dating back to the time of the French voyageurs and trappers.*

310

Hazelnut Drop Cookies

Yield: 4 dozen
½ pound hazelnuts, chopped
4 egg whites, stiffly beaten
1¾ cups confectioners' sugar, sifted

Preheat oven to 350 degrees F. Fold together nuts, egg whites, and confectioners' sugar. Drop by slightly rounded teaspoons on buttered cookie sheets. Bake 9 to 10 minutes. Remove from sheets at once.

> *Channahon, named for the Indian word which means "meeting of waters," is located near the juncture of the Du Page and the Des Plaines Rivers. An early lock system was built here to accommodate barges traveling the waterways. The town was first settled by immigrant workers on the Illinois-Michigan Canal in the 1840s.*

Fudge Cookies

Yield: 4 dozen
1 cup brown sugar
1 cup sugar
1½ cups (3 sticks) butter
½ cup milk
1 cup semi-sweet chocolate bits

2 cups rolled oats
½ cup chopped nuts or salted
  peanuts
½ cup coconut (optional)

Bring sugars, butter, and milk in a heavy pan to a boil, stirring occasionally. Boil 2 minutes. Remove from heat. Add remaining ingredients. Beat until thick. Drop from teaspoon onto waxed paper. Let cool.

> *Frankfort was named for Frankfort-am-Main in Germany by the German immigrants who originally settled it. Although the village was laid out in 1842, it was not granted official status until 1879.*

Kiss Cookies

Yield: 4 dozen
½ pound (2 sticks) butter, at room
  temperature
½ cup sugar
2 cups sifted flour
1 teaspoon vanilla extract

1 cup pecans, ground
1 14-ounce package chocolate candy
  kisses
1 cup confectioners' sugar

Preheat oven to 375 degrees F. Cream butter and sugar. Beat in flour, vanilla, and pecans. Chill. Wrap 1 teaspoon dough around each kiss and bake on an unbuttered cookie sheet for 12 minutes. Roll cooled cookies in confectioners' sugar.

> *Lake Forest, one of Chicago's most gracious and wealthy suburbs, was settled as early as 1835. One of its main thoroughfares, Deerpath Avenue, had actually been a path for deer and buffalo to Lake Michigan.*

Date-Cheese Cookies

Yield: 3 dozen

½ cup (1 stick) butter, at room temperature
4 ounces cream cheese, at room temperature
1 cup sifted flour

⅛ teaspoon salt
10 ounces pitted dates
½ cup walnuts or pecans
Confectioners' sugar

Cream together butter and cheese. Sift together flour and salt. Add to first mixture; stir until mixture becomes smooth. Chill several hours or overnight. Preheat oven to 375 degrees F. Slit dates and insert nuts; press dates closed. Roll out chilled dough to ⅛ inch thickness in confectioners' sugar. Cut dough in strips 1½-by-3½-inches. Put a stuffed date on the center of each strip; roll up. Sprinkle with confectioners' sugar. Arrange folded side down on a cookie sheet. Bake 15 minutes.

Berwyn, chartered as a city in 1908, is known for its streets lined with "Bohemian Bungalows." Ogden Avenue, one of the early plank roads, angles through this residential community.

312

Carrot Cookies

Yield: 2 dozen

¾ cup butter, at room temperature
1 cup sugar
1 egg
1 cup cooked, mashed carrots
1 teaspoon vanilla extract

½ teaspoon lemon extract
2 cups sifted flour
2 teaspoons baking powder
½ teaspoon salt

Preheat oven to 350 degrees F. Cream butter and sugar; add egg; beat well. Stir in carrots and flavorings. Sift dry ingredients and mix into batter. Drop by teaspoonfuls on a buttered cookie sheet. Bake for 12 to 15 minutes.

Wheaton, the home of the 1920s football idol "Red" Grange, was incorporated as a village in 1859. Its name comes from Warren and Jesse Wheaton who were its first settlers in 1831.

Almond Butter Balls

Yield: 7 dozen
¾ cup butter
1 cup firmly packed light brown
   sugar, sieved
1 egg
2 cups sifted flour
1½ teaspoons baking powder

¼ teaspoon salt
1 teaspoon vanilla extract
¼ teaspoon almond extract
¼ cup sugar
1 pound blanched almonds

Preheat oven to 400 degrees F. Cream butter and brown sugar thoroughly. Beat in egg. Stir in sifted dry ingredients. Add vanilla and almond extract. Shape dough in two long rolls. Cut in small even pieces. Roll pieces into balls. Dip in sugar. Place on unbuttered cookie sheets. Press one half almond into each ball. Bake 8 to 10 minutes.

Western Springs was settled by Quakers in the mid-nineteenth century. The town's name was chosen to reflect the abundant supply of water made available by natural springs. It was incorporated as a village in 1893.

Ginger Crackles

Mrs. Franke of New Baden in Egypt reports that this cookie has pleased the men in her family for as long as she can remember.

Yield: 2½ dozen
1 cup (2 sticks) butter, at room
   temperature
2 cups brown sugar, firmly packed
1 egg, well-beaten
1 cup molasses
4 cups sifted flour

½ teaspoon salt
2 teaspoons baking soda
2 teaspoons ground ginger
1 teaspoon vanilla extract
1 teaspoon lemon extract
Sugar for dusting

Cream butter; gradually add brown sugar. Blend in egg and molasses. Beat until light and fluffy. Sift together dry ingredients. Gradually blend in creamed mixture. Dough should be soft but not sticky. Add vanilla and lemon extracts. Chill until it can be handled (about 4 hours). Preheat oven to 350 degrees F. Shape into balls 1½ inches in diameter. Place on unbuttered cookie sheet. Do not flatten. Bake 12 to 15 minutes or until brown. Sprinkle with sugar.

—*Louise Scherer Franke*

The Bridge over the Fox River—Aurora

Downhome Fudge

Yield: 5 dozen

2 2-ounce squares unsweetened chocolate
½ cup water
1 cup sugar
1 cup firmly packed brown sugar

½ cup evaporated milk
3 tablespoons butter
1 teaspoon vanilla extract
1 cup walnuts or pecans, chopped

Mix together chocolate and water in 2-quart saucepan. Cook over low heat until chocolate is melted. Add sugars and milk; stir well. Cook to soft ball stage. Add 3 tablespoons butter and vanilla. Cool to lukewarm, about 110 degrees F. Beat until mixture loses its high gloss; add nuts. Pour in a buttered 8-by-8-by-2-inch pan. Cut in 1-inch squares when cool.

> *Plainfield became a town in 1869, but in 1790 it had started out as a trading post owned and operated by a French entrepreneur named Du Pazhe. The Du Page River, which borders Plainfield on the west, bears the anglicized name of this early French merchant.*

Butterscotch Peanut Butter Fudge

Yield: 2 dozen

2 cups butterscotch chips
1 14-ounce can sweetened
   condensed milk
16 large marshmallows, quartered

½ cup chunky peanut butter
1 teaspoon vanilla extract
Pinch salt

Combine butterscotch pieces, condensed milk, and marshmallows. Cook and stir over low heat until marshmallows and butterscotch melt. Remove from heat; stir in peanut butter, vanilla, and salt until blended. Pour into a buttered 8-inch square pan. Chill. Cut into squares.

315

> *Posen was named by its Polish immigrant founders for the Polish city Poznan. It was incorporated as a village in 1900.*

Chewy Dates

Yield: 4 dozen

1 7¼-ounce package pitted dates
1 cup walnuts or pecans
2 4-ounce cans moist coconut

½ cup firmly packed brown sugar,
   sieved
1 egg

Preheat oven to 350 degrees F. Put dates and nuts through food chopper. Add 1 can coconut, brown sugar, and egg. Mix well. Form in finger shaped pieces about 1¼ inches long. Cut remaining can of coconut in shorter shreds; place on waxed paper. Roll date pieces in coconut. Put on lightly buttered cookie sheets. Bake 10 minutes.

> *Riverside was planned as a suburb in 1869. "The village in a park" was designed by Frederick Law Olmstead who also planned Manhattan's Central Park. It was incorporated in 1875.*

Rhubarb Chew

Yield: 6 servings
1 cup sifted flour
¾ cup uncooked oatmeal
1 cup brown sugar
½ cup (1 stick) butter, melted
1 teaspoon cinnamon

4 cups chopped rhubarb
1 cup sugar
2 tablespoons cornstarch
1 cup water
1 teaspoon vanilla extract

Preheat oven to 350 degrees F. Mix first five ingredients until crumbly. Press half the mixture into a buttered 8-inch square pan. Cover crumb mixture with diced rhubarb. Combine sugar, corn-starch, water, and vanilla and cook until thick and clear. Pour over rhubarb. Top with remaining crumbs and bake for 1 hour. Serve warm with whipped cream.

> *Lyons is located on the Chicago Portage between the great water systems to the east and west. Its village seal reads "Founded 1673; incorporated 1888; then and now gateway to the West."*

Divinity

Yield: 4 dozen
5 cups sugar
1 cup light corn syrup
1 cup boiling water

3 egg whites, beaten stiff
⅓ cup chopped pistachio nuts
⅓ cup chopped maraschino cherries

Mix together sugar, syrup, and water. Cook over medium heat until soft ball stage. Slowly pour 1 cup syrup over egg whites, beating constantly. Cook remaining syrup until syrup forms hard and brittle threads when small amount is dropped in very cold water. Add slowly to egg white mixture. Beat until candy holds its shape. Add nuts and cherries. Pour in an 11-by-7-by-1½-inch buttered pan. Cut in 1-by-1¾-inch bars.

> *Wilmette is the world center of the Baha'i faith which promotes universal brotherhood. The domed shape of the white Baha'i Temple rises gracefully at the edge of the suburb's Lake Michigan shoreline.*

Cream Candies

Yield: 4 dozen

2 cups sugar
½ cup heavy cream
½ cup milk

1 tablespoon light corn syrup
3 tablespoons butter
1 teaspoon vanilla extract

Mix together sugar, cream, milk, and syrup in 3-quart saucepan, over low flame. Stir until sugar is dissolved. Cook until soft ball stage. Cool to lukewarm. Add butter and vanilla. Beat until thick and creamy. Pour into a buttered 9-by-5-by-2¾-inch loaf pan. Cut in 1-inch squares when cool.

> *The academic character of Evanston was spoofed by a pundit who claimed that if one threw a stone into Fountain Square, in the heart of the village, he "would probably hit an intellectual, and that would probably be a good idea." Although it was settled earlier, the founding of Northwestern University predated the incorporation of the village in 1873.*

Chicolate-Nut Delights

Yield: 5 dozen

2 tablespoons butter, at room
temperature
1 cup peanut butter
1 cup sifted confectioners' sugar

1 cup minced dates
1 cup minced walnuts
2 ounces paraffin
3 cups semi-sweet chocolate chips

Cream together butter, peanut butter and sugar. Stir in dates and nuts. Pat into an 11-by-7-by-1½-inch pan. Chill 3 hours. Form into 1-inch balls. Melt paraffin over medium flame. Add chocolate; melt. Dip balls, one at a time, in chocolate mixture. Place on waxed paper.

> *The University of Chicago was founded in 1890 by the American Baptist Education Society. John D. Rockefeller's generosity to its establishment and maintenance occasioned the students to sing his praises in the jingle—*
> *"John D. Rockefeller, wonderful man is he,*
> *Gives all his spare change to the U. of C."*

Heavenly Hash

Yield: 2 dozen

1½ pounds melting milk chocolate
1½ pounds marshmallows, cut up

1½ cups English walnuts, in coarse
 pieces

Melt chocolate in saucepan over low heat. Stir. Turn off heat; add nuts and marshmallows; stir until coated. Pour into a buttered 9-by-13-inch pan. Cool until hardened. Loosen from pan. Cut into pieces.

> *Morris was named for Isaac N. Morris, a commissioner for the Illinois-Michigan Canal. It was platted as a port town in 1842 for the newly constructed waterway.*

Pecan Pralines

Mrs. Hunter of Freeport in Rolling Northwest says that this is a "very old Southern recipe. It was made in our house only at Christmas time. Pecans were picked and shelled for candy."

Yield: 36 pieces

2 cups light brown sugar
¼ cup water

4 tablespoons butter
2 cups pecan halves

Mix sugar, water, and butter in saucepan. Cook until it threads. Add pecan halves. Drop on waxed paper by spoonfuls.

—*Georgia (Mrs. LeRoy) Hunter*

> *The term "The Loop" was first coined to identify the area circumscribed by Chicago's cable car lines in the 1880s and not by the pattern of the elevated train tracks.*

Cocoa Candies

Yield: 30 pieces

½ cup (1 stick) butter
2 cups sugar
1 cup heavy cream
3 cups quick cooking oatmeal

¾ cup peanut butter
3 tablespoons cocoa
1 teaspoon vanilla extract

Mix butter, sugar, and cream together in a saucepan and boil for 1 minute. Mix oatmeal, peanut butter, cocoa, and vanilla in a large bowl. Add boiled mixture and blend thoroughly. Drop by the spoonful on waxed paper. Cool.

> *Several legends hover around the name Peotone. One of the more popular bits of lore holds that Peotone was so named by a railroad inspector. The legendary inspector randomly combined letters contained in the names of stops on the railroad. It was incorporated as a village in 1869.*

Mocha Candied Nuts

Yield: 3 cups
1½ cups beet sugar
1 tablespoon corn syrup

½ cup warm, strong coffee
2½ cups mixed nuts

Place first 3 ingredients together in saucepan. Cook to soft ball stage: 240 degrees F. Remove from heat and add mixed nuts. Stir gently until creamy. Pour onto buttered cookie sheet; separate nuts with fork. Cool.

> *Summit was named for its location surmounting the ridge on the watershed between the St. Lawrence and Mississippi River systems. The town is traversed by Archer Avenue, the road built to transport material and laborers for the construction of the Illinois-Michigan Canal. Workers on the canal first settled Summit which incorporated as a village in 1890.*

Peanut Brittle

Yield: 1 pound
1½ cups sugar
¼ pound (1 stick) butter
½ cup light corn syrup

12 ounces salted peanuts
1 teaspoon baking soda

Melt the first three ingredients in an electric skillet at 400 degrees F. Add peanuts and stir 7 minutes. Remove from heat; add baking soda and stir well. Pour onto a buttered cookie sheet. Cool. Break up and store.

> *Stickney lies astride the Chicago Portage between the Chicago and Des Plaines Rivers. Tucked away in Mt. Auburn Cemetery here is the burial ground of Chinese immigrants from the early 1900s. Stickney became a village in 1913.*

Walnut Clusters

Yield: 3 dozen

4 tablespoons butter, at room
  temperature
½ cup sugar
1 egg
1½ teaspoons vanilla extract
2 1-ounce squares chocolate, melted

½ cup sifted flour
¼ teaspoon double action baking
  powder
½ teaspoon salt
2 cups coarsely chopped English
walnuts

Preheat oven to 350 degrees F. Cream butter and sugar. Beat in egg and vanilla. Mix in chocolate. Sift dry ingredients and add to mixture. Stir in walnuts. Drop by teaspoonfuls, 1 inch apart, onto buttered cookie sheets. Bake 10 minutes.

> *Park Forest is an example of the planned suburban development which drew large numbers of urbanites after World War II. Established as a village in 1949, its population trebled within ten years.*

320

Layered Meringues

Yield: 10 servings

6 egg whites
⅛ teaspoon salt
1½ cups sugar
1½ teaspoons vanilla extract, divided
1 teaspoon vinegar
2 cups heavy cream, whipped
½ teaspoon vanilla extract
2 tablespoons sugar

3 cups seedless green grapes,
  washed and drained
2 cups black grapes, washed,
  drained, and seeded
2 1-ounce squares semi-sweet
  chocolate
1 cup walnuts, halved

Preheat oven to 275 degrees F. Beat egg whites and salt until stiff peaks are formed. Add sugar gradually; beat well after each addition. Beat in 1 teaspoon vanilla and vinegar; continue beating 10 minutes. Cover cookie sheets with heavy brown paper. Drop meringue by tablespoons onto brown paper, making 18 oval mounds, 4-by-1½-by-1½ inches. Bake 45 minutes. Reduce heat to 250 degrees F, bake 15 minutes or until delicately firm. Cool on rack. Into whipped cream, fold ½ teaspoon vanilla and sugar. *To serve:* On large cake plate, arrange 5 or 6 meringues in a 9-inch ring. In center, lay 3 or 4 meringues, slightly crushed. Cover with half of cream mixture and grapes. Add 1 square chocolate which has been shaved with a vegetable peeler to form curls. Top with ½ cup walnuts. Repeat to form a second layer of meringues and topping. Chill until served.

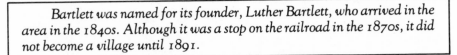

> *Bartlett was named for its founder, Luther Bartlett, who arrived in the area in the 1840s. Although it was a stop on the railroad in the 1870s, it did not become a village until 1891.*

Food For The Gods

Mrs. Franke of New Baden in Egypt says, "The recipe was given to me by my grandmother, Hilda Scherer, of Mascoutah. She told me the recipe was at least 250 years old when her mother handed it down to her."

Yield: 12 servings
6 eggs
2 cups sugar
2 cups crushed soda crackers
2 teaspoons baking powder
1 pound English walnuts, chopped
½ pound dates, chopped

Preheat oven to 350 degrees F. Separate eggs and reserve yolks for another purpose. Beat whites stiff, gradually adding the sugar. Gently stir in crackers and baking powder. Fold in walnuts and dates. Pour into a buttered and floured 13-by-9-inch pan and bake for 35 to 40 minutes until very lightly browned. Cool. Serve with whipped cream.

—*Louise Scherer Franke*

> *Westmont became a village in 1921. Bricks made from the clay deposits around the village were used to rebuild Chicago after the Great Fire in 1871.*

Frank Lloyd Wright House—Oak Park

Illinois Gingerbread

Yield: 1 loaf

½ cup (1 stick) butter, at room temperature
2½ tablespoons grated orange rind
½ cup brown sugar, packed
3 eggs, well beaten
2¾ cups flour, sifted
1 teaspoon baking soda
½ teaspoon salt

2 tablespoons ground ginger
1½ teaspoons cinnamon
1 teaspoon mace
1 teaspoon nutmeg
1 cup molasses
¼ cup orange juice
¼ cup brandy

Preheat oven to 350 degrees F. Cream butter, orange rind, and sugar. Blend in eggs and beat. Sift together flour, baking soda, salt, and spices. Add to creamed mixture alternately with molasses, orange juice, and brandy. Pour into a buttered and floured 8-by-12-by-2½-inch pan. Bake 35 minutes.

Pioneer Gingerbread

Mrs. Brooks of Hampton in Rolling Northwest says about this recipe, "I came across it in an old clipping of my husband's grandmother. The clipping said the recipe came from Germany in the late 1700s—also said the pioneer women would open the door occasionally causing the gingerbread to fall. They believed this made it chewy."

Yield: 12 servings

½ cup sugar
½ cup (1 stick) butter, at room temperature
1 egg
1 cup honey
2½ cups sifted flour

½ teaspoon salt
1 teaspoon baking soda
1 teaspoon cinnamon
1 teaspoon ground ginger
½ teaspoon cloves
1 cup boiling water

323

Preheat oven to 375 degrees F. Cream sugar and butter. Beat in egg and honey. Sift together flour, salt, soda, cinnamon, ginger, and cloves. Add to honey mixture alternately with boiling water. Bake for 20 minutes in a lightly buttered 9-by-13-inch pan. Reduce heat to 350 degrees F. and bake 10 to 15 minutes more. Open oven door occasionally causing gingerbread to fall.

—Mrs. Eugene Brooks

Soft Gingerbread

Mrs. Lanphere of Monmouth in Land Between the Rivers says, "This recipe came from Mrs. Louisa Long who was born October 2, 1838, and died January 25, 1927. As a child I sometimes visited in the Long home. Their home was heated with wood and on a cold winter evening the smell of wood smoke carried through the neighborhood. The story was that when she saw the men starting for the house for their noon meal she would stir up this gingerbread, and it would be ready for dessert when the meal was served. Their kitchen had a pitcher pump at the sink, a well-polished black cookstove, and a rocking chair with a blue and white checked gingham cushion on the seat."

Yield: 8 servings
1/4 cup sugar
1/2 cup molasses
1 large egg, beaten
1 1/2 cups flour, sifted
1/2 teaspoon salt

1 teaspoon ground ginger
1 teaspoon baking soda
2 tablespoons butter
1/2 cup hot water

Preheat oven to 350 degrees F. Beat the sugar and molasses into the egg. Sift together the dry ingredients. Melt the butter in the hot water and stir into the flour mixture. Beat in egg mixture. Pour into an 8-inch buttered square pan and bake for 35 minutes or until done.

—*Mrs. Robert D. Lanphere*

Marengo, like the chicken dish of the same name, was so called to commemorate one of Napoleon's more famous battles. It is one of the world's biggest producers of mousetraps.

Cereal-Nut Bars

Yield: 2 dozen
1 cup sugar
1 cup milk
1 cup light corn syrup

2 cups crisp rice cereal
5 cups corn flakes
2 cups salted peanuts

Mix together sugar, milk, and syrup. Cook over medium heat. Stir until sugar is dissolved. Cook until soft ball stage. Remove from heat; beat until smooth. Pour syrup over cereal and nuts; mix well.

Pour into a buttered 12-by-9-by-2-inch pan. Cut in pieces when cool.

> Long Grove began its existence as Muttersholtz when postal service was first dispatched in 1847. The name change took place in 1894. Since its incorporation as a village in 1956, Long Grove has become a treasure trove for antique hunters and boutique fanciers.

Six Layer Bars

Yield: 2 dozen
½ cup (1 stick) unsalted butter
1 cup graham cracker crumbs
1 cup flaked coconut
1 12-ounce package chocolate chips
1 cup chopped walnuts
1 14-ounce can condensed milk

Preheat oven to 350 degrees F. Melt butter in 9-by-13-inch pan. Add one layer each of graham cracker crumbs, coconut, chocolate chips, and walnuts. Drizzle milk over the top. Bake 25 minutes. Let cool and cut in bars.

> Arlington Heights was named Dunton after one of its first developers when the settlement began in the mid-nineteenth century. The Arlington Park Race Track, which opened in the 1920s, draws many onlookers and participants to watch the Sport of Kings each year.

Persimmon Pudding Squares

Yield: 6 servings
1¼ cups persimmon pulp
2 eggs, beaten
1 cup milk
2 tablespoons butter, melted
1 cup sifted flour
¾ teaspoon baking soda
½ teaspoon salt
½ teaspoon cinnamon
¼ teaspoon nutmeg
¾ cup sugar

Preheat oven to 375 degrees F. Mix pulp and eggs. Add milk and butter. Sift together the dry ingredients and stir into the liquid ingredients. Add more milk if necessary to make a soft batter. Pour into a buttered 8-by-8-2-inch pan and bake for 45 minutes. Cut into squares and serve with whipped cream.

> Crystal Lake was incorporated as a village in 1837. Settled by Beman Crandall in 1836, it was once occupied by Sauk and Fox Indians.

Rhubarb Squares

Yield: 2 dozen

½ cup sugar
½ cup chopped pecans or almonds
1 tablespoon butter, melted
1 teaspoon cinnamon
1½ cups brown sugar
¼ pound (1 stick) butter, at room
  temperature

1 egg
2 cups flour
1 teaspoon baking soda
½ teaspoon salt
1 cup sour cream
1½ cups rhubarb, chopped

Preheat oven to 350 degrees F. Combine sugar, nuts, butter, and cinnamon until crumbly for topping. Cream brown sugar with butter; add egg. Sift together flour, soda, and salt; add to creamed mixture alternately with sour cream. Stir in rhubarb. Pour into a buttered and floured 9-by-13-inch pan. Sprinkle with topping. Bake for 50 minutes. Cut in squares.

> *Plano became a city in 1865. It is located near the site of a devastating massacre of 300 Fox Indians by French soldiers in 1730.*

326

Pecan Surprise Squares

Yield: 3 dozen

1 18½-ounce package yellow cake
  mix
¼ pound (1 stick) butter, at room
  temperature

4 eggs
½ cup brown sugar
1 teaspoon vanilla extract
2½ cups pecan halves

Preheat oven to 350 degrees F. Set aside ⅔ cup dry cake mix. Combine remaining cake mix, butter, and 1 egg. Press into a buttered 9-by-13-inch pan. Bake for 15 minutes. Combine brown sugar, 3 eggs, and vanilla; beat until blended. Pour mixture into baked crust and top with pecans. Bake for 30 minutes or until set.

> *Bensenville, established as a village in 1894, has experienced a considerable amount of economic growth as a part of the expansion of the communities surrounding the O'Hare Airport complex.*

Chocolate Cherry Squares

Yield: 3 dozen
1 cup flour
¼ teaspoon salt
⅓ cup brown sugar, packed
½ cup unsalted butter, at room temperature
1 cup semi-sweet chocolate chips
1 8-ounce jar cherries, drained
2 tablespoons chopped pecans

Preheat oven to 350 degrees F. Combine flour, salt, and sugar. Cut in butter. Form into a ball and press into an unbuttered 8-by-8-by 2-inch pan. Bake for 20 minutes. Cut into squares while still warm. Melt chocolate chips and place a small amount of melted chocolate on each square. Top with a cherry and cover with more chocolate. Sprinkle with nuts.

> *Skokie originally bore the name Niles Center. It was incorporated as a village in 1888. Since World War II the village's population growth has been so extensive and steady that residents refer to it as "the world's largest village."*

Pecan Roll

Yield: about 48 slices
2 cups sugar
1 cup firmly packed brown sugar
½ cup light corn syrup
1 cup evaporated milk
1 cup pecans, coarsely chopped

Mix together sugars, corn syrup, and milk in a 3-quart saucepan. Stir until sugar is dissolved and until soft ball stage is reached. Cool to lukewarm. Beat until creamy. Let rest. Shape in rolls 1 inch in diameter when firm enough to handle. Roll in pecans; chill to harden. Slice when firm.

> *Westchester was the unrealized dream of Samuel Insull. Although the village was planned for a population boom when it was incorporated in 1925, the Great Depression extinguished all hope for its development. After World War II it revived and it is now a thriving residential community.*

Coconut Gems

Yield: 24 pieces
2 packages active dry yeast
¼ cup warm water
3 cups flour
⅓ cup plus 1 tablespoon sugar
1 cup (2 sticks) butter

⅔ cup evaporated milk
4 egg yolks
1⅓ cups flaked coconut
4 egg whites, whipped stiff

Soften yeast in warm water. Combine flour and 1 tablespoon sugar into a mixing bowl. Cut in butter until mixture resembles coarse crumbs. Add evaporated milk, egg yolks, coconut, and yeast; beat until smooth. Toss dough on floured surface until no longer sticky. Divide dough in half. Roll out on surface sprinkled with ⅓ cup sugar to an 18-by-6-inch rectangle. Spread each rectangle of dough with ⅓ of meringue; reserve remainder. Starting with 18-inch side, roll up jelly roll fashion. Cut each roll into twelve 1½-inch slices. Place, cut side up, in well buttered 2½-inch muffin cups. Spoon reserved meringue in mounds on top of each roll. Let rise in warm place until light and doubled in size, about 15 minutes. Preheat oven to 375 degrees F. Bake for 15 minutes.

328

> *Kenilworth became a village in 1892. Sir Walter Scott's novel provided the inspiration for its name as well as those of many of its streets.*

The Western Springs Water Tower

329

Jimsonweed—Native Flower

Sweet Potato Pie

Yield: 1 9-inch pie

2 cups mashed sweet potatoes
½ cup sugar
¼ teaspoon salt
4 tablespoons butter, at room
  temperature
¼ teaspoon cinnamon
¼ teaspoon nutmeg

2 eggs, beaten
¼ cup seeded raisins
2 cups heavy cream
1 unbaked 9-inch pie shell
Whipped cream for topping
2 tablespoons pecans or walnuts

Preheat oven to 350 degrees F. Beat sweet potatoes in a large bowl.
Add sugar, salt, butter, cinnamon, and nutmeg, mixing well. Add
eggs, raisins, and cream. Pour into an uncooked 9-inch pie shell and
bake until firm, about 1 hour. When pie is cold, spread with
whipped cream and sprinkle with nuts.

> *Waukegan began as a trading post dubbed Petite Fort by French
> traders in the seventeenth century. When it was incorporated as a village in
> 1849, the name was officially changed to Waukegan, which, in Potowa-
> tomi, means "trading post."*

Raisin Pie

Yield: 1 9-inch pie

1⅓ cups seedless raisins
2 cups hot water
1¾ cups sugar
4 tablespoons flour
1 egg, well beaten

Juice and rind of 1 lemon
¼ teaspoon salt
1 tablespoon butter
Rich pastry for 9-inch pie and lattice
  top

Preheat oven to 400 degrees F. Wash raisins and soak in hot water
for one hour. Add other ingredients and mix. Cook in double boiler
until thick. Cool. Pour into pastry-lined 9-inch pie pan and cover
with criss-cross strips of pastry. Bake in oven for 10 minutes; then
turn oven down to 350 degrees F. and bake until browned.

> *Paul Cornell, early developer of Hyde Park admittedly chose the name
> of that gracious community on the Hudson with the intent of projecting an
> aura of future charm and elegance around the swampy and sandy land he
> was trying to promote on the south side of Chicago.*

French Cherry Pie

Yield: 1 9-inch pie
3½ cups pitted sour cherries
¼ teaspoon red food coloring
¼ teaspoon almond extract
¼ cup flour
3 tablespoons cornstarch

1¼ cups sugar
¼ teaspoon salt
2 9-inch unbaked pie crusts
1 tablespoon milk

Preheat oven to 400 degrees F. Place cherries in bowl. Add food coloring and extract. Sift together dry ingredients; add to cherries and mix thoroughly. Turn into pie pan lined with crust. Cover with perforated top crust; crimp edges. Brush top crust with milk. Bake 45 minutes. Cool on wire rack.

> *LaGrange was linked to Chicago by the Burlington Railroad in 1862 although it was not chartered as a village until ten years later. The Annual Pet Parade here draws many spectators from the whole Megalopolitan area.*

Peach-Coconut Pie

Yield: 1 9-inch pie
1 envelope unflavored gelatin
¼ cup cold water
2 eggs, separated
¾ cup sugar
¼ teaspoon salt
⅔ cup heavy cream
2 cups minced fresh peaches

½ cup coconut
1 tablespoon lemon juice
1 9-inch baked pie shell
1 cup heavy cream
2 teaspoons sugar
½ teaspoon vanilla extract
½ cup coconut

Soften gelatin in water. Mix together egg yolks, ¾ cup sugar, salt, and cream. Cook, stirring constantly, until mixture coats spoon. Stir in softened gelatin. Chill until thick. Fold in peaches, coconut, and lemon juice. Beat egg whites until stiff. Fold into gelatin mixture. Pour into pie shell. Chill until firm. To serve, whip cream stiff with 2 teaspoons sugar and vanilla. Spread on pie. Top with coconut.

> *Glen Ellyn was first called Prospect Park. Although one of Glen Ellyn's interesting historic features is the remnants of Stacy's Tavern from stagecoach times, perhaps its most unique claim to historic fame was the discovery of the well-preserved bones of mastedon in the 1960s.*

Fruit Pie

Yield: 6 to 8 servings

Crust

1 cup quick oats
1 cup flour
½ cup sugar

¼ teaspoon cinnamon
Salt to taste
¼ pound (1 stick) butter, melted

Filling

2 cups rhubarb, peeled and cubed
2 cups apples, pared, cored, and
   sliced
1 cup strawberries, washed and

   stemmed
2 tablespoons flour
¾ cup sugar
½ teaspoon nutmeg

Mix together crust ingredients and press into a 9-inch pie pan, setting aside one cup for topping.

Preheat oven to 350 degrees F. Mix together filling ingredients and fill crust; sprinkle on topping. Bake 45 minutes.

332

> *Calumet City was settled as early as 1840 by Dutch farmers who raised produce on truck farms in the outlying areas of the growing metropolis. This area and its way of life provided the inspiration for Edna Ferber's novel, So Big.*

Butterscotch Pie

Yield: 1 9-inch pie
2 tablespoons butter
1 cup sugar
6 tablespoons cream
1 rounded tablespoon flour

1 cup light cream
1 egg, beaten
1 9-inch unbaked pie shell

Preheat oven to 400 degrees F. Brown butter in saucepan. Add sugar and cream and cook together 5 minutes. Then add flour, 1 cup cream, and egg. Pour in pie shell and bake for 25 minutes. Cool and serve with whipped cream.

Pecan Pie

Yield: 1 9-inch pie

Crust

1 cup sifted flour	6 tablespoons butter or shortening
¼ teaspoon salt	3 tablespoons water

Filling

3 eggs	⅓ cup butter, melted
⅔ cup sugar	1 cup dark corn syrup
⅓ teaspoon salt	1 cup pecan halves

Preheat oven to 375 degrees F. Sift together flour and salt; cut in shortening. Add water all at once and mix into flour mixture. Mixture will be crumbly. Roll out to fit 9-inch pie pan. Flute edge. Beat together eggs, sugar, salt, butter, and corn syrup. Mix in pecans. Pour into pastry lined pan. Bake 40 to 50 minutes. Cool.

Coffee Filbert Chiffon Pie

Yield: 1 9-inch pie

⅓ cup chopped filberts	1¼ cups strong, hot coffee
1 9-inch pie shell, unbaked	3 eggs, separated
1 envelope unflavored gelatin	½ cup heavy cream
¼ cup strong, cold coffee	1 teaspoon vanilla extract
1 cup sugar, divided	¼ teaspoon cream of tartar
¼ teaspoon salt	½ cup heavy cream, whipped
1 square 1-ounce semi-sweet chocolate	¼ cup chopped filberts, toasted

Preheat oven to 425 degrees F. Press filberts into pie shell. Bake 10 to 12 minutes; cool and set aside. Soften gelatin in cold coffee 5 minutes. Blend ½ cup sugar, salt, and chocolate into hot coffee; stir until chocolate melts. Beat egg yolks slightly. Stir a little hot mixture into yolks; slowly add yolks to hot mixture in saucepan. Cook over low flame, stirring constantly until mixture boils. Remove from heat. Stir in softened gelatin until dissolved; cool. When mixture is partially set, beat until smooth. Beat heavy cream until stiff; add vanilla. Fold into gelatin mixture. Add cream of tartar to egg whites; beat until stiff. Add remaining sugar; continue beating until glossy. Fold into gelatin mixture. Refrigerate until almost firm. Spoon into filbert pie shell. Chill until set. Garnish with whipped cream and toasted filberts.

> *The name Elmhurst was inspired by elm trees which lined one of the main routes into the town. Early residents had decided on the name Cottage Hill to commemorate the cottage-hotel which had served Chicago travelers as early as 1843. In 1870 the name was permanently changed to the present one.*

334

Lemon Custard Cheese Pie

Yield: 1 9-inch pie

1 cup sugar	1 cup milk
3 tablespoons flour	1 tablespoons butter, melted
Grated rind and juice of 1 lemon	Pinch salt
2 egg yolks	2 egg whites, stiffly beaten
1 cup creamy cottage cheese	1 9-inch pie shell, unbaked

Preheat oven to 350 degrees F. Mix sugar, flour, lemon juice, and rind. Add egg yolks, cheese, milk, and melted butter; then fold in the stiffly beaten egg whites to which a pinch of salt has been added. Pour into unbaked 9-inch pie shell and bake for 35 minutes.

> *Robbins, established as a village in 1917, was named for its founder, Eugene S. Robbins. This southern suburb was originally settled by Blacks who came from the South looking for work and non-urban housing in Megalopolis.*

Apple Custard Pie

Donnie Jones of Collinsville in the Bottom says this recipe is from 1870 at least and was handed down from her grandmother to her mother to her.

Yield: 1 9-inch pie

¾ cup sugar
¼ cup flour
⅛ teaspoon salt
1 egg, beaten slightly
3 cups apples, pared and cut in

½-inch cubes
½ teaspoon vanilla extract
1 cup sour cream
1 9-inch pie shell, unbaked

Topping

⅓ cup butter
⅓ cup flour

¼ cup sugar
1 teaspoon cinnamon

Preheat oven to 400 degrees F. Sift together dry ingredients. Stir into egg. Fold in remaining ingredients. Pour into pie shell. Bake 30 minutes. Remove from oven; sprinkle with topping. Return to oven 10 minutes longer.

Cut butter into flour; add sugar and cinnamon. Mix to a crumbly mixture for topping.

—Donnie Jones

335

> *Ravinia Park, named after the ravines which undulate to the lake, began as an amusement park. In 1910 the affluent residents of the area bought the park with the idea of turning it into a summer music center. The park still provides an amazing array of musical events each summer ranging from jazz, to opera, to folk music, to ballet.*

Custard Pie

Mrs. Robinson of Romeoville in Megalopolis says that this is her mother's recipe and has been "in the family going on 100 years. My mother was always expected to bring the custard pie to all pie suppers and church socials. It is my favorite recipe."

Yield: 1 9-inch pie

2½ cups scalded milk (half and half may be substituted)
4 eggs, beaten
½ cup sugar
¼ teaspoon salt
1 teaspoon vanilla extract
¼ teaspoon nutmeg
1 9-inch pie shell, unbaked

Preheat oven to 400 degrees F. Add milk to eggs. Add remaining ingredients and pour into pie shell. Bake for 15 minutes. Reduce heat to 350 degrees F. and bake for 20 to 25 minutes. Pie is done when inserted knife comes clean.

—*Madge Robinson*

> *Elgin became the Midwest center for the dairy industry in the latter half of the nineteenth century. It was here that Gail Borden developed the process of condensing milk.*

Cookie Pie

Mrs. Schramm of Freeport states that this recipe was made by her aunt to the delight of all the family. She writes, "We kiddingly 'fight' over whether someone else's piece of pie is bigger than the others'; and my aunt often 'hides' a second cookie pie to make sure everyone gets a fair share."

Yield: 8 servings

1½ cups crushed chocolate wafer cookies
¼ cup sugar
4 tablespoons butter
1 cup scalded milk
3 beaten egg yolks
½ cup sugar
¼ teaspoon salt
1 tablespoon unflavored gelatin
¼ cup cold water
1 teaspoon vanilla extract
3 egg whites, beaten stiff
½ pint heavy cream, whipped
Grated unsweetened chocolate for garnish

Mix crushed cookies, sugar, and butter. Press into a 10-inch pie tin. Cook scalded milk, egg yolks, sugar, and salt in a double boiler.

Dissolve gelatin in water and add to mixture. Let cool. Fold vanilla, egg whites, and cream into cooled mixture. Refrigerate and sprinkle grated chocolate on top.

—*Sharon Klontz Schramm*

> *Half Day was a stopping point on the early roads crossing the northern part of the state. As the story goes, its name is derived from the translation of Aptakisic, a Potowatomi Indian chief, whose tribe inhabited the region.*

Winter Pie

Winter pie has been handed down in Anna Belle Crumer's family of Collinsville in the Bottom over many years. It was an early Illinois winter favorite when no fresh fruits were available.

Yield: 1 9-inch pie
2 cups light brown sugar, packed
⅓ cup unsalted butter, at room temperature
3 eggs
½ cup heavy cream
½ teaspoon vanilla extract
Pinch salt
1 9-inch pie shell, unbaked

Preheat oven to 375 degrees F. Cream the butter and sugar. Add eggs and beat. Add cream, vanilla, and pinch of salt. Pour into pie shell and bake 40 to 50 minutes or until set.

—*Anna Belle Crumer*

> *Hillside was settled by German immigrants in the mid-nineteenth century. Limestone from its quarry built many Chicago houses, churches, and public buildings in the latter half of the nineteenth century. It became a village in 1905.*

Standard Pie Crust

Yield: 2 9-inch crusts
1½ cups sifted flour
½ teaspoon salt
½ cup (1 stick) butter or shortening
5 tablespoons cold water

Sift together flour and salt; cut in butter or shortening with pastry blender. Add water. Mix into flour mixture. Divide dough in half. Form one half in a flat circle; roll out to fit a 9-inch pie pan. Roll remaining dough for top crust 2 inches larger than pie pan. Perforate top crust on pie; fold extra crust under edge of bottom crust; press together. Crimp edge. Bake according to pie recipe.

Oatmeal Pie Crust

Yield: 1 9-inch crust
1½ cups quick-cooking oatmeal
6 tablespoons butter, melted
¼ cup confectioners' sugar

Preheat oven to 350 degrees F. Combine ingredients and press into a 9-inch pie tin. Bake for 10 minutes. Fill with your favorite pre-cooked filling.

338

Egg Pie Crust

Yield: 1 9-inch crust
6 tablespoons butter
1¼ cups flour, unsifted

¼ teaspoon salt
1 egg, slightly beaten

Preheat oven to 400 degrees F. Cut butter into flour until crumbly. Mix in salt and egg. Stir with fork until dough holds together. Shape into a ball. Roll out dough on lightly floured board. Fit into a 9-inch pan. Prick dough all over with fork. Bake 12 minutes, or until golden. Fill with a favorite pre-cooked filling.

Crust for Ice Cream Pies

Yield: 2 9-inch crusts
1 11½-ounce box chocolate wafers
1 8-ounce package broken pecans
¼ pound (1 stick) butter, melted

Crush wafers in a large bowl. Stir in nuts and butter. Divide in half and press firmly into 2 9-inch pie pans. Fill with home made ice cream.

> *Brighton Park's fortunes soared when it became the location for a mill producing explosives for quarrying stone. The Brighton Park Race Track, popular in the mid-nineteenth century, was owned and operated by Chicago's colorful mayor, Long John Wentworth.*

Baked Graham Cracker Crust

Yield: 1 9-inch crust
1 cup graham cracker crumbs
¾ teaspoon flour
¼ cup sugar
⅓ cup butter, melted

Preheat oven to 400 degrees F. Combine crumbs, flour, sugar, and melted butter. Mix well. Pat mixture onto bottom and side of 9-inch pie pan. Bake 8 minutes. Fill with desired pre-cooked filling.

> *The original building of the Art Institute of Chicago is one of the many legacies of the 1893 World Columbian Exposition. The building has been enlarged several times and houses a fine Oriental art collection as well as the best Impressionist and Post-Impressionist collection outside of France.*

A Megalopolis Scrapbook

Bread Pudding

Yield: 6 servings
2 cups cubed dry bread
3 cups heavy cream, scalded
3 eggs, beaten
¾ cup sugar

¼ teaspoon salt
¾ teaspoon cinnamon
⅓ cup white raisins
⅓ cup coarsely chopped pecans

Preheat oven to 350 degrees F. Soak the bread in the cream in a 1½-quart casserole. Blend egg, sugar, salt, and cinnamon and stir into bread mixture. Fold in the raisins and pecans. Place casserole in a shallow pan of water and bake for 60 minutes or until a knife comes out of the center clean. Serve with heavy cream.

> *Zion was founded at the turn of the century by John Alexander Dowie, a Scots preacher. When it was incorporated as a city in 1902, all activities were in accordance with the tenets of Dowie's religious beliefs. Blue Laws were so stringent that for years trains were not allowed to stop in Zion on Sundays.*

Pineapple Bread Pudding

Yield: 6 servings
½ cup (1 stick) butter, melted
1½ cups sugar
2 eggs, beaten
½ cup milk

1 12-ounce can pineapple chunks, drained
4 cups bread cubes, trimmed

Preheat oven to 350 degrees F. Combine ingredients in a 2-quart casserole. Bake for 35 minutes or until golden brown on top.

> *Roselle was settled at the end of the Black Hawk War. It received its present name from Roselle Hough, who came to the region in 1855 to operate a flax mill on the nearby creek.*

Cognac Pflaumenpudding

Mrs. Turner of Riverside in Megalopolis says that this plum pudding is the highlight of their holiday celebrations.

Yield: 4 to 6 servings

1 30-ounce can purple plums
2 envelopes unflavored gelatin
½ cup cold water
¼ cup sugar
1 teaspoon grated lemon rind
¼ cup lemon juice

⅓ cup plum or cherry brandy
¼ teaspoon cinnamon
1 teaspoon vanilla extract
½ cup chopped almonds
½ cup heavy cream, whipped

Drain plums; reserve and measure liquid. Pit and purée the plums in a blender or through a food mill. Soften gelatin in cold water. Heat 1¾ cups plum liquid and sugar to the boiling point, stirring frequently; remove from heat. Stir in softened gelatin until dissolved. Stir in 1⅔ cups plum purée, lemon rind, juice, brandy, cinnamon, and vanilla. Pour into 1½-quart mold which has been rinsed with cold water. Chill until firmly set, about 2 to 3 hours. Unmold on a serving platter. Garnish with almonds and whipped cream.

—*Rita Turner*

> *Gage Park derives its name from Henry Gage, an early truck farmer in this once-agricultural section of the southwest side of Chicago.*

Plum Pudding

Mrs. Metzger of Collinsville in the Bottom says that this treasured recipe came from her Grandmother Adams who was married in 1897 in Brighton, Illinois. The family has served the pudding each Christmas for eighty-four years.

Yield: 1½ quarts

1 teaspoon baking soda
1 tablespoon warm water
2 cups flour
1 cup seedless raisins
1 cup currants
1 cup chopped almonds
½ cup citron
4 eggs, well beaten

1 generous cup sugar
1 teaspoon ground cloves
2 teaspoons cinnamon
½ teaspoon nutmeg
1 teaspoon salt
1 cup milk
2 cups breadcrumbs
1 cup finely ground beef suet

Hard Sauce

1 cup sugar
½ cup (1 stick) butter, at room
    temperature
1 egg

½ cup hot water
½ teaspoon nutmeg
2 ounces bourbon

Dissolve soda in warm water and set aside. Flour fruit thoroughly, reserving rest of flour. In another bowl mix the eggs, sugar, spices, and salt. Add milk and stir in the fruit, nuts, breadcrumbs, and suet. Add the soda and the rest of the flour. Combine carefully. Pack in a 2-quart mold and steam for four hours. Serve with Hard Sauce.

To make Hard Sauce, cream the butter and sugar. Stir in remaining ingredients and cook in a double boiler, stirring constantly until thickened.

—*Lois Welch Metzger*

Woodstock was incorporated as a city in 1852, the same year that its post office opened its doors. Extensive restoration is an ongoing process here where the lovely old historic Opera House dominates the main town square.

Fudge Upside-Down Pudding

Yield: 6 sevings
1 cup sifted flour
2 teaspoons baking powder
½ teaspoon salt
¾ cup sugar
6 tablespoons cocoa, divided
½ cup milk

1 teaspoon vanilla extract
2 tablespoons butter
1 cup chopped pecans or walnuts
1 cup firmly packed brown sugar
1¾ cups hot water

Preheat oven to 350 degrees F. Sift together flour, baking powder, salt, sugar, and 2 tablespoons cocoa. Stir in milk, vanilla, and butter. Pour into a buttered 2-quart glass baking dish. Sprinkle with mixture of nuts, brown sugar, and remaining cocoa. Pour water over entire batter. Bake 45 minutes. Let cool 10 minutes before inverting on plate. Serve with whipped cream.

Romeoville, settled as early as 1835, was so named to go with Juliet, the original name for Joliet. It was incorporated as a village in 1895.

Apple Pudding

Yield: 6 servings

2 eggs
1½ cups sugar
5 tablespoons flour
2½ teaspoons baking powder

¼ teaspoon salt
1 cup chopped pecans
1 cup chopped apples
1½ teaspoons vanilla extract

Preheat oven to 325 degrees F. Cream eggs and sugar. Add remaining ingredients to the egg and sugar mixture. Put into a well buttered 8-by-8-inch baking dish. Bake 40 to 45 minutes. Serve with whipped cream.

> *Oak Brook has been synonomous with polo and the Paul Butler family since the early twentieth century. Large land holdings of the family have been developed into residential areas and business and industrial complexes, including the lucrative Oak Brook Mall.*

Date Compote

Mrs. Cramer of McConnell says, "The first year my parents were married, 1923, my mother had a big Christmas dinner and she served Date Compote. It had been in her family for years. Some of our relatives still serve this at their yearly Christmas dinner. It is rather rich but very good, so small portions are ample."

Yield: 8 to 10 servings

1 pound dates, minced
2 cups water
1 cup sugar

Dash salt
¾ cup pecan or walnuts
Whipped cream for topping

Cook dates, water, sugar, and salt over low heat until thick and soft. Cool and fold in nuts. Spoon into individual servings dishes and top with whipped cream.

—Mrs. Harry Cramer

> *Barrington in northwest Cook County was established as a village in 1865. Quaker settlers from Great Barrington, Massachusetts, gave the town its name.*

Bibliography

Adams, James N., *A List of Illinois Place Names*. Springfield, Illinois: Illinois State Library, 1968.

Alvord, Clarence Walworth, *The Illinois Country 1673-1818*. Chicago: Loyola University Press, 1965.

Angle, Paul M., *Illinois Guide and Gazetteer*. Chicago: Rand McNally & Company, 1969.

Carpenter, Allan, *Illinois, Land of Lincoln*. Chicago: Children's Press, 1968.

Counties of Illinois: Their Origin and Evolution (Illinois Secretary of State's Office Pamphlet). Springfield, 1977.

Dixon, Alan J., *Illinois Blue Book 1977-1978*. Springfield: State of Illinois, 1978.

Feeney, Agnes M. and John L. Leckel, *The Great Chicago Melting Pot Cookbook*. Virginia Beach/Norfolk: The Donning Company/Publishers, 1980.

Holt, Glen E. and Dominic A. Pacyga, *Chicago: A Historical Guide to the Neighborhoods*. Chicago: Chicago Historical Society, 1979.

Illinois: A Descriptive and Historical Guide. Chicago: A. C. McClurg and Co., 1947.

Horrell, William C., Henry Dan Piper and John W. Voight, *Land Between the Rivers, The Southern Illinois Country*. Carbondale and Edwardsville: Southern Illinois University Press, 1973.

Humphrey, Grace, *Illinois, The Story of the Prairie State*. Indianapolis: The Bobbs-Merrill Company, 1917.

Knack, Ruth Eckdish, *Preservation Illinois: A Guide to State and Local Resources*. Springfield: Illinois Department of Conservation—Division of Historic Sites, 1977.

Koeper, Fredrick, *Illinois Architecture: From Territorial Times to the Present*. Chicago: The University of Chicago Press, 1968.

Masters, Edgar Lee, *Spoon River Anthology*. New York: Macmillan Publishing Co. Inc., 1962.

Morrison, Olin Dee, *Illinois, Prairie State*, Vols. III and IV. Athens, Ohio: E. M. Morrison, 1964.

Plucker, Lina S. and Kaye L. Roehrick, *Brevet's Illinois Historical Markers and Sites*. Sioux Falls: Brevet Press, 1976.

Siegal, Arthur, *Chicago's Famous Buildings*. Chicago: University of Chicago Press, 1974.

The Weekend Book—A Guide to Small Adventure in Illinois. (Illinois Department of Commerce and Community Affairs Pamphlet), 1980.

Index

346

347

348

349

350

351

Agnes M. Feeney and John L. Leckel also wrote *The Great Chicago Melting-Pot Cookbook* which combined ethnic cuisine and cultural tidbits for 20 nationalities found in the Chicago area. They have written food articles for both *Gourmet* and *Chicago* magazines. Ms. Feeney studied painting and drawing at several schools of Italian art, and two of Mr. Leckel's television programs have been nominated for Emmys. Their artistic ability is demonstrated by the numerous delightful line drawings which help reflect the unique flavor of Illinois.